Deeper Competency-Based Learning

We would like to dedicate this book to the many students, teachers, school leaders, and colleagues who have supported us in our personal learning journeys over the years. This book is a result of the many trials, tribulations, successes, and failures that have now brought us to this time and place with the hope that we can make a difference for the next generation of educators. Know that you are in this book—in mind, in spirit, and in practice.

Deeper Competency-Based Learning

Making Equitable, Student-Centered, Sustainable Shifts

Karin Hess
Rose Colby
Daniel Joseph

Foreword by Barbara Bray

FOR INFORMATION:

Corwin
A SAGE Company
2455 Teller Road
Thousand Oaks, California 91320
(800) 233-9936
www.corwin.com

SAGE Publications Ltd.
1 Oliver's Yard
55 City Road
London EC1Y 1SP
United Kingdom

SAGE Publications India Pvt. Ltd.
B 1/I 1 Mohan Cooperative Industrial Area
Mathura Road, New Delhi 110 044
India

SAGE Publications Asia-Pacific Pte. Ltd.
18 Cross Street #10-10/11/12
China Square Central
Singapore 048423

Publisher: Jessica Allan
Senior Content Development Editor: Lucas Schleicher
Associate Content Development Editor: Mia Rodriguez
Production Editor: Andrew Olson
Copy Editor: Amy Hanquist Harris
Typesetter: C&M Digitals (P) Ltd.
Proofreader: Barbara Coster
Indexer: Integra
Cover Designer: Scott Van Atta
Marketing Manager: Deena Meyer

Library of Congress Cataloging-in-Publication Data

Names: Hess, Karin J., author. | Colby, Rose, author. | Joseph, Daniel A., author. | Corwin (Firm)

Title: Deeper competency-based learning : making equitable, student-centered, sustainable shifts / Karin J. Hess, Rose L. Colby, Daniel A. Joseph.

Description: Thousand Oaks : Corwin, 2020. | Includes bibliographical references and index.

Identifiers: LCCN 2020003583 | ISBN 9781544397061 (Paperback : acid-free paper) | ISBN 9781544397078 (ePub) | ISBN 9781544397085 (ePub) | ISBN 9781544397092 (PDF)

Subjects: LCSH: Competency-based education—United States. | Competency based education—Curricula. | Educational innovations—United States. | Educational change. | Teachers—In-service training. | Teaching—Methodology.

Classification: LCC LC1032 .H47 2020 | DDC 370.110973—dc23
LC record available at https://lccn.loc.gov/2020003583

This book is printed on acid-free paper.

22 23 24 10 9 8 7 6 5 4 3 2

List of Figures and Tables

Contents

Visit the companion website at
http://resources.corwin.com/DeeperCompetencyBasedLearning
for downloadable resources.

Deeper Competency-Based Learning

We would like to dedicate this book to the many students, teachers, school leaders, and colleagues who have supported us in our personal learning journeys over the years. This book is a result of the many trials, tribulations, successes, and failures that have now brought us to this time and place with the hope that we can make a difference for the next generation of educators. Know that you are in this book—in mind, in spirit, and in practice.

Deeper Competency-Based Learning

Making Equitable, Student-Centered, Sustainable Shifts

Karin Hess
Rose Colby
Daniel Joseph

Foreword by Barbara Bray

FOR INFORMATION:

Corwin
A SAGE Company
2455 Teller Road
Thousand Oaks, California 91320
(800) 233-9936
www.corwin.com

SAGE Publications Ltd.
1 Oliver's Yard
55 City Road
London EC1Y 1SP
United Kingdom

SAGE Publications India Pvt. Ltd.
B 1/I 1 Mohan Cooperative Industrial Area
Mathura Road, New Delhi 110 044
India

SAGE Publications Asia-Pacific Pte. Ltd.
18 Cross Street #10-10/11/12
China Square Central
Singapore 048423

Publisher: Jessica Allan
Senior Content Development Editor: Lucas Schleicher
Associate Content Development Editor: Mia Rodriguez
Production Editor: Andrew Olson
Copy Editor: Amy Hanquist Harris
Typesetter: C&M Digitals (P) Ltd.
Proofreader: Barbara Coster
Indexer: Integra
Cover Designer: Scott Van Atta
Marketing Manager: Deena Meyer

Printed in the United States of America

Library of Congress Cataloging-in-Publication Data

Names: Hess, Karin J., author. | Colby, Rose, author. | Joseph, Daniel A., author. | Corwin (Firm)

Title: Deeper competency-based learning : making equitable, student-centered, sustainable shifts / Karin J. Hess, Rose L. Colby, Daniel A. Joseph.

Description: Thousand Oaks : Corwin, 2020. | Includes bibliographical references and index.

Identifiers: LCCN 2020003583 | ISBN 9781544397061 (Paperback : acid-free paper) | ISBN 9781544397078 (ePub) | ISBN 9781544397085 (ePub) | ISBN 9781544397092 (PDF)

Subjects: LCSH: Competency-based education—United States. | Competency based education—Curricula. | Educational innovations—United States. | Educational change. | Teachers—In-service training. | Teaching—Methodology.

Classification: LCC LC1032 .H47 2020 | DDC 370.110973—dc23
LC record available at https://lccn.loc.gov/2020003583

This book is printed on acid-free paper.

22 23 24 10 9 8 7 6 5 4 3 2

Contents

Visit the companion website at
http://resources.corwin.com/DeeperCompetencyBasedLearning
for downloadable resources.

List of Figures and Tables

Chapter 3

Chapter 4

Foreword

In *Deeper Competency-Based Learning*, the authors write that moving the system toward more authentic ways of measuring student growth is necessary, but it takes time. Forty-nine states now have policies in place to enable schools to move to competency-based education (CBE). So why is it taking so long for schools to shift from teacher-centered to learner-centered classrooms?

Rose Colby's deep knowledge of CBE, combined with Karin Hess's expertise in assessment design and Dan Joseph's school-based coaching strategies for personalized learning, provide both a blueprint and guide for what we need to answer that WHY. This book starts with the working definition for CBE and the HOW that connects with your school's WHY. The authors then guide you from a traditional educational system to CBE that is transformational with organizational shifts. These shifts include the need for a profile of the graduate that describes future readiness, which is addressed with examples of profiles from different states.

Since the world is changing, work and education are impacted. According to the World Economic Forum report titled *The Future of Jobs*, by 2022 automation will displace about 75 million jobs worldwide. On the other hand, technology will create an estimated 133 million new jobs. With the information about job loss and the need for different skills, there is an urgent need to improve educational systems and a need for people to know their WHY for learning new skills throughout their lives.

Our children need to be prepared for an uncertain future. To make it even more complicated, too many learners of all ages are not prepared for today. Multiple pathways are needed in a system that moves them to being future-ready for the challenges they will face, not only in higher education and the workforce but in every part of their K–12 experiences.

Throughout *Deeper Competency-Based Learning*, the authors provide HOW to support a culture with the organizational shifts grounded in the principles of equity with special consideration for assessment policies and practices, including mapping competencies across a K–12 learning continuum leading to graduation. They weave into each chapter resources for designing, implementing, and sustaining multiple pathways needed for your students' K–12 experiences and include a number of downloadable tools for each stage of the journey.

The work of educators is challenging. Changing systems is big. But you *can* make this happen for your school and classroom. This is the book all educators need to transform teaching and learning. As you read through this book, ask yourself and reflect on these questions:

- WHAT is competency-based education, and what does that mean for you now?

- WHY would you want to adopt a learner-centered, competency-based model?

- HOW can you get started and then design, implement, and sustain the transformation?

You can do this. Our children are ready for change and need to be future-ready. What you learn from this book will inspire you and challenge you to go deeper, ask more questions, and rethink every aspect of what school means and what it means to be a leader, a teacher, and a learner. Our roles are changing because the world is changing. As educators, we have to design environments that empower agency, so all learners take ownership of the pathways that prepare them for their future as global citizens in a more equitable society.

Barbara Bray
Creative Learning Strategist
Author, *Make Learning Personal* and *How to Personalize Learning*
Podcast Host, *Rethinking Learning*

Acknowledgments

We are grateful to the many educators whom we have worked with and learned from over the years. We would like to thank colleagues who have provided input on ideas presented in this book or gave of their time to give us feedback on early drafts, including Paul Leather, Chris Sturgis, Barbara Bray, and Ellen Hume-Howard, as well as the many educators who have worked with our tools and provided feedback or shared how they have customized them.

We've guided the work of many CBE teams through processes similar to what is described in these chapters, with most of our in-depth work with schools in New Hampshire, Maine, Vermont, Illinois, Michigan, South Carolina, Colorado, Iowa, Arkansas, Washington, DC, and Virginia. We would like to express a special thank you to the educators who were willing to share their reflections, insights, and examples of their work in this book.

- Jillian Corey (Humanities Teacher) and Joe Bowe (Humanities Teacher), Manchester School of Technology, Manchester, New Hampshire

- Steve Rothenberg (CTE Director) and Tom Mungovan (Graphics Arts Instructor), Concord Regional Technical Center, Concord, New Hampshire

- Megan Delaney (Instructional Coach), Jennifer Moore (Teacher), and Patrick Hardy (Principal), Proviso East High School, Maywood, Illinois

- Angelique Hamilton (Project Administrator, Curriculum and Instruction), Illinois State Board of Education

- Damarr Smith (Project Manager of Competency-Based Education) and Roshaun Bowen (SEL Instructional Specialist), Chicago Public Schools, Chicago, Illinois

- Kirsten Soroko (Curriculum and Instruction Coordinator), Pinkerton Academy, Derry, New Hampshire

- Erik Lasky and Lisa Balata (Administrators), Ridgewood High School, Norridge, Illinois

- Mandy Cyr (Director of Instruction and Innovation), Biddeford School Department, Biddeford, Maine

- John Freeman (Superintendent), Pittsfield School District, Pittsfield, New Hampshire

Finally, we would like to express our deep gratitude to the staff at Corwin with whom we have worked most closely—Jessica Allan, Lucas Schleicher, Mia Rodriguez, Andrew Olson, Amy Hanquist Harris, and Scott Van Atta. They have been supportive in representing the essence and intent of our work and responsive to helping us think through our questions and clarify our ideas.

PUBLISHER'S ACKNOWLEDGMENTS

Corwin gratefully acknowledges the contributions of the following reviewers:

Miriam A. DeCock, EdS
High School Language Arts Instructor
iForward
Grantsburg, Wisconsin

Kelly VanLaeken
Director of Curriculum, Instruction, and Assessment
Gananda Central School District
Walworth, New York

About the Authors

For more than a decade, Karin Hess, Rose Colby, and Daniel Joseph have been actively supporting schools in making the transition to competency-based education. In doing so, they have become convinced of the need for practical new tools, strategies, and models to support schools as they shift to learner-centered, competency-based education. Their passion for this important work inspired this collaboration and the writing of this book.

Karin Hess, author of the Hess Cognitive Rigor Matrix, is a former classroom teacher and school administrator with over 40 years of deep experience in curriculum, instruction, and assessment. Dr. Hess is recognized internationally as a leader in developing practical approaches for using cognitive rigor, depth of knowledge, and learning progressions as the foundation for curriculum design and assessments at all levels of assessment systems, from developing local assessment systems to state-level, grade-level standards and test specifications for large-scale state assessments. Over the years, she has contributed to Maine's early thinking about how to structure requirements for assessing high school graduation exhibitions and has provided technical assistance to *Science Exemplars* in the development and annotation of K–8 science performance tasks (www.exemplars.com), to the Center for Collaborative Education's Quality Performance Assessment (QPA) initiative, and to Benchmark Education's *Ready to Advance* curriculum for PreK, using learning progressions in curriculum and assessment design. Her most recent publications include a chapter in the second edition of *Fundamentals of Literacy Instruction and Assessment, Pre-K–6* (Hougen & Smartt, 2020) and Corwin's *A Local Assessment Toolkit to Promote*

Deeper Learning: Transforming Research into Practice (2018). Karin's ongoing CBE work has included guiding the development and implementation of New Hampshire's K–12 Model Competencies and supporting school districts throughout the United States in creating and analyzing the effective use of performance scales and high-quality performance assessments for deeper competency-based learning.

Rose Colby is a nationally recognized competency-based learning and assessment specialist, assisting schools in designing high-quality competency, assessment, and grading reform systems in many states. She is a Talent Cloud Fellow for 2Revolutions, an education design firm. She is a contributor and member of the national Advisory Board for *Competency*Works, the national clearinghouse and resource for innovative practices in competency education. She has served as Competency Education Consultant for the New Hampshire Department of Education, supporting school districts as they develop their competency education systems, as well as designing and supporting the new state accountability pilot system, the New Hampshire Performance Assessment for Competency Education (NH PACE). She is an adjunct professor at Southern New Hampshire University in the Masters/CAGS program in competency education. Rose is the author of two books on competency education: *Competency-Based Education: A New Architecture for K–12 Schooling* (Harvard Education Press, 2017) and Corwin's *Off the Clock: Moving Education From Time to Competency* (2012).

Daniel Joseph is the founder of CBE Solutions, an organization that supports districts in the strategic transformational shift from traditional, time-based education to personalized, competency-based systems of teaching and learning. By promoting systems-level change, engaging shareholders, and building capacity through continuous improvement and aligned intentional instruction, districts can make the transformation to systems that promote achievement and equity for all students.

Daniel strives to provide the knowledge, tools, and processes to promote the depth of change needed to realize the vision of learning for all students. Daniel's practical experience in the arenas of public will, policy, and practice provides direction to schools working toward sustained growth and progress. His involvement with a state-level task force in Maine—the Proficiency-Based Diploma Strategic Task Force—provided support for the systemic change in both practice and policy. In addition to state-level engagement, Daniel also was the representative and building-based leader for his school district, which was part of the (ILN) Innovation Lab Network of the Council of Chief State School Officers (CCSSO). Prior to founding CBE Solutions, he supported districts across the country in developing personal mastery systems of learning for Marzano Research and Reinventing Schools Coalition. Daniel teaches graduate-level courses as an adjunct faculty member at Southern New Hampshire University and Saint Joseph's College of Maine.

Introduction

For a number of years, I have been saying that implementing CBE should be easier for the next wave of educators—that those of us who did the earlier work constructed pathways that others could ultimately follow. However, this has proven more difficult in practice than I predicted, as many of the early works on this topic only served to bring readers into the forest and lose them among the trees as the path petered out in the gloom. . . . Schools must attend to the larger elements of making big change in our public schools—addressing why this transformation is so important—if public education is to survive well into this century.

—Paul Leather, Director, Interstate Learning Community
National Center for Innovation in Education

For over ten years, **competency-based education (CBE)** has emerged not only as an innovation in education but as a true transformation of the traditional approaches to how we "do" school. Those tried and true trappings of the industrial model of traditional teaching and learning are no longer viewed as "modern" education as we approach the end of the first quarter of the 21st century. As a nation, we have simply outgrown the one-size-fits-all instructional and assessment practices of the past. Today, schools are embracing new models of teaching and learning that personalize a child's education, require evidence of **proficiency**, and lead to graduation from high school with future readiness for the workplace and further education. These new models of competency-based education seek to provide the learning opportunities for each child to be successful both in academics and personal development.

This pioneering work in school transformation has been advanced through collaborations among educators at the classroom, school, district, and national levels with a shared vision for more learner-centered schools. The successes of the schools we might call early adopters have informed and guided other schools in how to move their own schools forward with CBE. Because schools are transforming a one-size-fits-all model to something that must meet their unique needs, many different workable models are emerging organically. This makes the work of describing how to design new systems for teaching and learning difficult. CBE implementation can look very different from one school to the next. This is why we have included a variety of school-based scenarios to illustrate that point. In our experience, the most successful of schools may have different entry points into CBE, but they all stay true to their WHY. Having a clear purpose and vision for transforming schools becomes the cornerstone and focus of the decisions schools must make in forging their journey.

We call the CBE implementation process a journey simply because it will take a long time to get there—time to "unlearn" or strip away strongly held beliefs about the existing structures of teaching and learning and even the purpose for schooling in America today. As we watch the sunsetting of the No Child Left Behind era of high-stakes testing introduced in 2002 (Klein, 2015), we are moving toward more authentic ways of measuring student growth and learning over time. Educators ready to embrace the core beliefs of competency-based education, built on principles of equity for each student, are poised to begin an exploration that will transform their schools.

In 2012, nearly half of all states were designated as having no policies to support competency-based education. Now, according to an Aurora Institute report (Truong, 2019), the United States has reached a tipping point in recognizing the potential of competency-based education to transform K–12 education and providing policy to support these changes. As of December 2019, forty-nine states (with Wyoming being the exception) have some form of supportive policy or flexibility to allow competency-based learning.

State policies vary from state to state, with some states requiring that local school districts apply for waivers or credit flexibility in how credit is earned at the high school level for graduation.

The Aurora Institute (formerly iNACOL) categorizes and regularly updates the status of state CBE policies as *Advanced*, *Developing*, or *Emerging* to signify whether the state has permissive, enabling, or comprehensive state policy to advance competency-based education.

For example, *Advanced* means that the state has comprehensive policy alignment or has established an active state role to build educator capacity in local school systems for competency-based education. Seventeen states are now at the advanced stages of CBE implementation. One of these states is New Hampshire, which now uses a CBE model as part of its federal accountability system, using performance-based assessment, competency-based grading and reporting, and the state accountability assessment test once every three years.

The work of transforming to competency-based education is complex, requiring major shifts away from the conventional organizational structures of schools and away from many less effective teaching and learning structures toward student-centered classrooms. Our book explores these shifts in detail by sharing practical strategies, tools, and resources for sustainable implementation—moving your school from traditional teacher-directed learning to student-driven competency-based education.

APPLYING THE RESEARCH OF JOHN HATTIE TO CBE IMPLEMENTATION

In 2009, Professor John Hattie published *Visible Learning: A Synthesis of Over 800 Meta-Analyses Relating to Achievement.* This groundbreaking book synthesized the findings from 800 meta-analyses of 50,000 research studies involving more than 150 million students, and it built a story about the power of teachers and of feedback, thus constructing a model of learning and understanding by pointing out what works best in improving student-learning outcomes.

Since then, Hattie has continued to collect and aggregate meta-analyses to the Visible Learning database. His latest dataset synthesizes more than 1,600 meta-analyses of more than 95,000 studies involving more than 300 million students. This is the world's largest evidence base into what works best in schools to improve learning. *Visible Learning's 250+ Influences on Student Achievement* (Corwin, 2019) rank orders these factors from the ones having the greatest **effect size**—or impact on learning—to the least (meaning those with a negative impact, such as retention). For example, Hattie positions **collective efficacy** at the top of the list of factors that influence student achievement, finding it much more powerful and predictive of student achievement than the effects of a student's socioeconomic status, prior achievement, home environment, or parental involvement. When teachers believe that, together, they and their colleagues can impact student achievement, they share a sense of collective efficacy. Collective efficacy refers to "the judgments of teachers in a school that the faculty as a whole can organize and execute the courses of action required to have a positive effect on students" (Goddard, Hoy, & Woolfolk Hoy, 2004, p. 4).

As we have developed tools and strategies for long-term implementation of CBE, we've seen many correlations between Visible Learning's top-tier influencers and schools doing this work. In addition to developing and strengthening collective teacher efficacy (effect size = 1.39), we believe that well-implemented CBE systems also support the following:

- Teachers' engagement with cognitive task analysis (effect size = 1.29)

- Greater teacher clarity when setting expectations for learning and designing learning activities (effect size = 0.75)

- Developing students' ability to engage with tasks requiring that they transfer their learning (effect size = 0.86)

- Student use of self-reflection (effect size = 0.75)

- Strategy monitoring (effect size = 0.58)

- Metacognitive strategies (effect size = 0.55)

- Classrooms that personalize and deepen learning through timely, self-regulatory feedback (effect size = 0.66)

Therefore, throughout the book, we have referenced these influencers from Hattie's work as they relate to the changes that schools will engage in as they implement CBE and transform their schools (See Figure 0.1 on page 5).

TAKING TIME TO STOP AND REFLECT

We've written this book to promote CBE as a learner-centered system. So throughout the book's text, we have included thought bubble icons with reflection questions. We invite readers to use these as opportunities to pause, make personal connections, and to capture ideas and insights. CBE teams may want to share reflections with their colleagues as they develop and implement their evolving CBE systems.

STOP AND REFLECT

What is one question you have about CBE that you'd like this book to answer for you . . . and why?

_____

_____

_____

_____

FIGURE 0.1 Connecting CBE Implementation With Visible Learning Influencers

Collective teacher efficacy (1.39)

Teacher clarity when setting expectations and designing learning activities (0.75)

Teachers' engagement with cognitive task analysis (1.29)

Timely, self-regulatory feedback (0.66)

Students' ability to engage with tasks requiring that they transfer their learning (0.86)

Student use of self-reflection (0.75)

Student use of strategy monitoring (0.58)

Student use of metacognitive strategies (0.55)

CHAPTER OVERVIEWS

Chapter 1: The WHAT, the WHY, and the HOW of CBE

Chapter 1 is a primer for those beginning to explore CBE and who want to understand the quality design principles and the kinds of shifts schools must consider if they choose to embark on the journey.

- WHAT is competency-based education, and will it qualitatively change what we do now?

- WHY would a school want to adopt a competency-based model? Do *we* have a convincing WHY?

- HOW do we get started? HOW do we design, implement, and sustain this transformation? HOW will we know it's working?

An examination of the traditional education framework provides the launching point for deep systemic transformation to CBE based on fundamental principles of equity. This transformation requires the consideration of three kinds of shifts from traditional education to CBE. In this chapter, we share scenarios from schools who chose different entry points into the work based on their WHY. We introduce a CBE Readiness Tool for you to use and reflect on with colleagues as you consider your current status in the development of your own CBE system. We also begin the story of one school's CBE journey and visit with them several times in subsequent chapters.

Chapter 2: Making Organizational Shifts

In Chapter 2, we discuss the first of the three fundamental shifts in implementing CBE—organizational shifts. When a K–12 school district uses a community-based approach to develop the vision of their graduates, it is incumbent on that K–12 school district to refashion its organization to deliver on this new promise with the community. Four key dimensions in organizational shifts impact HOW school leaders support the new shared vision for teaching and learning. These organizational shifts are in the areas of policies, leadership, professional culture, and professional learning. To support learner-centered, competency-based education, schools must build a collaborative organizational culture that is mutually supportive among educators. This must be supported by state and local policies grounded in the principles of equity, with special consideration for assessment policies and practices. In order to support student learning in this new environment, it is necessary to support new learning for professionals through high-quality collaborative work as part of the school day.

Old paradigms of school schedules and time management within the day will be tested in support of these new learner-centered, competency-based teaching and learning methodologies. We will share the work of several different schools and districts in their work to develop and communicate their local vision of their graduates.

Chapter 3: Making Shifts in Teaching and Learning Structures

Chapter 3 introduces a variety of tools to enhance teacher collaboration in building new instructional and assessment approaches as schools "upgrade" their existing teaching—learning from the standards-based era or traditional curriculum approaches. In CBE, it is necessary to begin with developing high-quality, rigorous competencies that align with the profile of the graduate and then consider how to map competencies across a K–12 learning continuum leading to graduation. In addition to mapping academic expectations, incorporating the development and assessment of personal success skills embedded in performance assessment tasks is also critical. The focus of this chapter is on designing high-quality assessments that guide instructional decision-making while eliciting valid and reliable evidence and measures of student learning against academic and personal competencies. Specific strategies and tools (Appendix A and Appendix B) guide your work in designing rigorous K–12 competencies; creating performance scales to support assessment development, instructional planning, and progress monitoring; and developing and validating competency-based performance assessments.

Because of these instructional and assessment shifts, there is also a need for transparent communication with stakeholders about the expectations embodied in the competencies and student evidence that will demonstrate mastery. We offer several approaches to consider as part of the shift from traditional grading to evidence-based grading and reporting.

Chapter 4: Making the Shift to Student-Centered Classrooms

In Chapter 4, we move to the classroom to set out the parameters for making probably the most challenging CBE shift—from teacher-centered to more **student-centered learning** environments. The key elements of this shift will be in designing, implementing, and sustaining targeted core instruction that is personalized for students—essentially meeting each student where he or she is on the learning pathway—and then, moving them forward, shifting from the traditional teacher pacing of instruction to the student pacing of their learning. We also clarify what is meant by **"personalization"** and how it differs from individualization when planning instruction. Classroom shifts bring a greater need to incorporate personalized supports that include student goal setting; metacognition and reflection skills, especially of personal success skills; and peer and self-assessment strategies.

RESOURCES FOR DESIGNING, IMPLEMENTING, AND SUSTAINING YOUR CBE JOURNEY

Multiple pathways are needed across the K–12 continuum in order to design a CB system that meets students where they are and moves them to being future-ready for challenges they'll face in higher education and the workforce. To help your teams get started, a number of downloadable tools drawn from our own work (and discussed in each chapter) are provided in Appendix A and Appendix B to guide decisions and activities along the way. Appendix C provides suggested readings and web-based resources school teams can use to plan, design, implement, and reflect upon each incremental stage of their journey.

Finally, on our cover and throughout the book you'll see visuals of gears. The concept of a high-functioning system is that the parts work in harmony, like the interlocking gears of a well-oiled machine—working together to accomplish a task larger than any one part is designed to do alone.

We see the transformation to CBE as a new system requiring all levels—at the organizational level (leadership and management), the teacher level (instruction and assessment practices), and especially at the classroom level—to work in harmony. Making significant changes at one level of an educational system cannot be done without affecting the other levels in some way—slowing the systems change down or speeding it up. In our work, we find that if the gears at one level have not shifted in ways that support the other levels, systemic change is next to impossible to accomplish. Figuring out which gears will move your system forward will set you on a solid path.

We have seen many versions of competency-based learning goals. Some look like the skills checklists of the 1980s; others are more focused on deeper learning. Will your school choose to prepare students for the more rigorous path?

Our goal in sharing these practical tools and strategies is to support educators working together with the larger school community to find your WHY, and thus your WAY—the shifts needed to transform schools and have a greater impact on *deeper* student learning. This is collective efficacy at its very best!

FIGURE 0.2 Core Components of Competency-Based Education for Deeper Learning

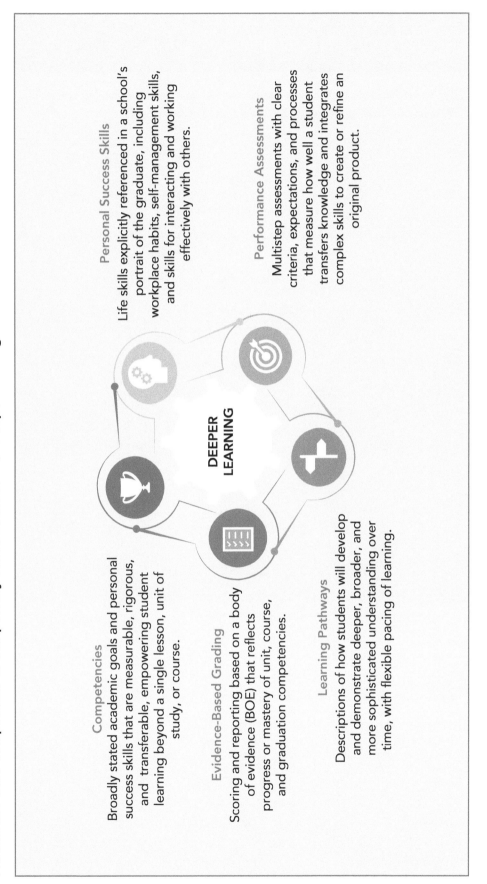

Personal Success Skills
Life skills explicitly referenced in a school's portrait of the graduate, including workplace habits, self-management skills, and skills for interacting and working effectively with others.

Performance Assessments
Multistep assessments with clear criteria, expectations, and processes that measure how well a student transfers knowledge and integrates complex skills to create or refine an original product.

Competencies
Broadly stated academic goals and personal success skills that are measurable, rigorous, and transferable, empowering student learning beyond a single lesson, unit of study, or course.

Evidence-Based Grading
Scoring and reporting based on a body of evidence (BOE) that reflects progress or mastery of unit, course, and graduation competencies.

Learning Pathways
Descriptions of how students will develop and demonstrate deeper, broader, and more sophisticated understanding over time, with flexible pacing of learning.

DEEPER LEARNING

STOP AND REFLECT

We've set the stage for building a system based on competencies of deeper learning. Why would—or should—your school want to take this journey?

_____

_____

_____

_____

_____

_____

_____

_____

_____

_____

_____

_____

_____

_____

_____

_____

_____

_____

_____

The WHAT, the WHY, and the HOW of CBE 1

We must convene around a set of strategies that
focus on dramatically changing the culture of our schools
and systems, the structures that are used to organize
schools and learning processes, and the very types of
learning experiences that students have throughout
their education.

—Chris Sturgis and Katherine Casey (2018a)

1.1 A HISTORICAL LOOK AT THE WHAT AND WHY OF COMPETENCY-BASED EDUCATION

Prior to 2011, the early pioneers in competency-based education (CBE) were generally trying to respond to the implications of being labeled a *failing school* under No Child Left Behind (NCLB). The penalties for not demonstrating an increase in the number of students meeting proficiency required that schools try harder to make the cut score. In general, schools that were labeled as *low performing* tried many different approaches over the years to "fix" the problem of low performance scores on annual high-stakes state tests. For some schools, fixing a failed system resulted only in continual failure. Out of the constraints imposed on these failing schools under NCLB, several schools realized they had to put aside test-driven teaching and learning and stop trying to fix what was broken in favor of reinventing a different approach that puts the learner at the center of

Brief Timeline of Factors Influencing the Evolution of CBE

2011—The "birth" of CBE: iNACOL hosts the first national meeting on CBE in Denver. A working definition of competency-based education is developed with participants at that meeting.

2011—iNACOL publishes a five-part definition of CBE to build a common understanding of CBE and promote performance-based, personalized learning.

2015—With the sunsetting of NCLB, the "Every Student Succeeds Act" inspires states to rethink assessment and higher expectations for every student.

2018—*Competency*Works publishes Quality Design Principles for CBE.

2019—*Competency*Works publishes an updated, seven-part definition of CBE. iNACOL is renamed the Aurora Institute.

the solution. Those early models of reinventing schooling in Chugach, Alaska (Sturgis, 2016), Adams 50 in Colorado (Sturgis, 2014), and Lindsay Unified in California (Sturgis, 2015) informed the thinking of many other public, private, and independent schools. Thus, their stories of success were shared widely.

In 2011, the International Association for K–12 Online Learning (iNACOL) called together early innovators from these spotlight schools to a gathering in Denver that today is recognized as the formal "birth" of CBE. Michael Horn, co-author of a new book on the influence of technology in disrupting education (Horn, Christensen, & Johnson, 2010) spoke at the Denver meeting, describing how new technologies and educational approaches were beginning to change the face of education. Around that same time, the national Council of Chief State School Officers (CCSSO) created the Innovation Lab Network (ILN) made up of a handful of states that were opting to further explore new approaches. At the forefront of curiosity was how a small state like New Hampshire had created a state policy that required high school students to demonstrate competency to gain credit for their courses rather than be granted credit for sitting through a course to earn Carnegie units. These early pioneers had no "how-to" manuals to guide them. They oftentimes looked to innovations happening in charter and independent schools that did not have the regulatory barriers found in public education. At that Denver assembly in 2011, these early innovators in CBE recognized that the reasons schools were moving away from traditional approaches to more diverse approaches was the very reason why, as innovators, they could not recommend to the field any one model, as several models were showing success. Thus, iNACOL launched *Competency*Works (www.competencyworks.org) to help build the field of K–12 CBE and create a knowledge-sharing hub to act as a clearinghouse for stories of innovation happening nationally. Teachers and leaders were invited to submit their stories in daily blogs.

Before long, several funding mechanisms came into play to fuel the emerging models. Private foundations such as the Hewlett Foundation, the Gates Foundation, and the Nellie Mae Education Foundation, as well as state grants, stepped forward to fund further innovation. Momentum was growing for CBE. When iNACOL established a strand of professional learning at its annual symposium, things really started humming nationally. This sparked what we see today—schools moving to CBE to varying degrees in almost all states.

In 2011, iNACOL published a working definition of CBE (Patrick & Sturgis, 2011), putting forward a five-part definition "designed to generate rich policy discussions on transforming the education system" (p. 7). That definition became a North Star for many school innovators, resulting in a variety of local CBE definitions and designs. Although the original five-part definition did hold the strong core of belief in learner agency, there was still a need for more guidance in making equity more explicit in the CBE definition. In October 2019, eight years after releasing the field's first working definition of competency-based education, *Competency*Works presented an expanded definition to reflect a deepened understanding in the field and to address the challenges of implementing student-centered learning models in K–12 education. While the 2011 working definition had five components, the revised and updated seven components express the field's greater understanding of the essential nature of student agency in building student motivation, engagement, lifelong learning skills, and depth of knowledge.

An Updated Definition for Competency-Based Education (Levine & Patrick, 2019)

1. Students are empowered daily to make important decisions about their learning experiences, how they will create and apply knowledge, and how they will demonstrate their learning.

2. Assessment is a meaningful, positive, and empowering learning experience for students that yields timely, relevant, and actionable evidence.

3. Students receive timely, differentiated support based on their individual learning needs.

4. Students progress based on evidence of mastery, not seat time.

5. Students learn actively using different pathways and varied pacing.

6. Strategies to ensure equity for all students are embedded in the culture, structure, and pedagogy of schools and education systems.

7. Rigorous, common expectations for learning (knowledge, skills, and dispositions) are explicit, transparent, measurable, and transferable.

Source: Reprinted with permission from iNACOL/Aurora Institute, https://www.inacol.org/. CC by 4.0 (https://creativecommons.org/licenses/by/4.0/)

STOP AND REFLECT

Referring to the updated definition of CBE, which features (1–7) are already beginning to become part of your school's WHAT in shifting to CBE?

_____

_____

_____

_____

_____

Quality Design Principles for CBE

This more robust definition will help field practitioners and system designers, especially with its focus on student empowerment, as we currently see some "less-than-high-quality" examples of the WHAT that some schools are touting as CBE. Definitions help in understanding the scope of CBE. In addition to evolving the original (2011) CBE definition, iNACOL (now renamed Aurora Institute) and *Competency*Works also sought out the advice and experience of national educators doing this work to tease out design principles for high-quality competency education. A draft of suggested quality principles for CBE was further refined at a National Summit on Competency Education in 2017, resulting in the publication *Quality Principles for Competency-Based Education* (Sturgis & Casey, 2018b). These design principles are meant to be the guardrails for high quality that every school should consider when designing CBE for its unique school community.

Often when school personnel begin the process of moving to CBE, they do so in response to particular "felt needs" within the school. These may include student academic performance, high dropout rate, high absenteeism from school, and issues of student or professional culture. When schools seek out CBE as a solution to a single problem, they may be so focused on solving their problem that they fail to see or understand the systemic nature of the shifts that are necessary throughout the system. The Quality Design Principles set forth by Sturgis and Casey bring attention to the systemic supporting principles to guide CBE designers.

1.2 CONSIDERING THE HOW THAT CONNECTS WITH YOUR SCHOOL'S WHY

The Quality Design Principles have three major components: (1) Purpose and Culture Design Principles; (2) Teaching and Learning Design Principles; and (3) Structure Design Principles.

As you look to your own school organization, think carefully about each of these key components. For example, you may find that your existing school culture may not tolerate rushing too quickly in making structural changes. Or you may rush into grading changes as a lever to move to CBE when instructional practices, competency alignment, learner agency, and assessment policies and practices have not changed. In all of this, schools must really know who they are before beginning this work. These Quality Design Principles are most important as schools begin to explore their WHAT, WHY, and HOW of CBE. Applying such design principles can take schools from making the same mistakes in trying to address issues of school reform, which, for the most part, were solutions to unsuccessfully fix an already broken system using a narrow focus of academic metrics.

The tools included in subsequent chapters of this book further strengthen these design principles to ensure a high-quality approach that embraces the core concepts in CBE. These tools will craft decision points that schools and districts must grapple with to begin this multiyear effort to transform their current traditional approaches. Most importantly, schools and districts must carefully leverage how their developmental entry point into CBE is further supported by work currently done in the district versus what is most needed to address an urgent issue of concern. For example, there may be an effort in a district to support professional learning in performance assessment; however, there may be an equity issue of immediate concern by virtue of a civil rights complaint.

Perhaps the first concern expressed by groups of educators who have taken on a passion for CBE transformation is this: How can we make teachers in our school buy into CBE? The simple answer to this question is you can't! Transforming traditional teaching and learning to CBE isn't like introducing a new math program to teachers. This transformation is not an additive to what currently is in place. Research is very clear in this area. There are four elements to scale and sustainability (Coburn, 2003):

1. **Depth**—The degree to which there is change in underlying assumptions about how students learn, the nature of subject matter, expectations for students, and what constitutes effective instruction and pedagogical principles (cf. *Educator Competencies for 21st Century Learning*)

2. **Sustainability**—Internal versus external development of reform by teachers

3. **Spread**—Norms of interaction become embedded in policy, not number of adopters

4. **Shift in Reform Ownership**—Providing meaningful professional learning opportunities for teachers and administrators

The implications of bringing a CBE transformation to scale with sustainability will further bring into question a school's ability to provide the time, talent, technology, and resources to support the effort. To be successful, teachers need not be "sold" a bill of goods in the hopes that they will support it. To be successful in scaling and sustaining this work, the transformation must be rooted in clear communication of the WHY, the WHAT, and the HOW of CBE and then in supporting teachers in collaborative efforts to do this work over time.

There are many reasons that may spark a school or district to consider moving to competency-based education. Most often when the topic is broached with parents and community members, they will often say that what schools have always been doing was good enough for them because they see themselves as successful adults. This actually represents one of the barriers that impedes measures to move forward with CBE. Many people truly believe this tenet, while others are distrustful of what schools choose to foist on parents and their children, all in the name of school improvement, such as higher test scores. As you consider moving to CBE, we ask that you take your time to consider your WHY. It may take you quite a while to clarify this within your school community. That discernment may happen with the community engagement around developing a profile of your graduates.

STOP AND REFLECT

As your school thinks about moving to CBE, take some time to consider your WHY. What is part of your WHY?

_____

_____

_____

_____

_____

One of the most convincing approaches in having a community accept moving to CBE is to debunk the perceived beauty and effectiveness of traditional teaching and learning as it is practiced in the 21st century. One thing that can be said of traditional education is that it pretty much looks the same everywhere. Again, some people would argue that is an asset, and many would argue it is a liability as schools in different communities have students, teachers, and community members that are becoming increasingly more diverse.

1.3 START BY EXAMINING THE TRADITIONAL EDUCATION FRAMEWORK

The Drivers of Traditional Education

Let's look a bit more closely at the components of traditional education (Table 1.1). This should help you ascertain where your particular school is strongly traditional or where your school has made some initial steps to CBE. The main drivers of traditional education are curriculum, instruction, assessment, and grading.

TABLE 1.1 The Main Drivers of Traditional Education

Curriculum	Instruction	Assessment	Grading
• Standards-based curriculum, Grades K–8 • Course content-driven curriculum, Grades 9–12, with some alignment to high school content standards • Fixed by grade level or course (general, honors courses, etc.) • Coverage of all standards or content expected for all students • Interventions based on fixed grade level or course curriculum for all students	• Often program or course driven (e.g., tracking, Honors and Advanced Placement courses; K–8 mathematics programs) • Emphasis on academic content knowledge and skills • Teacher-directed delivery of content and skills, with some differentiation • Projects, open-ended investigations, and performance assessments mostly optional and teacher designed	• Assessment practices vary by teacher • All students take same assessments at same time • Predominantly paper-and-pencil testing • Minimal or no assessments of deep learning • Formative assessment use varies by teacher • Summative assessments at end of chapters, units of study • Students move to the next unit regardless of test results	• Grading practices vary widely across K–12 continuum • Highly subjective among teachers, mixing academics with behavioral dimensions • Grades are generally averaged to arrive at the quarter, term, or end-of-year grade • Grades sometimes used as a criteria for participation in school events or "honor" status

STOP AND REFLECT

Are there additional "drivers" in your school's current system you'd add to the list in Table 1.1? How might these existing drivers impact the shift to CBE?

_____

_____

_____

_____

_____

With closer introspection, you may want to add some features of your school to the list in Table 1.1. Beyond the pillars of curriculum, instruction, assessment, and grading, schools should ascertain how their current practices provide equity for each child to be successful. An area for even greater discussion and introspection is a consideration for the inequity built into traditional schooling.

Competency education moves the traditional framework that has been in place for over a hundred years into the present and future. Before looking at that framework, it is important to consider the lenses through which you transform your schools. The lenses of equity and the culture of teaching and learning should be foundational philosophical orientations to any high-quality design for competency-based learning systems, and part of your school's WHY.

Educational Equity

Recognizing the potential negative impact of many drivers of traditional education, some schools are moving toward competency-based approaches to achieve more equitable outcomes for each student. **Educational equity** is defined as a measure of achievement, fairness, and opportunity in education. Fairness means that the factors specific to one's personal condition should not interfere with his or her potential of academic success. Achievement and opportunity require a comprehensive standard that applies to every learner in an educational system. These three factors are closely related and depend on each other for full implementation and sustained success of a competency-based educational system.

The work of the National Equity Project (www.nationalequityproject.org) further clarifies our understanding, stating that educational equity is achieved when each child receives what she or he needs in order to develop full academic and social potential. Working toward equity involves these steps:

- Ensuring equally high outcomes for all participants in our educational system and removing the predictability of success or failures that currently correlates with any social or cultural factor

- Interrupting inequitable practices, examining biases, and creating inclusive multicultural school environments for adults and children

- Discovering and cultivating the unique gifts, talents, and interests that every human possesses.

Educational equity is a powerful concept with deep implications for how we structure our schools, how learners access their education, and how learners (including teachers and school leaders) engage in and support academic learning and development of their own personal success skills:

Competency-based education is not a silver bullet, but it can be a powerful strategy for equity when it allows educators, leaders, and communities to collaborate and provide learners with the right supports at the right time,

foster learner voice and deepen learning and create systems of transparency
and continuous improvement needed to work toward success for all.
(Casey, 2018, p. 26)

Our inclusion of opportunities for personal (teacher and school leader) reflections
on their own learning while implementing CBE is meant to stress the importance of
becoming a learner-centered system at all levels of the system.

Equity should guarantee not only that each student will learn,
but that the learning generates sufficient, high-quality evidence
to indicate that every learner is future-ready for college and
careers. Therefore, the major shifts required to fully implement
and sustain an equitable, competency-based system must
provide continuity, coherence, and transparency across the
school culture and the structures and methods used to elicit,
gather, and interpret this evidence. We realize that this is a tall
order for most schools to accomplish. But in our work, we have
seen success when school teams are willing to stay the course
over several years with a clear vision of the desired destination.

> *An equity-oriented profession is designed to ensure all students thrive and experience the broader purpose of education: deep, relevant knowledge and the capacity for lifelong learning. Student learning and professional practice are multicultural and inclusive. Educators, learners, and communities form deep relationships and share power.*
> (Casey, 2018)

The equity framework presented in the report *Designing for
Equity: Leveraging Competency-Based Education to Ensure
All Students Succeed* (Sturgis & Casey, 2018a) raises the question, "How should we
think about equity in a personalized, competency-based system to ensure that every
student is indeed successful?" The equity principles outlined in the report provide
further guidance in how to collaboratively advance a vision for educational equity
as a "fair and just system where every learner—students and educators alike—is
thriving" (p. 5).

The equity framework is complex and comprehensive. It is intended to guide states,
districts, and school teams to consider how to design their CBE systems and shape
their discussions of WHY. As a starting point for your work, we illustrate some
aspects of these equity principles by sharing our school-based stories and applying
these principles in the design of our CBE tools and implementation strategies. We
also suggest taking a deeper dive into the full report—a little bit at a time—as your
work progresses.

Principles of the Equity Framework

The Equity Framework (Sturgis & Casey, 2018a) outlines nine principles that
support a transition to personalized, competency-based education. The principles
are organized under three broad domains: Purpose and Culture, Structure, and
Pedagogy. We've added a few concrete examples here to help your team explore how
to begin implementing parts of the equity framework.

Purpose and Culture

- ***Nurture strong culture of learning and inclusivity.*** We suggest starting with involving the school community in an "equity audit." Panorama (www .panoramaed.com) or Smith, Frey, Pumpian, and Fisher (2017, pp. 192–199) provide excellent guiding questions to engage both staff and students.

- ***Engage the community in shaping new definitions of success and graduation outcomes.*** We provide guidance (later in Chapter 1) for how schools can begin ongoing collaborative discussions to develop a vision articulating a profile of their graduates. CB assessment policies and practices can then be developed consistent with this vision, using CBE Tool 2.

- ***Invest in adult mindsets, knowledge, and skills.*** Chapter 2 explores how shifts in leadership roles and professional culture will ultimately lead to a more learner-centered organization. Adults engage in collective efficacy to design a system that supports a more collaborative professional culture.

Structure

- ***Establish transparency about learning, progress, and pace.*** Chapter 3 goes into great detail about how to develop aligned performance assessments of deeper learning (CBE Tools 5, 6, and 7) and how to employ evidence-based grading and feedback loops while building and verifying each student's body of evidence (BOE).

- ***Monitor and respond to student progress, proficiency, and pace.*** The development of performance scales (CBE Tool 6, Chapter 3) helps both teachers and students to understand that learning is incremental, happening along a continuum. In Chapter 4, we introduce ways to capitalize on formative uses of assessment, as well as student self-assessment and self-monitoring strategies.

- ***Respond and adapt to students using continuous improvement processes.*** We've included a variety of strategies and scenarios in each chapter illustrating how school leaders and teachers are learning to shift their roles so that students can learn to set personal and academic goals, direct their learning pathways, and reflect on their own learning and progress.

Pedagogy

- ***Ensure consistency of expectations and understanding of proficiency.*** We stress that broader expectations for deeper learning—competencies—must encompass both academic learning and the development of personal success skills. CBE Tools 1A–1E, 3, and 4 help your team to evaluate readiness for developing and implementing clear, measurable, and rigorous competencies. These tools help you to align your profile of the graduate with the development of competencies and adoption of high-quality assessment tools, methods, and policies.

- ***Develop shared pedagogical philosophy based on learning sciences.*** Through collective efficacy, the adults in the system also become learners in this process as they adopt new perspectives on learning and develop new approaches to instruction and assessment. Chapter 3 outlines protocols for five important implementation "pit stops" that serve to help the system recalibrate with the expectations described in the profile of the graduate.

- ***Support students in building skills for agency.*** CBE Tool 12 is one example of the many strategies presented in Chapter 4 that promote student-directed learning and student agency.

The call to communities and educators to build systems of teaching and learning that are designed for educational equity is what we like to call the "Whatever it takes!" approach. Sometimes, when faced with barriers in working through designs for CBE, we have to fall back to the "whatever it takes" mode of action.

Comparing Traditional Education With Distinguishing Characteristics of CBE

One approach when working toward equity in schools is to start by considering the ten flaws of traditional education that have led to systemic inequity (see Table 1.2, adapted from Casey & Sturgis, 2018a, pp. 11–12). This can begin a powerful discussion of WHY for teachers, administrators, school boards, and community members. With this examination of your current system, it is much easier to understand the WHAT of CBE's distinguishing characteristics.

The distinguishing features of CBE on the right side of Table 1.2 represent the WHAT of CBE. However, moving to CBE is not additive. It is transformational. Transformational means that the shape or form and the way we do business fundamentally changes or shifts. This work becomes the HOW of CBE. How you choose to engage in this work will depend on your school community and a decision to determine your portal of entry into this work.

Entry Points Into CBE

There are many ways for a school or district to get started on its CBE journey. We have worked with schools that wanted to begin by developing performance assessments of deeper learning and then later developed descriptions of learning that evolved into academic competency statements. Others began by examining

TABLE 1.2 Ten Flaws of the Traditional System and Distinguishing Characteristics of CBE

Comparison of the Traditional Education System With Competency-Based Education		
	Ten Flaws of the Traditional System	**Distinguishing Features of CBE**
Outcomes	Focuses on a narrow set of academic outcomes emphasizing academic skills, memorization, and comprehension of content. Fails to recognize that student success is dependent on a full range of foundational skills (including social-emotional skills) and the application of skills.	Focuses on a broad and holistic set of student success outcomes that includes deep understanding and application of academic content knowledge and personal success skills that prepare students for college, career, and lifelong learning.
Mindset	Based on a fixed mindset—that people's abilities are innate and immutable. Ranks and sorts students, creating "winners" and "losers," perpetuating patterns of inequality in society.	Builds upon a growth mindset—that learning and performance can improve with effort. Demonstrates belief that all children can learn with the right mix of challenges and supports. Takes responsibility for all students mastering deeper learning expectations. Requires shared vision, collaborative approach, flexibility to be more responsive, and commitment to continuous improvement.
Culture	Emphasizes compliance and order in school culture. Relies upon a bureaucratic, hierarchical system that perpetuates traditional (teacher–student) roles, cultural norms, and power dynamics.	Nurtures empowering, inclusive cultures of learning. Values agency for students and adults with distributed leadership. Recognizes safety and belonging are important to learning.
Reliability	Permits high degrees of variability in how educators, schools, and districts determine proficiency. Students are held to different standards within courses, schools, and districts.	Ensures consistent expectations and definitions of what it means to master knowledge and transferable skills. Builds educator capacity to calibrate judgments of student mastery (e.g., grading, body of evidence) and hold all students to the same high standards.
Learning Infrastructure	Offers opaque learning objectives and performance expectations with limited information for students about the learning cycle. Students receive grades with little guidance on what is needed to do to better and without opportunities for revision. Varies in teacher expectations of what high achievement means.	Values transparency (community, parents, students), setting clear and measurable expectations of what is to be learned—the level of performance required for mastery—and how students are able to make progress.

Comparison of the Traditional Education System With Competency-Based Education		
	Ten Flaws of the Traditional System	**Distinguishing Features of CBE**
Grading	Uses academic grading practices that can often send mixed messages and misleading signals about what students know by reflecting a mix of factors, including behavior, assignment completion, and getting a passing grade on tests, not student learning.	Communicates progress in ways that support the learning process and student success. Closely monitors growth and progress of students based on their learning pathway, not just grade level. Evidenced-based grading and scoring supports students in communicating their progress in learning academics and applying transferable skills.
Advancement	Time-based. Batches students by age and moves them through the same content and courses at the same pace. Advances students to the next grade level after a year of schooling regardless of what they actually learned.	Advances students based on attainment of learning expectations (mastery) through personalized learning pathways. Provides instruction until students fully learn the concepts and skills and then advances them after demonstrating mastery. Uses additional support, not retention.
Supports	Targets support to students when academic or behavioral needs are identified as significantly above or below the norm (special education, gifted, etc.).	Designs timely and differentiated instruction and support. Provides daily flex time and time for students to receive strategic scaffolding before and after semesters.
Pedagogy	Delivers a single curriculum to all students based on age, grade, or course sequence. Emphasizes covering the curriculum each year. Fails to ground learning and teaching in the learning sciences—what we know about how children learn.	Draws upon learning sciences to inform pedagogical principles for students and adults. Takes into consideration student-directed pathways in designing instruction. Increases motivation, engagement, and effort through research-based strategies.
Assessment	Emphasizes assessment for summative purposes to verify what students know. Conducts one-size-fits-all assessments at predetermined times or at the end of the unit. Administered to all students at the same time and in the same format on the same content.	Embeds formative and summative assessment in a personalized learning cycle (including peer and self-assessment). Performance assessment aligns to expectations for transferring (academic and personal skills) knowledge to challenging new contexts. Clarifies students' next steps for individual learning pathways. Informs educator professional learning.

whether or not their existing programs were equitable for all students. Did they have high expectations for each student and provide adequate supports to help every one of them succeed? Still other schools began with the broader perspective of personalization so that all teachers—not just core content teachers—would become invested in the long-term changes about to be made. Regardless of the initial entry point, schools have a variety of reasons to begin this journey.

It is here that we begin to follow the journey of one school in particular—the Manchester School of Technology (MST), located in Manchester, New Hampshire. MST is one of twenty-two regional career and technical education centers (CTE) in New Hampshire that have been offering two- and three-year programs to sophomores since 1982. Students from high schools in surrounding communities arrive at the start of each day at MST for specialty programming in their elected CTE program (e.g., building trades, graphic arts) and return to their home schools at the end of the day. In 2012, MST opened its doors to a group of Manchester freshmen who wanted an alternative to the traditional high school approach found in the other comprehensive high schools in the city. This group of entering freshmen experienced the emerging competency-based, project-based learning approach wherein their career exploration and academics would be integrated throughout their high school experience. Jillian Corey and Joe Bowe are humanities teachers who helped to shape the school's multiyear journey to CBE. Throughout the remaining chapters of this book, we will share their reflections on MST's transformation story.

Scary, but Possible

The mandate was clear. Competency-based education and project-based learning were the vision for students enrolling at the Manchester School of Technology High School. With three weeks until welcoming the first class of students, our feelings were a mixture of fright and excitement. But with the knowledge and training that followed, we began to see that this paradigm shift was certainly doable—still scary, but possible.

It was not only possible but potentially awesome for us as professional educators. We recognized the possibility of increased authentic student engagement and ownership of learning. These benefits came from a new grading system, physical learning environment, and culture, as well as a new perspective on the roles in education of students and teachers. Our classroom was flipping!

— Jillian and Joe

STOP AND REFLECT

How are you currently thinking about engaging in this work? How have you—or will you—determine your portal of entry into CBE?

_____

_____

_____

1.4 SHIFTS IN MOVING FROM TRADITIONAL EDUCATION TO CBE

The major shifts in moving from traditional education to CBE happen at three levels within the school system: at the organizational level, at the teaching–learning level, and at the classroom level (see Figure 1.1). For example, for CBE classrooms to become more student centered, policies at the organizational level and corresponding teaching–learning structures need to shift in support of the changes coming to classrooms.

Each of the three major shifts have several different dimensions that we will examine in depth in the following chapters. A summary of the dimensions of each shift and how they differ from traditional education is outlined in Tables 1.3, 1.4, and 1.5. As you examine the different dimensions of the CBE shifts, you may notice that your school or district tends to be more traditional for some of these dimensions and more progressive toward CBE in others. This is a great vantage point for asking yourselves what portal of entry is best for your school to explore more formally in your transition to fully systemic, learner-centered, sustainable, competency-based education.

FIGURE 1.1 Major Shifts in Moving From Traditional Education to Competency-Based Education

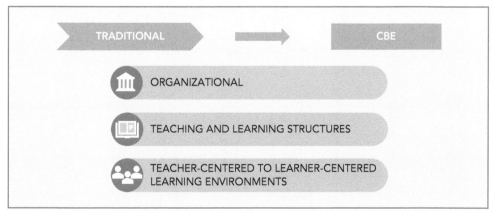

TABLE 1.3 Major Organizational Shifts: Moving From Traditional Education to Competency-Based Education

Major Organizational Shifts: Moving From Traditional Education to Competency-Based Education		
Dimension	**Traditional Education Descriptor**	**Shift to**	**Competency-Based Education Descriptor**
Policy	Policies constrain teaching and learning to cohort-driven, time-based models for school structure without flexibility or opportunity to learn in various learning environments, such as blended, online, and community-based learning opportunities.	→	Local policies support the vision of the graduate—anytime, anyplace learning is supported; equity scan and review has taken place; proficiency is valued over time and place; and collective bargaining supports whatever it takes to reach the vision of the graduate. Assessment policies and instructional support aid implementation of more complex and integrated learning tasks and evidences.
Leadership	Leadership is a hierarchical structure with fixed job roles and responsibilities.	→	Leadership roles are expanding to include teacher roles. Top-down hierarchy is flattened to respect teacher leadership voice and role in supporting new paradigms in student learning.
Professional Culture	Professional culture reflects top-down hierarchy with little collaborative decision-making at the school or teacher level. Teachers are mostly isolated in their work roles.	→	Teachers take ownership for professional learning that advances schoolwide CBE implementation, working collaboratively with peers. School schedules support collaborative work groups within the school day.
Professional Learning	Professional development is directed through central office via whole-group training. Professional goal setting is generally individual with hours of activity accrued as evidence for further licensure.	→	Professional goal setting by collaborative groups is prioritized. These groups focus their protocol-driven work on professional learning that supports the shift from teacher-directed to personalized student learning. Collaborative groups meet frequently to develop and pilot new strategies and to examine student artifacts of learning.
	Class scheduling isolates teachers within their work environments. Professional work is constrained to after-school work hours and student-free sessions for inservice.	→	Priority in school scheduling allows collaborative work groups to meet regularly. These groups have open communication with administrators who facilitate and provide support with resources to accomplish group learning goals for their students.

STOP AND REFLECT

Do you see a logical entry point for making organizational shifts?

TABLE 1.4 Major Teaching and Learning Shifts: Moving From Traditional Education to Competency-Based Education

Major Teaching and Learning Shifts: Moving From Traditional to Competency-Based Education			
Dimension	Traditional Education Descriptor	Shift to	Competency-Based Education Descriptor
Academic Competencies	Academic content is defined by course or grade level standards. High school graduation is dependent on time-based credit accumulation.	→	A well-articulated, coherent K–12 system of rigorous academic competencies is supported—but not limited—by standards. Graduation requirements include demonstrating both academic and personal skills competencies.
Personal Success Skills Competencies	Individual student progress is undefined or randomly integrated into instruction by individual teachers and rarely assessed.	→	Locally determined personal success skills and dispositions are identified and assessed by students against a developmental continuum of skill sets leading to the graduation expectations, or the POG. Social-emotional learning is integrated into authentic academic learning. Policies and practices are supported by learning sciences research (e.g., learning is through social interaction, metacognition, and self-reflection).
Performance Assessments	Assessments are mainly summative, paper-and-pencil chapter or unit tests of variable quality and quantity based on teacher discretion. Use of performance assessment is optional.	→	Performance tasks and project-based learning identify academic competencies integrated with personal success skills and are based on higher depth-of-knowledge (DOK) performance levels. Some assessments are co-designed with or by students.
Evidence-Based Grading	A variety of subjective grading procedures occur teacher to teacher across the K–12 continuum. Grading is generally based on the average of scores. A 100-point scale predominates middle and high school grading.		Proficiency descriptions are articulated using holistic proficiency scales that guide assessment task and scoring rubric design. Determinations of proficiency are established collaboratively and anchor the collection of artifacts (body of evidence) used for K–12 grading.

☁ STOP AND REFLECT

Where are the greatest challenges and opportunities for your school in shifting teaching and learning structures? Where might there be resistance?

TABLE 1.5 Major Student-Centered Classroom Shifts: Moving From Traditional Education to Competency-Based Education

Major Student-Centered Classroom Shifts: Moving From Traditional Education to Competency-Based Education			
Dimension	Traditional Education Descriptor	Shift to	Competency-Based Education Descriptor
Core Instruction	Curriculum is assigned by grade level and is often specifically sequenced and program driven.	→	Students have different entry points into learning and advance along a progression of performance levels in the identified K–12 learning continuum. Instructional approaches are fluid and influenced by student input.
Pace	Pacing is based on whole-class completion of units of instruction.	→	Multiple pathways allow a learner to move forward in her or his learning progression when proficiency is demonstrated.
Assessment and Feedback	Results from formative assessments tend to be graded and recorded, rather than used to advance learning. Grades are used as the evidence for learning, promotion, or the need for interventions.	→	A balanced system of assessments offers a variety of ways to interpret and support progress. Assessment data are used formatively to improve learning and inform instruction. Students actively engage with assessment processes, responding to timely, ongoing feedback.
Student-Centered Learning	Instruction is teacher directed; academic content coverage is prioritized through whole-class instruction. A whole-class learning model predominates with some small-group differentiation to address struggling learners.	→	Student voice and choice give rise to student agency, informing where and how students can access and demonstrate learning. Learning environments expand beyond traditional classroom walls. Peers engage and support each other's learning. Professional resources support diverse student learning needs.
Student Support	Special education and interventions are fixed by policy, time, place, and student assignment.	→	Intervention systems are replaced by flexible systems of student support, meeting students where they are in their learning and providing scaffolding to take them to the next performance level.
Body of Evidence	Course progression and advancement are reflected in grade averages that are communicated with report cards and transcripts.	→	Equity-designed reporting systems accurately communicate student learning with evidence from a mix of performance assessments. Policies describe how students build a sufficient, valid, and reliable body of evidence.
Classroom Culture	Individual teachers subjectively determine and develop their own classroom culture.	→	Democratic classrooms rely on student input and ownership of their learning environment and guidelines for engagement in their learning.

STOP AND REFLECT

Which of these indicators mesh with your current understanding of student-centered classrooms? Are there any surprises?

1.5 GETTING STARTED ON YOUR CBE JOURNEY

If knowing your WHY shows you the way, then knowing the profile and characteristics each of your students will demonstrate upon graduation is the best place to get started. So often—for purposes of accreditation agencies and school handbooks—faculty are the main contributors to local school goals. Although faculty should have an important voice in shaping the profile of the future-ready graduate, the parents, students, and community members should also have a voice. This work is so important that some states have put forward a model profile of the graduate for districts to emulate. In fact, South Carolina and Virginia have created very similar profiles of the graduate.

Developing a Future-Ready Profile of the Graduate (POG)

The South Carolina State Board of Education (2020) adopted a profile of its graduate in 2015 that requires them to have world-class knowledge to include meeting rigorous standards in language arts and math for career and college readiness, as well as proficiency in multiple languages; science, technology, engineering, mathematics (STEM); arts; and social sciences. In the area of world-class skills, the graduate is required to demonstrate creativity and innovation; critical thinking and problem solving; collaboration and teamwork; skill in communication, information, media, and technology; and knowledge of how to learn. In addition to these world-class characteristics, each graduate should demonstrate life and career characteristics that include integrity, self-direction, global perspective, perseverance, work ethic, and interpersonal skills. Note that this profile includes both academic competencies and personal success skills—the very essence of CBE (see www.ed.sc.gov).

Another state, Virginia, layers in several pieces to its profile of the graduate. Virginia expects graduates to be life-ready during their educational experience. It is expected that in this experience each student will accomplish the following:

- Achieve and apply appropriate academic and technical knowledge

- Attain and demonstrate productive workplace skills, qualities, and behaviors

- Build connections and value for interactions with diverse communities

- Align knowledge, skills, and personal interests with career opportunities

The POG further includes expanded expectations in content knowledge, workplace skills, community engagement and civic responsibility, and career exploration with the expectation that across these areas students are using critical and creative thinking, collaboration, communication, and citizenship (Cave, 2016).

← **Teacher Clarity: Expectations for Learning**
(Effect Size = 0.75)

Additional profiles of a graduate can be found at www.portraitofagraduate.org and in Appendix C.

Getting Started With a Profile of the Graduate: One School in Vermont

In 2014, Vermont adopted new Education Quality Standards requiring schools to have proficiency-based graduation requirements (PBGRs) to determine progress and graduation readiness for students graduating in 2020 and for each subsequent graduating class. Proficiency-based graduation soon became the focus of conversations and confusion as many high schools began to explore what this might look like in their schools.

Karin was asked to meet with one Vermont high school staff at the end of the school year to lay the groundwork for the anticipated transition and to plan for the initial work, which would begin over the summer. To kick off the first whole-school PBGR discussion, teachers were each given a 3 x 5 card and asked to write down three things they expected all students graduating from their high school to know and be able to do. Cards were collected, and responses were then tallied and categorized. Of course, there were many content-specific differences, but several broad and more general ideas also surfaced: communication skills, problem-solving skills (in different content areas), and developing inter- and intrapersonal skills (students knowing their strengths and challenges, knowing how to advocate for themselves, how to work with others, etc.). Small groups then each took different ideas and developed a short rationale—WHY each skill set would be important for their graduating seniors, no matter what path they took after high school.

The information generated in this two-hour session was used as the starting point for summer work with a representative group of teachers from the high school. Their task was to further develop statements of proficiency and identify the kinds of evidence students *could* generate to demonstrate meeting the proficiency during their high school years. While this task may sound simplistic on the surface, it took several days and many large charts with extensive discussions and editing before the teachers ended up with their first version of PBGRs, which fell under four broad categories.

Under each category, draft PBGR statements emerged and were numbered, for a total of eleven. Then, to test whether this "vision" was even possible to implement, they listed examples of current and proposed curricular activities that would generate evidence of proficiency. In Table 1.6, you'll see a partial draft of this early work that continued to evolve as the school built its new PBGR system over the years with input from staff, parents, students, and community members.

(Continued)

(Continued)

TABLE 1.6 A Vermont School's Early Draft of Proficiency-Based Graduation Requirements

Student Develops as a Person	Student Develops as a Thinker	Student Develops as a Communicator	Student Develops as a Scholar and Autonomous Learner
#1 *Each student develops an understanding of his or her own strengths and weaknesses and learning styles and applies this knowledge in identifying goals, setting priorities, and managing progress and future planning.* Examples: • Community service-type activities; involvement as a community member • Career/ed planning • Individual learning plan (ILP) • Fitness goals (PE class) • Personal interest surveys • Student-led parent conferences • Outside activities based on personal interests (volunteerism, citizenship)	#4 *Each student uses inquiry and research to acquire, analyze, synthesize, and evaluate information and ideas, using evidence to solve problems and justify conclusions.* Examples: • Science: inquiry projects • ELA: sophomore research paper • Math: investigate parabolic motion, using statistical analyses • Civics: analyze current events • Humanities: round table	#5 *Each student effectively uses math, science, and technology to find, organize, and communicate information for a variety of purposes.* Examples: • Use of media to convey ideas: presentations, etc. • Digital portfolio with performance tasks and investigations	#11 *Each student demonstrates the achievement of a personally identified goal that documents her or his skills, knowledge, and enduring understanding as an autonomous learner.* Examples: • Depth of content/ real-world standards and content • Document new learning • Communicate with expert or mentor (internship, part-time job) • Apply habits of mind • **Extended learning opportunities** (ELO) • Evidence-based portfolio

Today, this school's PBGR system looks quite different from the earlier version in Table 1.6, but it still reflects many of the same values; and in 2020, for the first time, graduates have digital portfolios that document evidence of proficiency across multiple areas of learning.

Whether you develop a profile of your graduate at the school or district level, community involvement is critical. Often, school boards and parents fall into the security of thinking that how we have always done school will grow their students into future-ready graduates. However, a new profile of their graduates should center the conversation on the need to do things differently. For example, many profiles of the graduate describe future readiness to include collaboration skills. What are the design principles that include collaboration instructionally and in a balanced assessment system across each of the grade levels in the K–12 continuum?

This essential question, fashioned around each of the characteristics identified for a future-ready graduate, should be used by multiple working groups when transforming a school or district. Remember, creating the CBE infrastructure is the HOW in this transformation; and every teacher, every parent, and the community at every grade level must have a deep investment in bringing each learner to her or his future readiness upon graduation . . . whatever it takes.

How do you know where to start this work? The best approach is to first use the lens of equity to determine where the flaws are in your current system. That work may raise up the most pressing course of future action for you. While you go through a process to develop a profile of your graduate—which could take up to a year—you can begin to build capacity for the design principles of CBE, to network with other schools at different phases of their work, and to build understanding within your community of the three major shifts that the school or district will be moving through over the coming years of developmental work.

☁ STOP AND REFLECT

Does your school already have a POG? How are you using it to guide your work? If not, how might you start developing a POG?

Core Components of Competency-Based Education: A CBE Readiness Tool

A CBE readiness tool—Core Components of Competency-Based Education (CBE Tools 1A–1E)—is included in its entirety in Appendix A (and see Figure 1.2) for ongoing self-reflection and collaborative action planning as you work through the many parts of CBE and set the gears in motion. Five CBE core components are included in the CBE readiness tool: Competencies, Personal Success Skills, Performance Assessment, Learning Pathways, and Evidence-Based Grading.

Three phases of implementation are described across multiple dimensions for each of the five CBE components:

- **Phase 1—Initiating:** District has begun to examine its existing system and identify where shifts in teaching and learning are needed.

- **Phase 2—Emerging:** District is beginning to develop and deploy competency-based systems and structures and is monitoring shifts in teaching and learning to measure impact.

- **Phase 3—Implementing:** District uses an ongoing feedback cycle to design, evaluate, and revise all core components of CBE for equitable and deeper learning.

FIGURE 1.2 Cutaway of CBE Tool 1A**: Core Components of Competency-Based Education**

CBE Tool 1A	Core Components of Competency-Based Education: CBE Readiness Tool			
Component 1: Competencies Develop a K–12 continuum of rigorous competencies describing how students will apply or transfer essential knowledge, skills, and dispositions across the grades leading to graduation.				
Focus	**Phase 1: Initiating**	**Phase 2: Emerging**	**Phase 3: Implementing**	**Where is your school now? What are possible next steps?**
Leadership	Graduation requirements are policy driven. Curriculum and course offerings are used to develop scope and sequences by course or content area.	Articulated profile of a graduate (POG) is developed with input from staff and shared with community stakeholders. Graduation requirements, curriculum, college and career pathways are not yet aligned to POG.	Articulated profile of a graduate (POG) is developed with input from staff and community stakeholders. Graduation requirements are clearly articulated and integrated into curriculum and college and career pathways.	
Instruction and Assessment	Learning outcomes are clear and articulated by course or grade level. Instructional design emphasizes application of knowledge and skills described in state-adopted standards.	Learning outcomes are clear and articulated by course and standards-based curriculum. K–12 academic competencies are adopted but not incorporated into instruction or assessment design.	Learning outcomes emphasize competencies that include application and creation of knowledge, along with the development of important personal skills and dispositions. Instruction and assessments support and measure competencies.	
Learner Culture	Interpersonal skills are expressed as personal behaviors. Students are aware of these skills and monitored by teachers.	Interpersonal and intrapersonal competencies are developing and evidenced by students when they monitor and reflect on these skills.	Interpersonal, intrapersonal, and learning competencies include explicit, measurable, transferable learning objectives that empower students to have input into their learning path.	
Organizational Structures	The system is driven by "seat time" and whole-class instruction with some differentiation and remediation. Departments and grade-level teams with content expertise guide the delivery of instruction.	The structure and schedule allow for teacher collaboration and flexible grouping of students. School structures and systems are developing new pathways for students to advance to the next level of learning.	Structures and scheduling support collaboration in creating multiple pathways and academies that integrate standards and skills into core competencies aligned to career readiness standards and postsecondary expectations.	

As you begin to examine the current system across many different dimensions of CBE, you will be able to identify areas you may want to address immediately and others that are longer-term goals. The reality is that schools find themselves at many different levels of implementation depending on when and how they started this work and what they have already accomplished to date. When using this tool throughout your action-planning processes, think about defining the scope of involvement of stakeholders. For example, will you begin by engaging the whole school or district? Or will you begin with piloting a few shifts at a grade span or content area? There is not only one way to approach this work, except to get started.

← Collective
Teacher Efficacy
(Effect Size = 1.39)

STOP AND REFLECT

You may want to refer to CBE Tool 1A (Appendix A) as you respond to this question: What are some areas you are "ready" for and want to address immediately? What will be included later in the process?

_____

_____

_____

_____

_____

_____

_____

_____

_____

_____

_____

_____

_____

_____

2 Making Organizational Shifts

///

Mobilizing collective action to focus on the process of learning changes relationships and develops new pedagogical practices, which in turn pushes the structures to change. It is crucial to recognize that shifting to a focus on the process of learning represents a change in culture.

—Michael Fullan, Joanne Quinn, and Joanne McEachen (2017)

CBE Requires Four Major Organizational Shifts

1. Policy Shifts at the State and Local Levels

2. Shifts in Leadership Roles Within the Organization

3. Shifts in Professional Culture

4. Shifts in Professional Learning

This chapter provides an in-depth discussion of each of the four organizational shifts that educational leaders must become deeply involved with during the multiyear transition to competency-based education (CBE). Without setting these shifts in motion, CBE implementation is not sustainable, especially if there is a turnover in school or district leadership. Even the best teachers cannot shift the organization by themselves, no matter how hard they work. The good news is that these shifts are not solely the responsibility of a few school administrators. Shifting the organization means building **leadership density** throughout the system (Hess, 2000).

2.1 ORGANIZATIONAL SHIFT 1: POLICY

In the traditional model, many policies at the state and particularly at the local level constrain teaching and learning to cohort-driven, time-based models of school structure. This includes length of day and number of days in the school year. There often is little flexibility within the framework of a standard grade-level curriculum that paces across the school year. Local policies may be restrictive, requiring attendance policies that affect whether a student can pass a course or issuing requirements in the length of time assigned as homework at different grade levels. As mentioned earlier, today most states have enacted greater flexibility for how students can earn credits to meet graduation requirements and have implemented some innovation in the use of credit-bearing learning opportunities.

However, the degree to which these regulatory state policies allow local-level innovation varies from state to state. An excellent resource for district and school leaders to understand the policy environment for these shifts is *Fit for Purpose: Taking the Long View on Systems Change and Policy to Support Competency Education* (Patrick, Worthen, Truong, & Frost, 2017). This resource is especially helpful in understanding how policy change is intrinsically connected to understanding CBE using the perspective of systems change. We once again have to move our mindset from the "fix-what-is-broken" thinking to making deep, significant changes in our organizational structure. These changes should be grounded in policies that enable these transformational systemic changes. Because so many states have begun moving toward CBE, local districts must update their policies to reflect new state policies that best enable CBE. For example, if a state policy that affects high schools states that students must demonstrate mastery of competencies for a course, then students can't fail the course due to a local attendance policy when mastery is shown through competency-based assessments.

It is important for local school boards and committees to examine their policies in anticipation of final board approval for local changes in moving to CBE. For example, CBE Tool 2 walks you through developing an assessment philosophy and establishing supportive policies for CBE assessments.

Local policies should be enacted to support the profile of the graduate that the school district adopts. One significant shift in the area of policy is for collective bargaining to also support the profile of the graduate. Greater flexibility must be enacted through contract negotiations that prioritize the future readiness of learners as well as the needed school resources and professional learning supports to enact the shifts toward CBE.

One approach in mapping policy decisions is to plan policy changes that correspond to the phases of development of the district's move to CBE. Because this work in a district is very organic, some pieces of the work may take longer or some work that was planned and anticipated to take a long time in development may move

---

STOP AND REFLECT

Does your state have policies in place to support this work? Do they align with your existing local polices?

_____

_____

_____

_____

---

along smoothly. Areas for policy development not found in traditional school policy are assessment and instructional support in aiding the demonstration of more complex and integrated learning tasks and evidences that will now be required of all students. Districts will have to think beyond the usual earned-credit and credit-recovery policies to consider policy language that supports more complex evidence found in balanced assessment systems in CBE. Some schools may even enact policies that require a final competency-based capstone experience. Such a defense of learning may in fact have to meet *Competent* or *Proficient* demonstration of mastery before a high school diploma is granted. Such capstone experiences require both a demonstration of academic performance as well as evidence that the student has met the criteria for graduation in his or her personal success skills. The New York Performance Standards Consortium (n.d.) requires graduating students to complete graduation-level written tasks and oral presentations, known as PBATs (performance-based assessment tasks), including an analytic essay on literature, a social studies research paper, an extended or original science experiment, and problem-solving at higher levels of mathematics. There are thirty-eight high schools in this consortium. Students must also take and pass the English/Language Arts Regents Examination, which is required of all students in New York State. However, it is the only Regents exam required. Schools may add on additional PBAT tasks, for example, in the creative arts, foreign language, and supervised internships.

The PBATs use common scoring rubrics both for the academic competencies as well as the personal success skills. In addition, outside evaluators sit in on the assessment panels to ensure validity and reliability in scoring. The policy implications for such advanced practices in CBE are significant when compared to the traditional examination and grade point requirements found in most traditional school district policies relevant to high school graduation. Therefore, revisiting and revising policies related to local assessment, grading, and determining **competency** are essential.

Key Policy Decisions: Guidelines for Developing a Competency-Based Body of Evidence (BOE)

Determining whether or not students have met competency-based (CB) requirements for grade advancement or graduation requires a fresh look at the evidence students will produce (e.g., products, performances, self-reflections on learning) to demonstrate their learning. This is very different from a policy establishing a minimum number of Carnegie units acquired by each student taking required courses (and exams) during Grades 9–12. These policy decisions must be grounded in *what each student has learned* during Grades 9–12 and what types of "evidence" will demonstrate learning.

The following are four common approaches a CB school district might choose to use in making decisions regarding whether or not students have met **proficiency** (or proficiency-based graduation requirements [PBGRs]). These approaches are far more complex than counting courses passed and averaging grades! In the end, you may find that a combination of methods works best for reporting student progress in your school.

- **Standard setting**: Standard setting is typically used when there is one assessment, such as a state assessment or a common local benchmark assessment (e.g., end-of-course exam). Educators collaboratively review scores from the range of scores generated by the test and then set "cut" scores to denote score ranges for performance levels, such as *Advanced*, *Proficient*, *Approaching*, and *Basic*. Using this method for every CB assessment would be too time consuming and unmanageable. However, standard setting could be included as part of a school district's overall approach to CB decision-making when all students might be taking a small number of **common assessments** in academic courses that will be included in a larger BOE.

- **Mathematical**: Mathematical methods use a common formula to aggregate assessment results (from multiple assessments) on performance indicators over time. While this approach may save time, the precision and accuracy in truly describing student learning over time is at best questionable. We *do not* recommend using a mathematical formula.

- **Moderation**: The moderation method is used in Queensland, Australia's, school-based assessment program wherein schools are responsible for collecting evidence of student work, judging that work based on the standards, and submitting sample work to external moderation panels (Allen, 2012). This method involves using a generalized (common) rubric with a representative collection of **portfolios** that include some common assessment tasks and some unique pieces of evidence. A "moderation" panel then creates sample portfolios that represent different performance levels (at, above, and below proficiency). The sample portfolios are used by teacher teams for calibration purposes when comparing their students' portfolios to the exemplar portfolios. Your school might consider using this method for one aspect of CB decision-making if students are required to develop digital portfolios, create capstone projects, or complete graduation exhibitions.

- **Body of evidence**: A body of evidence contains student work samples—some common and some unique—and other evidence of learning (e.g., assessment data using evidence-based grading, test scores, mentor feedback, student reflection pieces).

Evidence is more precise than any formula.

—*Pathways to Proficiency*
(Gobble et al., 2017, p. 129)

Collective
Teacher Efficacy
(Effect Size = 1.39)

Student work samples are placed and sometimes replaced in the student's individual BOE, which might be organized using digital portfolios. BOE guidelines are created as to what types of evidence, what quality of evidence, and what to look for in determining that there is "sufficient" evidence of proficient performance. Questions such as, "Does this only represent the student's best work, or is it representative of typical and consistent work over time?" must be answered and clarified in the CB policy. Once a common set of criteria has been defined (such as in a holistic rubric or portfolio scoring guide), teams of educators review BOE evidence to make decisions that will be reported to parents and students. We recommend starting your policy discussions using a BOE approach and regularly verify its validity and effectiveness.

Establishing policies and guidelines about CB decisions will take collaboration time and some "experimentation" with feedback loops built in to make guidelines defensible to parents and community, fair and equitable for all students, and meaningful yet manageable for staff. Your policies will be based on your profile of the graduate and articulate how the CBE system supports that vision. These characteristics are critical for systemwide consistency and objective CB reporting:

1. The agreed-upon intended content, rigor, and scope of CB learning goals

2. How competencies will be assessed and *be accessible* to all students

3. What types of evidence and work products may be included in a student's BOE (e.g., replacement assessments, student-designed assessments)

4. How much evidence will be considered to be "sufficient" in determining proficiency

STOP AND REFLECT

What are your current policies for grading and reporting? Are they consistently implemented throughout the grades and across content areas?

_____

_____

_____

_____

_____

A district grading policy for CBE should be in place for all teachers to (objectively) assign grades in the same way. Teacher to teacher, an understanding of evidence-based grading practices[1] and how to develop and use valid CB assessments and determine proficiency are critical. This means that personal grading practices must be set aside and replaced with research-based approaches that eliminate teacher-to-teacher variability and subjectivity in grading (adapted from Colby, 2017). Holistic proficiency scales (see Figure 2.1), developed collaboratively by teacher teams, provide guidance in how to examine evidence across multiple student work samples (e.g., performance assessment tasks, group projects, student reflections) to determine not only a grade but to describe student performance in relation to meeting one or more competencies (e.g., _Advanced, Beyond, Competent, Not Yet_, or _Insufficient Work Shown_). These grading categories do not include failing grades. Instead, the grade may suggest that more evidence—and probably more strategic support—is needed in order for the student to demonstrate competency.

Figure 2.1 illustrates a sample holistic proficiency scale with connections among the local assessment and grading policies, the decision-making holistic rubric, and the underlying role of performance scales and CB performance assessments

---

[1] Chapter 3 addresses evidence-based grading and assessment development in depth.

FIGURE 2.1 Sample Holistic Proficiency Scale

Local Assessment and Grading Policies describe the types of assessments that assess both basic skills and deeper learning.[2] They also provide guidance in how to interpret student work samples. Policies are consistent with using student evidence to assign evidence-based grades.

⬇

Sample Holistic Proficiency Scale:
It describes levels of performance based on multiple pieces of evidence, not grade averages.

Report Card Grade	A	B	C	NYC	IWS
Performance Level	Advanced Competency	Beyond Competent	Competent	Not Yet Competent	Insufficient Work Shown
Performance Descriptor	Competency-based performance assessment scores demonstrate that the student can analyze and synthesize course content within the discipline and can initiate and extend understanding to other disciplines or real-world contexts.	Competency-based performance assessment scores are a mixture of evidence of *Competent* and some *Advanced Competency* Scores.	Competency-based performance assessment scores consistently demonstrate both basic skills and the application and transfer of essential content and skills.	There is evidence of many basic skills mastered. Competency-based performance assessment scores are inconsistent in demonstrating the ability to apply and transfer essential content and skills.	There is insufficient evidence in the student's body of evidence to determine proficiency.

Competency-Based Performance Assessments assess deeper learning (competencies) and incorporate multiple standards. Assessments are designed based on levels described in performance scales for each competency.[3]

used to generate evidence. The ultimate goal is to have well-designed holistic proficiency scales that can be used across content areas and grade levels.

2.2 ORGANIZATIONAL SHIFT 2: LEADERSHIP

Traditional leadership structures, roles, and responsibilities in K–12 education generally follow a hierarchical structure, which has not changed over many decades.

---

[2] Developing local assessment policies and assessment philosophies is discussed later in Chapter 2.

[3] Chapter 3 describes in detail how to develop CB performance scales and performance assessments.

What we question now about these structures is the fact that leaders and roles within traditional education settings may not be appropriate or effective in supporting competency education. Part of the transformation to CBE requires new vision for what is needed to lead the transformation to CBE. How traditional leadership roles will change as the school transforms is a fundamental question that should be addressed early in the process.

Pittsfield Middle/High School in New Hampshire developed a robust extended learning opportunities (ELO) program to offer a more varied learning opportunity for their small student body. As more and more students engaged in these community-based learning opportunities, it became clear that they needed a school-based coordinator to build community relationships and oversee each student's academic progress in these competency-based learning experiences. They did not have the ability to add staff, so they thoughtfully reexamined the role of their school counselors. This began a deep study into how the functions of their schools were networked. With that realization, they redefined leadership roles and responsibilities and created new job descriptions that cross-walked the functions among the leadership team. Today, the school no longer has a principal because most of the traditional duties of the principal were subsumed in new school protocols. Problem-solving in the school is handled by faculty and interested parties using a logic model process. The important governance of the school is handled through a student-led, community-based council. The administrative team now includes a director of student services, a director of college and career readiness, a dean of instruction, a dean of maintenance, and a director of intervention.

How one school chooses to handle its leadership structure may not be a model for every school. However, the many years that it takes to transform to CBE cannot be owned by one single visionary leader. Administrators change, teachers move on—what holds the transformation process together? Teachers. Teachers doing this work every day alongside administrators create a pace and understanding for the work that is sustained as leaders and staff members change over time (Coburn, 2003). Formally raising the traditional role of teacher to teacher-leaders in this process is critical to successful implementation of CBE. There are new and emerging roles for teachers beyond the role of a traditional classroom teacher. Some recent teacher roles emerging in support of CBE include competency education coaches at different levels (elementary, middle, and high school), communications directors, ELO coordinators, and community engagement coordinator positions.

STOP AND REFLECT

Who are the CBE leaders in your district? What new roles would you like to create as you move forward?

_____

_____

_____

_____

2.3 ORGANIZATIONAL SHIFT 3: PROFESSIONAL CULTURE

Typically, in traditional education systems, professional culture reflects a top-down hierarchy with little collaborative decision-making at the staff or student level. Professional development that is offered is often directed through the central office through whole-group training. The theme of the training throughout a school year is generally determined by the central office, leaving many experienced teachers within the district with the sense that a new superintendent brings along new initiatives, and when the superintendent leaves, a new initiative is begun with the new person. In districts with frequent changes in leadership, teachers are left weary, having to switch priorities in their teaching. Such an approach to the professional workplace culture simply can't support the time and professional learning at all levels of the system that is necessary for a move to CBE that requires thoughtful planning over a period of years.

Like our students who come to their learning with their individual assets and liabilities, so do our teachers have their own professional experiences they bring to their instructional roles. Each teacher has assets and liabilities that are likewise unique. Learning new instructional strategies that support CBE is not a top-down, whole-group learning experience. Moving to learner-centered teaching strategies, new approaches to assessment and grading, and understanding the competency framework is learning that is done by each teacher based on what she or he knows, current practices, and what may need to be learned. And, as with most learning, it should be socialized by teachers working together collaboratively. The traditional workday schedules in education support the work of providing time for a single teacher to prepare for one classroom of students. Today's schoolhouse is very different. We have been calling on teachers to do so much more than what the fixed schedules ask of them. If we want our teachers to design and prototype new learning opportunities for their students, shouldn't we provide this work time as part of their school day, allowing them to work together? There is great power when a grade-level team has control of their time during the day so that they can flexibly group students and allocate time for project-based learning, provide student supports and interventions, and advance their own collaborative work needed to support their learning designs for their students. The shift for school leaders—and this includes teachers—is to create a new and better professional culture that reorganizes the time resources during the workday so that teachers can collaborate.

One strategy that enables a shift in professional work culture is to create a master schedule that is based on student needs and not the needs of the adults in the building. This is a courageous step to take. When creating new schedules, we suggest providing phase-in time as the year progresses, because you will undoubtedly find things you want to tweak over and over again. The traditional notion of creating a schedule in the summer that stays in place for a whole school year is unnecessary and impractical until you have many of your system's CB components solidly in place. Any alternative scheduling approaches you experiment with must consider ways to encourage teacher collaboration and flexible student grouping as you work to redesign how you use time and resources. Remember that scheduling changes are unique to your system and will require collaborative planning as well as giving yourself permission to do it over when you figure out what will work better. We suggest taking an approach such as Stack and VanderEls use (2017, pp. 133–147) to guide collegial discussion and ongoing planning.

When moving to CBE, school roles and functions must also evolve. However, change is often met with inertia, resistance, and barriers. Whether this change is embraced heartily or is met with negativity, it is experienced by all shareholders. Here is what Jillian and Joe experienced at MST.

Leaders Letting Go

Our excitement about competency-based education and all of the possibilities it held was not without challenge. Our excitement was challenged by parent, student, and staff misconceptions about the

(Continued)

(Continued)

tenets of competency-based education. There was systemic oppression regarding a legacy learner management system, funding, infrastructure, and technology, to name a few. Our community was simply not prepared to embrace the possibility of change.

We were on an island. With limited resources, we had to create ways to adapt our CBE practice for our students. Not the least of immediate issues were adapting to student pace, shifting from old learning paradigms, and pushback from often the most vocal group . . . the naysayers. With support from our principal, we were given the trust and freedom to learn how to practice CBE alongside of our students. We asked students to take more responsibility for and engage more thoroughly in their education. In return, we committed to let go.

—Jillian and Joe

💭 STOP AND REFLECT

When and how do teachers and leaders engage in reflection? How do colleagues know what people are thinking and feeling as systems move through stages of transition?

_____

_____

_____

_____

_____

2.4 ORGANIZATIONAL SHIFT 4: PROFESSIONAL LEARNING

Most teacher advancement is based on credits earned as part of degree programs. But how do we recognize teachers moving forward on their own to learn the latest teaching and learning strategies in CBE? These teachers have a passion they exercise daily with their learners, but they are often left unrewarded by their district's traditional methods of moving teachers forward on their compensation scales. As districts move from traditional education to CBE, so must there be accommodations within collective bargaining agreements. It is in the interest of all concerned to have teacher union representatives weigh in continually throughout the reform process. Partnering with teacher associations along the way strengthens the work.

We must recognize that teachers are also learners and will need to explore new strategies and examples with their colleagues as they create a profile of the graduate and "reset" their thinking on the best way to "cover" curriculum in a CB school. Much like our students, when we ask our teachers to own their learning and we give them the time, resources, and guidance, they will own it. There are many resources for professional learning available without cost, including Learn Next (www.getinspired.2revolutions .net/explore), which is a toolbox of resources to transform teaching practices. Teams of teachers or individual teachers can customize their professional learning, creating their own learning progression in many CBE-related topics that include the following:

- Personalized learning

- Competency-based learning

- Deeper learning

- Tech-enabled learning

- Learner agency

- Assessment for learning

- Broader definition of success

- Safe and supportive environments

- Using data

- Powerful planning

How do we engage all staff in new learning? If school leaders are serious in creating the professional environment to provide teachers both the time and risk-free environment, schedules need to change. Lack of time for learning and collaboration is a real barrier to this work and one that requires courage from administrators to lead this shift—moving from centralized, one-size-fits-all adult learning to a more powerful accelerator in how we ask the entire system to become learner-centered.

How can building-level administrators set aside their current building schedules based on adult preferences to move the learning time to one that allows teachers to work together to support student learning . . . whatever it takes.

STOP AND REFLECT

What would your school look like if it were learner-centered?

_____

_____

_____

_____

_____

2.5 DEVELOPING CBE ASSESSMENT POLICIES AND PRACTICES

Examining Your Current Local Assessment System (LAS)

In addition to determining guidelines for building a BOE for each student, the following is one of the first policy questions that school and district leadership teams must address as the organization shifts to CBE: What is already in place systemwide (assessment philosophy, competency-based assessments, protocols and quality controls, etc.), and what is needed to support the changes we're thinking of making in order to assess competencies with fidelity? Often, teachers will discover that when they begin to use competency-based performance assessments, there are few or no local assessment policies or practices in place that support teacher collaboration time for developing and validating the quality of assessments or for examining and evaluating student work products.

Four critical components make up high-quality comprehensive **local assessment systems** (Hess, 2018), listed here:

1. Technically sound assessments of academic achievement and assessments of district-based goals for learning (e.g., community service)

2. A theory of action that illustrates how curricular programs, instruction, assessments, and assessment data interact

3. Adequate protocols, professional development, and leadership supporting implementation of assessment principles and practices

4. Explicit and well-coordinated mechanisms (feedback loops) for managing assessments, assessment results, and addressing student and program needs

Leadership teams can use a protocol developed by Hess (2018, Tool #28) to guide discussions as they examine their beliefs about what to assess, how (and how often) to assess, and how to use assessments and assessment data. Now renumbered for ease of use with this book, our **CBE Tool 2** contains five indicators of a comprehensive assessment system with related discussion questions for examining the quality and comprehensiveness of your assessment system.

STOP AND REFLECT

Review the discussion questions in **CBE Tool 2.** Which question would be a good starting point for your school to reexamine assessment policies, and why?

_____

_____

_____

_____

_____

Indicators of a *Comprehensive* Local Assessment System (Hess, 2018)

1. The LAS is comprehensive: It includes varied assessment formats with high technical quality, supports professional learning and leadership, and describes well-coordinated feedback mechanisms for use and management of assessments and assessment data.

2. The competency-based assessment philosophy is supported by coherent and well-articulated policies and practices.

3. Communications with stakeholders identify how learning expectations (competencies) for all students relate to assessment types, purposes, and uses.

FIGURE 2.2 Cutaway of CBE Tool 2: Discussion Questions—Examining Local Assessment Systems

CBE Tool 2	Discussion Questions—Examining Local Assessment Systems (LAS)

LAS Indicator 1: *Do we include these key components in our local assessment system? How comprehensive is our system?*

To what degree does our system . . .

- include technically sound assessments of academic achievement and explicit or shared district-based goals for learning (e.g., proficiencies/competencies, transferable skills, community service);

- illustrate how assessments and assessment data interact;

- provide adequate protocols, professional development, and leadership regarding implementation of assessment principles and practices; and

- establish explicit and well-coordinated mechanisms (feedback loops) for managing use of assessments, assessment data or results, and using data to address individual student needs?

Aces (what's useful and relevant right now):

Spaces (where do we need work; what are the gaps):

LAS Indicator 2: *Is our (proficiency-based) assessment philosophy supported by coherent policy and practices?*

4. Processes ensure that assessments and what is included in each student's body of evidence are of high quality.

5. A comprehensive district implementation plan (multiyear action plan) includes supports and strategies for short- and long-term implementation goals.

Collective Teacher Efficacy (Effect Size = 1.39)

While CBE Tool 2 is designed to guide the thinking and action planning by school leadership teams, an easy way to begin your policy discussion with teachers is to have a whole-school brainstorming session to generate individual beliefs about the role of assessment in a CBE system. Before using the guiding discussion questions in CBE Tool 2, we generally begin this brainstorm by placing three large charts in the room. (Each high school department, content area, or grade level has a set of charts.) The headings on charts would look something like the ones that follow. We've added some of the typical responses that we've seen when working with faculties. Think about how you would respond to these three focus questions.

WHAT should we assess?	HOW and HOW OFTEN should we assess?	What are my beliefs about WHY we use assessments?
Sample responses: Skills, procedures Oral, written, demonstration-type products Concepts Problem-solving, critical thinking Transfer to novel situations Deeper thinking (DOK[4] levels 3 or 4) tasks	**Sample responses:** Age-appropriate assessments Observation, conferencing, unit tests, problem-solving performance tasks Peer and self-assessment, self- reflection Allow for retakes Student choices and self- or group-designed projects	**Sample responses:** Formative assessment drives learning and instructional decisions. Students are involved (student-led conferences). Assessment FOR learning is what will create student growth. Common assessments provide checks in system for agreed-upon expectations. How we currently grade needs to change.

Teachers in each group (by content area or grade level) write one idea on each chart. If a person agrees with an idea already on the chart, he or she simply puts a check mark after it. It will quickly become apparent where there is agreement and where there may be some conflicts within or across groups. The following are a sampling of actual comments generated by different high school departments answering similar questions.

MATH

Our Assessment Beliefs

- Promote growth mindset
- Mastery of content
- Should provide opportunities for what is assessed on college-readiness tests (SAT, etc.)

What should we assess?

Skills, conceptual understanding, ability to apply, cumulative knowledge

What should grades reflect?

Mastery of content, ability to transfer

SOCIAL STUDIES

What should we assess?

- Authentic learning
- Application of content knowledge
- Development of citizenship skills
- Collaboration with others (local and beyond)
- Integration of technology
- Connecting past—present events, primary sources

Balance between skills, transfer, content, analysis

(Continued)

[4] Depth of knowledge (DOK) is used to illustrate examples of deeper understanding. DOK and the Hess Cognitive Rigor Matrices are used in Chapter 3 to guide development of performance scales and performance assessments; see also Glossary and Appendix B.

(Continued)

WORLD LANGUAGE

What should we assess?

- Build student portfolios
- Measure growth in student's interpretation (reading, listening) of language, interpersonal skills, and presentation skills (writing, speaking)

Hold all students accountable for similar expectations districtwide and analyze student work districtwide.

💭 STOP AND REFLECT

What are your beliefs and values about assessment? Is there a shared understanding in your school about WHY and HOW we use assessments?

_____

_____

_____

_____

_____

Ideas generated from the school staff and school leaders can then be analyzed and used to draft a local CBE assessment philosophy. Taking the time to discuss and collaboratively write a brief narrative to clarify what you assess, how you assess, and for what purposes you assess is well worth the time. It sets the course for all future assessment work, professional learning activities around assessment literacy, and policy development related to use of assessments and assessment results.

Figure 2.3 provides an example of what a local assessment philosophy might include. As you can see by this example, an assessment policy does not have to be long, but it should capture what is most important in terms of your beliefs about the purposes for assessment. Then, it can be used to guide your assessment decisions and practices in the future.

After drafting a local assessment policy, school leaders can then use the guiding questions in **CBE Tool 2** to begin to determine what specific assessment practices are currently working well (the "Aces") and what is missing or needs to be

FIGURE 2.3 Sample Local Assessment Policy Statement

A Sample Local Assessment Policy Statement

Philosophy

At the _____ School, we are committed to using a variety of assessment tools to gather evidence of growth and learning. Assessment helps us to know our students and guide our instruction. Our goal is that our students will become critical thinkers, global citizens, and directors of their own learning pathways. Students are encouraged to reflect on their growth using consistent, quality feedback from teachers, peers, and outside experts as appropriate.

Rationale

- We will implement research-based best practices in assessment.

- We will align a schoolwide competency-based framework with our assessment practices and tools.

- Students will use assessment data to reflect on their learning and set goals for their own growth.

Objectives of Our Assessment System

- Support and encourage student learning by providing feedback on the learning process, as well as products of learning.

- Promote a deeper understanding of each subject area's content by encouraging student inquiry set in real-world contexts.

- Develop global skills and apply them in students' daily real-world activities.

- Promote positive student attitudes toward learning and provide opportunities for student reflection and growth.

- Assist students' development of critical thinking and self-evaluation skills and provide them with opportunities to self-direct their learning and inquiry.

- Employ assessment practices that are sensitive to cultural and linguistic diversity.

Learning Is at the Heart of Assessment

Assessment allows teachers to effectively modify or accelerate learning based on how the student performs. Our goal is to meet students where they are in the learning process and to close gaps, should the need arise. Instructors will use two primary types of assessment: formative and performance.

Formative assessments provide information needed to adjust teaching and learning while they are taking place. Formative assessments are **for** learning; teachers can select from a variety of tool (e.g., observations, Socratic seminar participation, reflections, journals, self- and peer assessments, homework, rough drafts, research outlines) in order to measure progress and determine supports that may be needed while learning is taking place.

Performance-based assessments allow each student to demonstrate mastery of the specific standards integrated with multiple skills and are scored with multicriteria rubrics. Performance tasks are developed for each unit and are intended to be challenging (DOK 3 or DOK 4). These assessments **of** learning provide evidence for evaluating individual and group achievement through an assortment of tools (e.g., exams, performance tasks, individual and group projects, presentations, internships).

TABLE 2.1 Summary Comments Generated by Team Members at Ridgewood High School Using CBE Tool 2: Discussion Questions—Examining Local Assessment Systems

LAS Indicator	Our "Aces"—What's Working Well	Our "Spaces"—What We Still Need to Work On
1 LAS Is Comprehensive	Students at Ridgewood High School use technology on a daily basis to enhance their learning. Through the emphasis of developing 21st-century skills, students are driven to gain real-world experience that will prepare them for college and careers. When the iPad was introduced to students at Ridgewood High School, teachers immediately noticed much higher levels of engagement as well as the opportunity to easily implement project-based learning. Through employing project-based learning, teachers are able to personalize instruction to meet all students' needs and ability levels. Part of project-based learning is allowing students the opportunity to demonstrate what they have learned through various applications to an authentic audience.	The teachers need to find the time to discuss and use assessment data, as well as use feedback loops for meaningful use of assessments and data.
2 Assessment Philosophy	Ridgewood teachers have worked together in developing a learning progression for the academic, innovation, and life skills our community values.	We are working on making the learning progression non–content specific, so they can be used in any class or experiences.
3 Expectations and Assessment Types	Our teachers have completed the Buck Institute PBL training for the last two years. They could use that training along with the learning progressions to create learning experiences and assessments.	Our teachers still need to use a wider range of assessments on a regular basis. PBL shouldn't be done only once a semester; it should be the most used way of assessing students. We need to communicate our expectations with the students, parents, and the community.
4 Body of Evidence	Our team has created an agreed-upon plan and performance scales that guide assessment development.	We need to determine how many pieces of evidence are needed to show mastery. And we need more checks for reliability and collaboration of assessments.
5 Implementation Plan	When designing professional development experiences for teachers and other members of the certified staff, who knows better about their areas of interest and growth opportunities than the teachers themselves? Over a decade ago, Ridgewood implemented the teacher-led Professional Development Committee (PDC) in an effort to support the needs of individuals and their professional goals. In fact, to ensure equity of voice for our teachers, members of the teaching staff remain on the planning committee to ensure their needs are met. Teachers actually developed the idea of creating specialized new-teacher meetings, and one of the first duties is to provide a multitude of professional development opportunities for iPad training and implementation in the classroom that exceeds well beyond substitution and ensures student-created projects that allow them to use their critical-thinking skills mixed with their innovative ideas.	We need to do a better job of documenting our work and circling back. We have been doing a good job of meeting students where they are, but not the best job of meeting teachers where they are.

Source: Used with permission from Lisa Balata and Eric Lasky.

eliminated or eventually replaced (the "Spaces"). Your collective responses will lead to the development of an initial CBE implementation action plan. The questions in **CBE Tool 2** will be used and revisited multiple times over several school years while designing and implementing the CB system. Most schools create plans that phase in various CB components by year, and often by content area. For example, all content area teachers might participate in professional learning in the same school year to better understand the WHY and the WHAT of competency-based education. Implementing the HOW will have to be done at a slower pace, with development and review of competencies laying the foundation for developing CB performance assessments in each content area. Some schools choose to work on content-based competencies first (e.g., ELA and math in the first year, science and social studies in the next year, and remaining subject areas in the third year). Other schools begin with competencies that all teachers will begin to develop in the same school year, such as ones addressing **social and emotional learning (SEL)**. There really is more than one way to approach CB implementation and development of new CB assessments. Professional learning and collaboration are integral to each phase. Good advice might be to go slowly at first so you can go faster and deeper later on. (For more guidance on using this tool, see also *A Local Assessment Toolkit to Promote Deeper Learning*, Hess, 2018 pp. 363–366.)

Table 2.1 shows a summary of comments that Erik Lasky and Lisa Balata, administrators at Ridgewood High School, in Norridge, Illinois, generated with their CBE team members using **CBE Tool 2**.

3 Making Shifts in Teaching and Learning Structures

Given that there are different types of learning goals, we need an associated variety of assessment types to gather valid evidence of learning. Think of assessment as analogous to photography. Like the results on a test, a picture can be informative; however, no single photo can provide a complete portrayal of a situation. To continue the analogy, what we need is a photo album of evidence on student learning, not a snapshot—a collection of multiple measures, appropriately aligned to different types of learning outcomes that matter.

—Jay McTighe (2018)

CBE Requires Three Major Shifts in Teaching–Learning Structures

1. Establishing Rigorous Goals for Learning (Competencies)

2. Using a Range of Performance Assessment Types

3. Measuring and Reporting Progress Based on Evidence of Learning

Now that we've explored the four organizational shifts that school leaders must focus on, we dive into the important shifts in teaching and learning practices found in competency-based (CB) schools. These structural shifts begin with how we establish rigorous goals for student learning (called competencies or proficiencies) and then consider how we assess more complex and personalized learning tasks (using a range of performance assessment types). Finally, we examine the shifts in how teachers approach grading (using *evidence-based* grading) and CB reporting (determining whether or not students have demonstrated mastery of multiple competencies). Any one of these structural shifts can take several years for educators to fully implement, so a multiyear, incremental phase-in plan is recommended. With any approach you choose, part of the plan needs to also include professional learning opportunities and collaboration time for school staff. Remember, competency-based education (CBE) is a learner-centered system in which even the adults will always be learning!

The two most promising entry points to making these shifts are to either begin with developing (or adopting and adapting) competencies or learning how to create and use CB performance tasks that will assess the more complex learning described in competencies. It's almost impossible to shift your school's grading and reporting practices before the first two gears of establishing rigorous learning goals and designing assessments begin to shift. For example, Gobble, Onuscheck, Reibel, and Twadell (2017) describe a thoughtful three-year implementation process for the shift to evidence-based grading in their school. Likewise, Sanborn Regional High School in New Hampshire also built its competency-based grading and reporting system over three years (Stack, 2012). We suggest that you go slowly at first. Lay the groundwork for what will be learned and assessed—and how it will be assessed—before tackling evidence-based grading and competency-based reporting.

3.1 ESTABLISHING RIGOROUS GOALS FOR LEARNING: COMPETENCIES

Whether your school will be developing competencies or adopting and adapting competencies that another group has created, it is important to consider how these broader and more rigorous competencies (and assessments of them) will—by necessity—shift instructional practices and ultimately how learning happens over time. It is our experience that each shift requires teachers to examine their current instructional, assessment, and grading practices against new models of assessment and student engagement (e.g., are students reflecting on their processes and products of learning; are students making choices to direct their learning). These analyses help everyone to connect their school's WHY with an actionable plan of HOW to accomplish it.

> ← Teacher Clarity:
> Expectations
> for Learning
> (Effect Size = 0.75)

CBE Tool 1A (Figure 3.1) provides a framework for school teams to examine where your school is now in having a K–12 continuum of competencies that require students to transfer essential knowledge, skills, and dispositions as they advance across the grades to graduation from high school. (The full version of CBE Tools 1A–1E is found in Appendix A.)

There are two kinds of competencies; some schools start with a focus on academics, while others choose a more personalized approach as their starting point. **Academic competencies** are drawn from established college- and career-readiness standards and course content, while **personal success skill competencies** are skills shaped locally using a combination of workplace habits and self-management skills (e.g., goal setting). Personal success skills can also include skills for interacting effectively with others (e.g., developing empathy and collaboration skills) and self-reflection skills. These skills are sometimes referred to

FIGURE 3.1 Cutaway of CBE Tool 1A: Analysis of K–12 Competencies Development

CBE Tool 1A	Core Components of Competency-Based Education: CBE Readiness Tool			
Component 1: Competencies Develop a K–12 continuum of rigorous competencies describing how students will apply or transfer essential knowledge, skills, and dispositions across the grades leading to graduation.				
Focus	Phase 1: Initiating	Phase 2: Emerging	Phase 3: Implementing	Where is your school now? What are possible next steps?
Leadership	Graduation requirements are policy driven. Curriculum and course offerings are used to develop scope and sequences by course or content area.	Articulated profile of a graduate (POG) is developed with input from staff and shared with community stakeholders. Graduation requirements, curriculum, college and career pathways are not yet aligned to POG.	Articulated profile of a graduate (POG) is developed with input from staff and community stakeholders. Graduation requirements are clearly articulated and integrated into curriculum and college and career pathways.	
Instruction and Assessment	Learning outcomes are clear and articulated by course or grade level. Instructional design emphasizes application of knowledge and skills described in state-adopted standards.	Learning outcomes are clear and articulated by course and standards-based curriculum. K–12 academic competencies are adopted but not incorporated into instruction or assessment design.	Learning outcomes emphasize competencies that include application and creation of knowledge, along with the development of important personal skills and dispositions. Instruction and assessments support and measure competencies.	
Learner Culture	Interpersonal skills are expressed as personal behaviors. Students are aware of these skills and monitored by teachers.	Interpersonal and intrapersonal competencies are developing and evidenced by students when they monitor and reflect on these skills.	Interpersonal, intrapersonal, and learning competencies include explicit, measurable, transferable learning objectives that empower students to have input into their learning path.	
Organizational Structures	The system is driven by "seat time" and whole-class instruction with some differentiation and remediation. Departments and grade-level teams with content expertise guide the delivery of instruction.	The structure and schedule allow for teacher collaboration and flexible grouping of students. School structures and systems are developing new pathways for students to advance to the next level of learning.	Structures and scheduling support collaboration in creating multiple pathways and academies that integrate standards and skills into core competencies aligned to career readiness standards and postsecondary expectations.	

STOP AND REFLECT

CBE can provide the design for integrating both academic and personal success skills. You may want to refer to CBE Tools 1A or 1B to respond to this question: How are you currently monitoring and measuring knowledge, skills, and dispositions for your learners?

_____

_____

_____

_____

_____

_____

in the literature as **social and emotional learning (SEL)** competencies and tend to vary more than academic competencies from school to school.

Once your school decides on an approach—development or adoption and adaptation of competencies—the competency design team will engage in several iterative processes to guarantee the quality and coherence of implementation described in this chapter. These collaborative processes include the following:

- Analyzing the K–12 competency continuum (CBE Tool 4)

- Analyzing the intended learning and rigor described in each competency (CBE Tool 3, CBE Tool 5, and the Hess Cognitive Rigor Matrices #1–#5D)

- Creating performance scales for each competency (CBE Tool 6)

- Designing CB assessments (CBE Tool 7) and embedding them within planned instruction (CBE Tool 8)

- Validating CB assessments (CBE Tools 9–10) and scoring rubrics (CBE Tool 11)

To support this work, Appendix C includes resources with examples of model competencies, and Appendices A and B have downloadable tools described throughout the book.

Academic Competencies

In traditional educational settings, academic content is defined by state-adopted standards, structured by content area and framed by grade level. Often, a standards-based curriculum is paced to the structure of the quarters and semesters of a traditional school year. A common profile of the teaching delivery for standards is a front-facing teacher who moves through units of study in whole-class fashion, with some degree of differentiation. Some of the most difficult long-term implementation shifts when moving to CBE are shifts in the structures of teaching in competency-based classrooms. Competencies move past standards in demanding that students show that they can transfer or apply the content and skills the standards demand. Shifting from content and skills acquisition to performance using content and skills is monumental. This instructional shift depends on establishing high-quality academic competencies and professional collaboration to create performance scales and assessment tasks that produce evidence to show whether a learner has met proficiency criteria demanded by the competency. A traditional "stand-and-deliver" worksheet approach to content acquisition simply falls short of what students will need for future college and career experiences. It takes time, professional learning, and opportunities for teacher collaboration during the school day to generate, practice, and study the instructional changes that support engaged student-centered learning in a competency-based learning environment.

Since academic competencies must articulate K–12 goals for learning, it is best to design them as a continuum in spite of the fact that individual teachers will only be using them at one grade level or grade span. For example, if a high school wants to start the competency journey, it needs to do so with a backward glance at what these competencies look like at earlier grades leading up to the high school courses. High school alone cannot be solely responsible for college and career readiness; therefore, it is important for high school teachers to develop their portion of the competency expectations, conferencing with elementary and middle school teachers. This vertical alignment work is critical for systemic success in the earliest planning stages.

When teachers at a school approach the work of creating their academic course competencies, not everyone needs to be involved in the process. The days of asking all teachers to sit to write curriculum—or now, competencies—is long over. Some teachers really enjoy this type of work and should work together in small groups to generate a "Version 1.0" of prototype competency statements for input from and discussion with their peers. We are fortunate to now have many groups that have created high-quality K–12 competencies, so it is possible to adopt and adapt published sets of competencies to further customize them at the local level. One example of high-quality academic competencies is the New Hampshire Model Competencies, created by representative groups of teachers in different content areas. While it is not mandatory for New Hampshire schools to adopt these competencies, doing so saves schools time because they can immediately begin to work with them.

Personal Success Skills Competencies

In traditional education, the personal skills reported out on a report card are locally chosen, often based on what teachers deem to be important for the particular grade level. These personal skills—sometimes called soft skills, dispositions, or study habits—are generally given a "rating" by the teacher. One can't really call it a grade because it is rarely documented systematically and generally not recorded over the semester (only put on the report card by the teacher at grading time). Such ratings tell little or nothing about how each personal characteristic is developing over time or what evidence (if any) is behind the ratings. Often, subjective ratings such as these are defined differently by different teachers. At the "other end" of the report card is the parent who just wants to know his or her child got good grades and is doing OK.

In the CBE classroom, these personal skills are intentionally built into teaching and learning every day. They are modeled by teachers and practiced by students. Personal success skills are drawn from the profile of the graduate and used by the student all along the way, as part of his or her personalized learning plan. When teachers develop and use **performance tasks**, they draw on one or more of these personal skills to incorporate into the performance expectations for students. For example, as part of completing an assessment task, learners regularly reflect on how (or how effectively) they are using a particular skill or work habit (such as collaboration, self-reflection) in their learning. This becomes the evidence a student has at hand for personal goal setting and progress monitoring, thus ensuring that these skills are documented and reflected on so that they continue to develop over time. What we do know from research about learning is that academic learning is deepened when skills for developing independence as a learner (e.g., metacognition and reflection, time management, critical thinking) are employed within academic learning tasks (Hess & Gong, 2014). As educators, we must design tasks and teach these skills all along the K–12 continuum of learning. As such, these skills are on a developmental continuum, not a fixed-age or grade-level performance expectation. (Resources with examples of personal success skills competencies can be found in Appendix C.)

← Teacher Clarity: Expectations for Learning (Effect Size = 0.75)

CBE Tool 1B (Figure 3.2) provides a framework for examining where your school is now in developing personal success skills competencies. (The full version of CBE Tools 1A–1E is found in Appendix A.)

FIGURE 3.2 Cutaway of CBE Tool 1B: Readiness Examination for Development of Personal Success Skills Competencies

CBE Tool 1B	Core Components of Competency-Based Education: CBE Readiness Tool			
Component 2: Personal Success Skills Dispositions, soft skills, and 21st century skills (critical thinking, problem-solving, collaboration, goal setting, etc.) articulate qualities that are essential for success in life and are integrated with academic learning.				
Focus	Phase 1: Initiating	Phase 2: Emerging	Phase 3: Implementing	Where is your school now? What are possible next steps?
Leadership	Current policies and practices (grading, discipline, etc.) lack an awareness of the importance of personal success skills in promoting academic success and overall well-being.	Policies and practices are aligned to the POG and revised to promote equity and personal learning skills in supporting students and staff.	Policies and practices reflect the POG and integrate personal success skills as indicators of competence for graduation.	
Instruction and Assessment	Student engagement and reflection opportunities are evidenced in some learning areas and situations.	Student engagement and reflection opportunities are being aligned to learning experiences and targeted personal success skills, leading to student goal setting and self-reflection.	Student engagement measures and reflection opportunities consistently monitor the learning experience, learning outcomes, and personal success skills.	
Learner Culture	Learning culture is teacher-centered and content-driven, where students are mostly compliant and passive learners. Personal success skills are not directly taught by teachers or consistently practiced by students.	Learning environments and interactions promote independent and collaborative learning opportunities for students to exercise voice and choice. Personal success skills are integrated with academics.	Learning environments and interactions are responsive to learner agency and are flexible in meeting students' learning needs, as articulated by the learners' goals and self-reflections. Learners emerge as confident and independent learners.	
Organizational Structures	Individual teacher grading practices sometimes emphasize different personal success skills (e.g., collaboration, study skills) when reporting on academic grades.	Personal success skills are aligned to the POG and identified school wide to promote learning for all students. School structures (team planning) are used to clarify a developmental continuum and disseminate common expectations.	School/district instructional delivery methods support the integration of personal success skills with academic learning. Educators co-design personalized learning activities and assessments consistent with the POG.	

> ### 💭 STOP AND REFLECT
>
> How do personal success skills reflect what might be included in the profile of the graduate (POG)? How might students integrate academic knowledge and skills with dispositions?
>
> _____
>
> _____
>
> _____
>
> _____

3.2 A RANGE OF PERFORMANCE ASSESSMENT TYPES

The No Child Left Behind (NCLB) era in education usurped a great deal of learning time in favor of preparing students for high-stakes tests that purportedly measured academic proficiency and ultimately ranked schools through various state-level reporting and accountability systems. What we do know now is that these large-scale tests can suck the joy out of both teaching and learning. Just ask students and teachers how they feel about these tests! One of the leverage points in moving to CBE is to have teachers take a fresh look at what it is that students need to know and do and how students need to prove that they have actually learned it. One "breakthrough" activity we've used is to simply put a well-written, rigorous competency before teachers and ask them how many ways they could ask students to demonstrate their knowledge. The next step is to develop one (or more) of these scenarios into a performance task that can generate the evidence a teacher needs to see in order to determine proficiency. Most educators will agree that this type of evidence collected over time is far more indicative of student learning. Yet the years of test prep and test taking have resulted in a distillation of local assessment strategies.

What Is a Performance Assessment?

Our everyday lives are filled with "authentic" **performance assessments**, such as making a cake, learning to ride a bike, getting a driver's license, or planning a family reunion. Unlike paper-and-pencil tests, performance assessments require the student to *do* something, not simply describe how to do it (e.g., swimming the length of the pool versus explaining how to swim the backstroke). With performance tasks, students understand the relevance of applying skills and concepts in a real-world situation (e.g., knowing that measuring accurately is important to the success of the cake). There is also an acknowledgment that multiple performance trials may be needed as students move from being a beginner to becoming proficient.

We'd probably agree that when students design and conduct a STEM (science, technology, engineering, mathematics) investigation or develop a capstone project, they are engaged in performance assessment. These examples require in-depth engagement with content, extended time and resources, and instruction along the way to help prepare students for designing and carrying them out. Sometimes, the instruction is accomplished with a community mentor or an internship outside of school. However, not all performance assessments need to take extended time or extensive teacher planning.

On a continuum from least to more complex performance assessments, capstones, extended learning tasks, and project-based learning live at the more complex end (see Figure 3.3). The final products of these multistage performance assessments probably developed with several smaller performance tasks embedded in them as the larger project evolved. Less complex performance assessments comprise the rest

FIGURE 3.3 The Performance Assessment Continuum

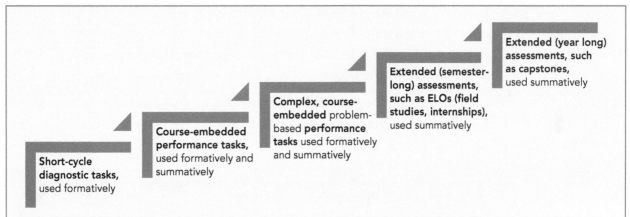

Short-cycle diagnostic tasks used formatively, such as running records in reading, "free writes" during a literacy block, or theater games that demonstrate acting techniques, do not take much time to administer, but they allow students to demonstrate subskills and concepts needed for more complex tasks. Because these tasks elicit clear and observable evidence, teachers can determine whether students are ready to integrate these skills into more cognitively demanding content or decide what additional scaffolding or instruction might be needed next. Tasks designed to be open-ended, rather than having correct answers, elicit thinking, reasoning, and misconceptions. This provides insights as to *why* students are confused or confirms that students are ready to move ahead, having mastered skills or concepts with less complex content.

Course-embedded performance tasks generally require one or more class periods to complete and are linked to ongoing instruction. Mathematics problem-solving activities, open-ended research prompts, and arts-based explorations are performance assessments that require students to apply multiple skills, strategies, and concepts in new ways. The cognitive demand for performance tasks can be reduced by using less-complex content or texts at first or allowing students to work together in small groups. Once students show that they can successfully complete a complex task with less-complex content, teachers can ask for the same skills and strategies to be employed with more challenging content or use of more sources. Course-embedded performance tasks can be used to provide formative, interim, or summative evidence within a unit of study or across a course as content and skills become more complex.

Extended multistage assessments may take as long as a semester or full year to research and develop, such as culminating group projects at the end of a unit of study (**project-based learning/PBL**), student-designed expeditionary learning opportunities (ELOs), community service projects, in-depth analyses of case studies in science or social studies, and capstone projects.

Source: Adapted from Hess, 2018, p. 133.

of the assessment continuum, informing instruction and building the foundation for deeper learning over time. We will revisit this assessment continuum in our discussion of performance scales later in the chapter.

Performance assessment invites critical and creative-productive thinking and often requires integration of more than one skill, concept, or strategy to reach a solution. Performance tasks also invoke opportunities for students to apply many personal success skills (e.g., collaboration, disciplined inquiry, academic perseverance). In our experience, professional collaboration in developing and using competency-based performance assessments is essential in moving away from "teaching to the test" and is far more accurate in determining student mastery. The CBE tools described later in the chapter were developed specifically for designing and validating CB assessments.

Assessment Form Follows Function

In CBE schools, students are required to transfer the knowledge and skills described in one or more academic areas (competencies) while integrating personal success skills, such as creativity, critical thinking, collaboration, or communication. CBE assessments document evidence of learning along a learning continuum (**learning progression**), providing important feedback to teachers that a student is either ready to move on to something more complex or needs more support and practice before advancing. "Teach them, test them, and move on" in a standards-based culture is now replaced in CBE by an assessment system that focuses on how learning develops over time, from being a novice to being an expert at something.

| Collective Teacher Efficacy (Effect Size = 1.39) |

→ **CBE Tool 1C** (Figure 3.4) provides a framework for examining where your school is now in developing competency-based assessments. (The full version of **CBE Tools 1A–1E** is found in Appendix A.)

☁ STOP AND REFLECT

What types of assessments are currently in use in your school? Do they include performance assessments? Does the use of assessments (e.g., in each content area) form a *continuum* for measuring progress toward deeper understanding?

_____

_____

_____

_____

FIGURE 3.4 Cutaway of CBE Tool 1C: Readiness Examination for Development of CB Performance Assessments

CBE Tool 1C	Core Components of Competency-Based Education: CBE Readiness Tool			
Component 3: Performance Assessments To determine a student's college and career readiness, the continuum of assessments rely on varied formats and multiple opportunities for students to demonstrate learning in authentic (real-world) tasks.				
Focus	**Phase 1: Initiating**	**Phase 2: Emerging**	**Phase 3: Implementing**	**Where is your school now? What are possible next steps?**
Leadership	Assessments of student learning are evidenced within courses and content areas and guided by policies (grading, graduation, etc.) and curriculum.	Policies support multiple and varied assessments, including rigorous assessments that capture student learning and mastery within a standards-based curriculum.	Timely, rigorous, and competency-based assessments capture student learning and mastery within and beyond the school-based environment.	
Instruction and Assessment	Standards are expressed as learning outcomes and are assessed in all content areas. Assessments are given to all students on the same day. Performance assessments are rarely used to capture evidence of deeper learning.	Rigorous competencies with learning outcomes are identified. Performance tasks are introduced as a part of a balanced assessment system used both formatively and summatively in most courses and content areas.	Rigorous competencies and learning outcomes are scaffolded and integrated across content areas. Performance assessments provide meaningful feedback and measure both academic and personal success skills to promote deeper learning.	
Learner Culture	Students are aware of the knowledge and skills that will be assessed. Students do not view most assessments as relevant to their learning because there is only one way to demonstrate what they know.	Performance assessments begin to align with the knowledge, skills, and dispositions that all students should acquire within and across content areas or courses. Learning can be demonstrated in a variety of ways.	Performance assessments align with academic and personal skills (e.g. collaboration, goal setting, social discourse). Learning is student driven and demonstrated in a variety of ways. Assessment evidence and feedback promote deeper learning.	
Organizational Structures	Grading methods are often limited by the student information systems (SIS). Grades are reported by traditional assessment types (e.g., exams, state assessments), methods (averaging), and timelines.	Teachers are given the time and tools to co-plan and co-develop common rigorous assessments, including performance tasks and projects.	District protocols guide consistent design and use of assessments and review of student evidence from competency-based performance assessments. Evidence informs instruction and student learning.	

3.3 EVIDENCE-BASED GRADING IN CBE SYSTEMS

Like most educators, we rarely questioned traditional (grading) practices despite what we know about growth in learning. These deeply embedded traditional practices continue to live in schools as they generalize descriptions of student performance and lump students into letter groups. "He's an A student" and "She's a C student" are comments that seem to have meaning in our schools, to our families, and in our judgements about what students know, understand, and do. These letter stamps operate like distinctions or labels. For better or worse, they denote each student's capacity and predict potential success. The truth is no one can really state what those letters stand for from classroom to classroom, school to school, or state to state.

—Gobble, Onuscheck, Reibel, and Twadell, 2017, p. 3

As education moved to the standards-based era, grading systems began emerging that more adequately reflected whether students met or exceeded the standards demanded by grade-level content. Much of the fair grading and reporting work heralded by Guskey and Brookhardt (2019), Marzano (2006), Wormeli, (2006, 2018), Feldman (2018), and O'Connor (2009) helped to shape the guidelines that schools use to rethink the traditional grading systems riddled with subjectivity and questionable ethical and fair grading practices. In CBE, however, meeting or exceeding an individual standard isn't enough to guarantee that students are proficient in reading or mathematics—meaning that they can apply their knowledge and skills by integrating multiple standards into more-complex tasks in future learning. Simply meeting low-level standards may also mean that the skills or concepts students memorize will be forgotten soon after they have taken a test. Well-written competencies are of a larger grain size (in scope and depth) than individual standards, integrating the skills of multiple, high-priority standards. Table 3.1 shows some of the similarities and differences between how standards and competences represent learning goals and possible assessment uses.

To illustrate differences between standards and competencies, consider that a mathematics performance task can assess standards describing math concepts, math skills and procedures, and several mathematical practices (e.g., constructing an argument, analyzing the reasoning of others). Several well-designed competency-based performance tasks in mathematics can apply these same skills, concepts, and practices in a variety of real-world contexts. Thus, evidence-based grades for assessments like these are connected to clearly defined learning objectives, do not average behavior with knowledge, and are focused on learning progress in demonstrating the competency (see Table 3.2). A student's portfolio would be able to show evidence of how understanding became deeper and more sophisticated over time while the student works to achieve mastery.

TABLE 3.1 Comparing Standards and Competencies

Standards	Competencies
• Written in "teacher" language (using educational terminology)	• Written in student-friendly language (I can . . .)
• Variable grain sizes, some encompassing broad ideas and others describing discrete skills	• Larger grain size, encompassing multiple standards (skills, procedures, concepts, application) in more-complex tasks
• Many in each grade-level and content area, making them less manageable to track individually	• Fewer overall in each grade-level or content area, making them more manageable to track student progress and reinforce
• Mastery on one standard does not mean that students can apply those skills or concepts in a variety of more complex tasks	• Lend themselves to comparable applications across courses and learning opportunities
• Varied applications across courses	• Assessments are used to determine whether students are ready to advance ("advance upon mastery") or get additional support
• Postassessments may not indicate "mastery" or time for a student to move on	• Describe deeper learning (DOK 3 and DOK 4), including transfer of skills and concepts and creation of knowledge
• DOK levels vary, with most standards written at DOK 1 or DOK 2 level	
• Must be combined in rich performance tasks to assess deeper thinking (DOK 3 or DOK 4)	

TABLE 3.2 Comparing Standards-Based Grading With Evidence-Based Grading

Standards-based grading is based on learning goals described in each content standard.	**Evidence-based grading** is based on learning goals described in competencies, which include both content and performance descriptors (how content knowledge is demonstrated).
Each standard is tracked during a school year. A student can be considered "proficient" if she or he scores high enough (above a set cut score) on an end-of-course exam assessing a sample of several prioritized standards or on multiple smaller assessments of the same standard.	Each competency is tracked, sometimes across grade levels, until a student's body of evidence (BOE) demonstrates sufficiency of evidence that the student has mastered those learning goals. Standards that support learning that underlies competencies are built into performance scales.
If more than one standard is assessed on a single test or assessment task, one grade is given per standard, based on test questions that address each standard.	Grades are given based on the sufficiency of evidence produced by a student using CB assessments. Evidence for a competency may come from tasks completed in multiple courses or content areas (e.g., writing portfolios with work samples across content areas).
Standards are criterion-based.	Competencies are criterion-based and may have had staff and community input into developing them.
Assessment criteria (skills and concepts) are communicated to students and parents ahead of time.	Assessment criteria (*application* of skills, concepts, and personal skills) are communicated to students and parents ahead of time.
Usually a set number of assignments are completed by all students.	The evidence produced is more important than the number of assignments completed. Students can demonstrate proficiency based on different, fewer, or more pieces of evidence.
Grades measure academic achievement only; or grades separate academic achievement from effort and behavior. No penalties or extra credit affect the grade given.	CBE systems can generate grades or performance descriptions for both academic and personal skills (e.g. work or study habits, self-regulation), based on how effectively they are applied to the processes and products of learning. No penalties or extra credit affect the grade given.
Selected assessments (tests, quizzes, projects, etc.) are usually averaged to determine an overall grade. Strengths and weaknesses based on assessments of individual standards might also be reported (e.g., an overall letter grade is given for science but identifies investigation skills as weaker than knowledge of science concepts).	More-complex tasks and most-recent assessments can be given greater weight. Students may have input into designing assessment tasks or on which assessment evidence in their BOE best reflects learning. Self-reflections also contribute evidence. CB reporting is based on accumulating evidence in the BOE and is not the same as a grade.
Emphasize the most recent evidence of learning when grading.	Students move from one level of learning to the next, based on understanding described in the competency and performance scales, without regard to time or pacing. Students are given multiple opportunities to demonstrate learning and replace lower grades. Evidence-based grades can consider both progress made and demonstrated mastery.

STOP AND REFLECT

Do teachers in your school teach, assess, and grade what you collectively value as the most important learning? Is the evidence collected giving teachers information related to where students are on their learning path toward competency?

_____

_____

_____

3.4 EVIDENCE-BASED GRADING
AND THE BODY OF EVIDENCE (BOE)

In traditional education settings, report cards and transcripts convey grades earned in each subject or course as the evidence for learning, regardless of how each teacher calculates them or what evidence of learning is included to arrive at a final grade. In many systems, the grades are then further used for other decision points for a student. For example, a grade may be used by a teacher to recommend a student for an honors course, for additional academic support, or for a student to qualify for social events or privileges within the school day. Traditional and standards-based grades are artificially constrained to units of time allotted for learning (e.g., a marking period) rather than the specific learning accomplished. At the end of the school year, a calculation of grades for each quarter of the school year might be used as an average to determine class rankings or decisions about promotion to the next grade. These mathematical calculations may seem precise on the surface (e.g., class rankings in high school can come down to hundredths of a point for a student's grade-point average [GPA]); but given the underlying inconsistencies in where the numbers originated and what was actually measured, they lack transparency and **validity**.

In CBE, this type of grade reporting is inadequate to communicate what the student has learned or, more importantly, what progress the student has made. In CBE, a year of learning in science might be mapped out with units of instruction addressing competencies based on the broader "**Big Ideas**" in science (e.g., systems, cause–effect, patterns) with the science competency on patterns being assessed in three units of study at different points across the year in different science courses (life science, physical sciences, or earth–space science). The work a student produces when addressing the competency on patterns becomes part of the student's BOE to show science learning over time, no matter which science course is taken. The grade that a student receives in a course in biology represents not only life science concepts learned and applied but also progress made in demonstrating learning about patterns or systems in science (two competencies addressed in the biology course). The same could be true of a student taking a physics or chemistry course, also addressing competencies of patterns and systems while applying different course-specific science concepts. Remember that the **learning targets** for a unit of study are smaller in scope than the broader learning goals articulated in competencies. Learning targets are written in student-friendly language as "I can . . ." statements, with a lesson or unit of study addressing some but not all of these. This means that a project or assessment completed for a unit of study generates both a grade (how well did the student meet the learning targets for this unit) and evidence for the BOE.

Students therefore have multiple opportunities within and across science courses to contribute evidence about understanding patterns in science (the competency).

CB reporting is based on evaluating the collection of work in the BOE and is not the same as an evidence-based grade a student might receive on one assessment during a given marking period or unit of study.

Multiple and varied assessments aligned along a learning progression (reflected in CB **performance scales**) generate work products and evidence-based grades used to determine overall performance on each competency at a given point in time. Again using our science example, each time a student demonstrates proficiency when knowledge of patterns is part of a unit of study in science, there will be pieces of evidence for teachers to objectively review to determine the demonstration of mastery for the patterns competency in science. Collecting a body of evidence based on scores derived from CB assessments becomes part of the data teachers use to evaluate progress on competencies for reporting purposes. Other CB data may be generated by students, outside mentors, experts in the field, and the like. This is why establishing policies about (1) the agreed-upon intended content, rigor, and scope of CB **learning goals**; (2) how competencies will be assessed and be accessible to all students; (3) what types of evidence and work products may be included in a student's BOE (e.g., replacement assessments, student-designed assessments); and (4) how much evidence will be considered to be "sufficient" in determining proficiency are critical for systemwide consistency and objective CB reporting.

STOP AND REFLECT

What types of evidence—of knowledge, skills, *and* dispositions—would constitute a BOE in each content area or course in your school?

_____

_____

_____

_____

_____

The real purpose of a report card is to communicate *ongoing* student progress in achieving agreed-upon learning goals. A CBE report card can communicate the level of proficiency for each competency in a variety of ways: using new definitions of what letter grades mean, providing numerical ranges for rubric scores that translate to letter grades, or replacing traditional *A*s, *B*s, *C*s, and *D*s with new numerical ranges (4.0, 3.0, 2.0, 1.0) or with descriptions such as *Advanced, Proficient, Approaching Proficiency,* and *Still Developing.* Performance-level descriptions such as these can also be built into performance scales for each competency, providing transparency and clarity in communicating what progress toward proficiency can look like. Often, a combination of numerical ranges and letter grades is used for reporting academic competencies, while the broader performance-level terms are used for reporting on personal success skill competencies. The only correct way to make this shift is to be thoughtful, equitable, and consistent within and across the school system.

Stack and VanderEls (2017, p. 78) suggest several shifts to consider in local grading practices when implementing CBE:

- Grades must reflect what students learn, not what they earn.

- Grading must consider the use and purpose of diagnostic testing, formative assessment, and summative assessment.

- Rubrics must replace the traditional 100-point scale (and eliminate averaging) with a smaller rubric scale based on three, four, or five points.

- Grades must separate academics from academic behaviors (e.g., neatness, participation, effort, meeting deadlines).

- Students must have the opportunity to reassess their work without penalty.

A system for evidence-based grading and competency-based reporting is not the engine that drives the transition from traditional education models to CBE. We have found that before new grading systems are created, teachers must learn how to develop CB performance scales, create performance assessments aligned with competency expectations for deeper learning, verify that guidelines in determining proficiency and the assessments used are valid and **reliable** in producing high-quality evidence of learning, and shift the focus of the classroom from teaching-centered to student-centered learning.

| Collective Teacher Efficacy (Effect Size = 1.39) | → | *Reread that last sentence because it explains why implementation will take you on a multiyear journey with potential roadblocks, detours, and required pit stops along the way!* |

CBE Tool 1E (Figure 3.5) provides a framework for examining where your school is now in developing competency-based assessments. (The full version of **CBE Tools 1A−1E** is found in Appendix A.)

FIGURE 3.5 Cutaway of CBE Tool 1E: Readiness Examination for the Shift to Evidence-Based Grading

CBE Tool 1E	Core Components of Competency-Based Education: CBE Readiness Tool			
Component 5: Evidence-Based Grading Scoring, grading, and reporting reflect students' progress toward unit, course, and graduation competencies.				
Focus	**Phase 1: Initiating**	**Phase 2: Emerging**	**Phase 3: Implementing**	**Where is your school now? What are possible next steps?**
Leadership	Grading and reporting policies and practices are different at the elementary, middle, and high school levels.	Grading and reporting policies support practices in standards-based grading. Competency-based assessments are graded but are not part of a larger body of evidence (BOE) for meeting graduation requirements.	Policies define the body of evidence (BOE) needed to demonstrate proficiency in relation to academic and personal skills competencies. CB reporting indicates student progress toward mastery of competencies.	
Instruction and Assessment	Grading and reporting are done within the context of a course or content area. Mathematical calculations and averaging generally determine grades.	Formative assessments provide a level of transparency to inform where a student is in relation to a particular learning outcome for a course or content area. Learning outcomes are tracked and measured relative to standards.	Formative assessment data provide the body of evidence used for instructional and learner feedback. Evidence informs where a student is in relation to a competency and whether the student is ready for a summative assessment.	
Learner Culture	Grading practices affect both positive and negative student attitudes toward learning and self-image.	Grading practices are more transparent to the learner, relative to progress in demonstrating skills described in standards.	The body of evidence informs pacing of learning, is responsive to addressing student needs, and promotes student reflection and ownership of learning experience and learning outcomes.	
Organizational Structures	Systems of scoring and reporting are aligned to course expectations, reporting policies, and school year timelines.	Systems of scoring and reporting are aligned to course and graduation requirements, standards-based reporting, and school year timelines.	Competency-based systems of building a student's BOE, scoring work samples, and reporting results inform graduation readiness relative to the POG.	

STOP AND REFLECT

Use the four focus areas in CBE Tool 1E (leadership, instruction/assessment, learner culture, organizational structures) to consider potential challenges and opportunities as you are making the shift to evidence-based grading.

_____

_____

_____

_____

_____

3.5 CBE DEVELOPMENT AND VALIDATION TOOLS AND PROCESSES

A term frequently used in the assessment world is *validity*. Simply put, a valid assessment is an assessment that assesses what it was intended to assess; elicits observable and measurable evidence linked to the intended learning goal(s); and, therefore, can be used to interpret what students have learned. Consider a science assessment that only asks students to interpret data displays in graphs and tables. Even if a student gets a high score on that assessment, we could not interpret the score to mean that the student is able to design and conduct science investigations. Likewise, we cannot assume that a student who can edit an essay can compose an essay; or that a student who is fluent with math facts can construct a mathematical argument.

FIGURE 3.6 The "Big Picture" of CBE: Possible Entry Points and Five Validation Pit Stops on Your Journey

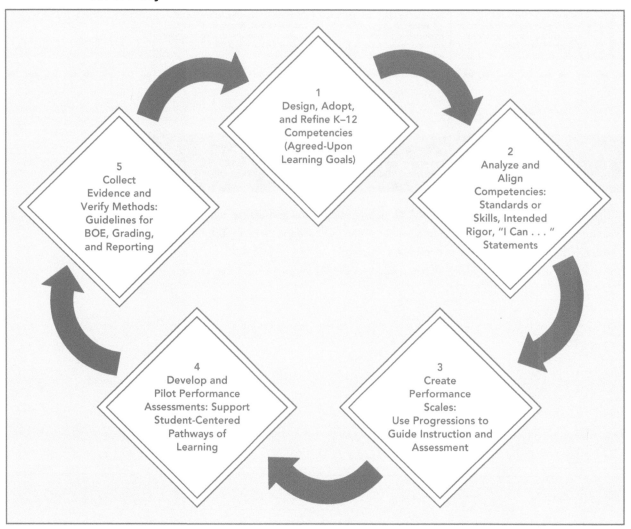

A valid and reliable CBE system is a system that builds in checks and balances to ensure clear communication of learning goals to all stakeholders (the profile of the graduate and K–12 competencies); fidelity of implementation among school staff (by instruction, grading, and reporting); and validity of purpose and use of practices employed. Do not assume that if your school has adopted an existing set of competencies that your work is done. Validation is essential along each phase of CBE implementation. Figure 3.6 illustrates the "big picture" of CBE implementation with possible entry points into your journey and critical validation "pit stops" you'll need to make and recalibrate as your system evolves. Use these five pit stops just as a race car driver would—not necessarily in a sequential manner, but as needed—to refuel, tune performance, and revisit before going on.

Validation Pit Stop 1: Design of K–12 Competencies—Clarity, Scope, Rigor, and Usefulness

Clear, agreed-upon expectations for K–12 learning are the foundation of your CBE system. They will only be relevant and useful when they guide instruction and assessment practices and illustrate how any child entering school will develop into your shared vision of the graduate. This includes academic and personal success skills competencies which must

1
Design, Adopt, and Refine K–12 Competencies (Agreed-Upon Learning Goals)

- **Be observable and measurable.** Vaguely written competencies will inhibit consistent instructional planning, use of assessments, and interpretation of assessment results throughout the school system. Your first validation question is, Can we measure this?

- **Be manageable in terms of grain size and number.** Having an excessive number of small-grained competencies for each grade level or content area or having too few that are broadly written (or vague) creates unnecessary management time and effort. In our work, we've suggested that there be no more than eight or nine competencies for teachers to be tracking across a school year, with fewer being mapped to each unit of study or project. Using individual standards (as many as twenty to thirty per content area) as competencies becomes unmanageable (too many to keep track of) or they are simply turned into low-level skills checklists and called competencies. Your next validation question is the "Goldilocks" test: Are our competencies too small-grained and too many, too large in scope and too vague, or just right in grain size and number to make them manageable?

- **Articulate increasingly more rigorous and sophisticated K–12 learning.** Learning is continuous and ongoing regardless of age or grade level. Competencies across grade spans or adjacent grade levels should clearly depict an underlying learning progression—how learning typically develops and becomes more sophisticated over time. True learning progressions (also called learning trajectories) are based on cognitive science and empirical research. Your validation questions: Can we see how learning will develop over time, building on earlier learning? Is there any research basis for our K–12 continuum?

- **Be valid.** Competencies are aligned with intended content (standards or skills) and rigor (DOK levels) and measured with performance assessments of comparable rigor. Assessments are equitable for all students, regardless of specific disabilities or learning needs. Your validation questions: Do our competency-based assessments measure deeper understanding? Are our assessments fair and equitable?

- **Provide instructional guidance.** Competencies describe what to teach along a K–12 learning progression. In doing so, competencies help teachers to consider how to strategically scaffold learning and measure progress along the way. Your validation question: Will competencies lead to deeper understanding over time that we can teach, support, measure, and report on?

When Karin was helping several schools in Illinois to develop personal success skills competencies, she realized that many of their early statements of these SEL competencies were lacking in rigor and were much too vague to validly measure consistently. Table 3.3 shows samples of her feedback and how some competency statements were revised to be clearer and more rigorous. The revised wording of the competencies also suggests how a performance scale might be developed to guide the teaching of skills and what evidence of learning to collect for the BOE.

TABLE 3.3 Revising SEL Competency Statements to Improve Clarity and Increase Rigor

Competency Statement Before Feedback	Sample Feedback on SEL Competency Statements	Competency Statement After Feedback
1. (Empathy) I can **recognize** the feelings and perspectives of others.	Simply "recognizing" feelings might be possible to assess but does not offer ways for students to make progress in using that information or transferring skills to new situations.	1. (Empathy) I can recognize, **respond to, and evaluate my responses to** the feelings and perspectives of others.
2. (Goal setting) I can demonstrate skills related to achieving my **personal and academic** goals.	Students might approach working on their personal goals very differently from how they approach academic goals. A suggestion was made to separate the types of goals and add student reflections on progress for each competency.	2a. (Goal setting) I can demonstrate **and reflect on** skills related to achieving my **personal** goals. 2b. (Goal setting) I can demonstrate **and reflect on** skills related to achieving my **academic** goals.

For the last decade, we have worked with state- and school-based teams to develop their own competencies, and we can tell you from experience that it is much easier to adopt and then adapt competencies to fit your system's needs than to start from scratch. Knowing what to look for in well-designed competencies provides guidance in how you might adapt or revise existing competencies.

For the purpose of locally validating the clarity, scope, intended rigor, and usefulness of local competencies, we provide three tools: The Hess Cognitive Rigor Matrices (CRMs); a Self-Evaluation Rubric for Examining or Revising Competency Statements (CBE Tool 3); and a tool to examine the Development or Analysis of Competency Statements Across Grades (CBE Tool 4). The full versions of CBE Tools 3–4 are included in Appendix A with links for downloading. The Hess Cognitive Rigor Matrices #1–#5D are found in Appendix B.

The following section describes the purpose and use of each CBE tool in developing high-quality competency statements.

Examining Rigor and Scope

When we speak of rigorous competencies and rigorous assessments, we mean that they are "cognitively" rigorous, not just something that is hard to learn. **Cognitive rigor** encompasses the complexity of the content, the cognitive engagement with that content, and the scope of the planned learning activity (Hess, Carlock, Jones, & Walkup, 2009). Therefore, the **cognitive demand** of a given learning goal describes the potential range of mental processing required to complete a task within a given context or scenario. Determining the intended cognitive demand of a learning or assessment task requires more than simply identifying the "verbs" and the "nouns" used in a standard. Teachers must consider both the content and the reasoning and decision-making required to interact with content to complete a task successfully. During instruction, the cognitive demand of highly complex tasks can be lessened using strategic scaffolding strategies (Hess, 2018) without significantly changing the constructs being assessed. This might include strategies such as "chunking" texts for a reading assessment, group data collection for a science investigation, and facilitated discussions as a prewriting activity.

Different models have been used to examine rigor, the most common ones being Bloom's Revised Taxonomy (Anderson et al., 2001) that describes types of thinking and Webb's **Depth-of-Knowledge** (DOK) levels (2002) that describe depth of engagement with content and task complexity. We prefer using the Hess **Cognitive Rigor Matrices** to validate the intended rigor and scope of learning expectations (competencies) because the CRMs integrate these two familiar models and expand them with examples for different content areas. There are eight content-specific CRMs (including fine arts, health and physical education, and career and technical education). Hess CRMs are used to validate the intended rigor of competencies, as well as the rigor assessed using CB performance assessments and scoring rubrics. A general rule of thumb for examining the intended rigor of competency statements is that they must be written at a DOK 3 or DOK 4 level in order to encompass deeper learning that cannot be assessed on pencil-and-paper tests. Skills checklists and many standards fall well short of DOK 3 thinking and understanding (see Table 3.4). Likewise, broadly written competency statements such as "Students will recognize empathy" are much too vague to determine any level of implied rigor.

The example of the Hess CRM for reading and listening (in Figure 3.7) describes a range of DOK levels that can guide both competency development and assessment task design. (To read more about the development and uses of the Hess CRMs, see Module 1 of *A Local Assessment Toolkit to Promote Deeper Learning*, Hess, 2018).

Examining Relevance, Alignment, Equity, and Opportunity to Learn
Use **CBE Tool 3**, Self-Evaluation Rubric for Examining or Revising Competency Statements, to analyze six aspects of well-written, rigorous competencies. **CBE Tool 3** goes into more depth on the ways a competency statement might be stronger or weaker in terms of aligning with relevant Big Ideas (and essential questions) of the content domain, representing prioritized standards, or being designed with equity and learning pathways in mind. Because this tool provides a range of descriptors for each dimension, schools can locate the current status of competencies for each dimension and see how they might revise wording to strengthen how competencies will be taught and assessed. **CBE Tool 3** is especially useful for schools that have adopted competencies without considering how they might adapt or strengthen them. The full version of **CBE Tool 3**, Self-Evaluation Rubric for Examining or Revising Competency Statements (Figure 3.8), is included in Appendix A and can be downloaded.

TABLE 3.4 Connecting DOK Levels and Transfer of Learning to Competency-Based Expectations

Connecting DOK Levels and Transfer of Learning to Competency-Based Expectations		
DOK 1	Demonstrating skills and knowledge in isolation or for specific situations	
DOK 2	Applying skills and concepts in a more generalized way, across contexts, but very much like the way they were taught (how to observe, summarize, compare, predict, organize data, etc.)	Near Transfer
DOK 3	Going deeper into issues, themes, and problems through inquiry and problem-solving; exploring how evidence can be used to support, defend, or refute alternative approaches, alternative solutions	
DOK 4	Generating new questions, in-depth insights, solutions, or applications that go beyond what was explicitly taught (investigating, triangulating evidence, uncovering competing perspectives, piloting ideas, reflecting upon, and revising)	Far Transfer

FIGURE 3.7 Cutaway of Hess CRM Tool #1: Reading and Listening

CRM Tool 1	Hess Cognitive Rigor Matrix (Reading CRM): Applying Webb's Depth-of-Knowledge Levels to Bloom's Cognitive Process Dimensions			
Revised Bloom's Taxonomy	**Webb's DOK Level 1 Recall and Reproduction**	**Webb's DOK Level 2 Skills and Concepts**	**Webb's DOK Level 3 Strategic Thinking/Reasoning**	**Webb's DOK Level 4 Extended Thinking**
Remember Retrieve knowledge from long-term memory, recognize, recall, locate, identify	• Recall, recognize, or locate basic facts, terms, details, events, or ideas explicit in texts • Read words orally in connected text with fluency and accuracy	Use these Hess CRM curricular examples with most close reading or listening assignments or assessments in any content area.		
Understand Construct meaning, clarify, paraphrase, represent, translate, illustrate, give examples, classify, categorize, summarize, generalize, infer a logical conclusion, predict, compare or contrast, match like ideas, explain, construct models	• Identify or describe literary elements (characters, setting, sequence, etc.) • Select appropriate words when intended meaning or definition is clearly evident • Describe or explain who, what, where, when, or how • Define or describe facts, details, terms, principles • Write simple sentences	• Specify, explain, show relationships; explain why (e.g., cause/effect) • Give nonexamples or examples • Summarize results, concepts, ideas • Make basic inferences or logical predictions from data or texts • Identify main ideas or accurate generalizations of texts • Locate information to support explicit/implicit central ideas	• Explain, generalize, or connect ideas using supporting evidence (quote, example, text reference) • Identify or make inferences about explicit or implicit themes • Describe how word choice, point of view, or bias may affect the readers' interpretation of a text • Write multiparagraph composition for specific purpose, focus, voice, tone, and audience	• Explain how concepts or ideas specifically relate to other content domains (e.g., social, political, historical) or concepts • Develop generalizations of the results obtained or strategies used and apply them to new problem-based situations
Apply Carry out or use a procedure in a given situation; apply or use in an unfamiliar situation or nonroutine task	• Use language structure (pre-, or suffix) or word relationships (synonym/antonym) to determine meaning of words • Apply rules or resources to edit spelling, grammar, punctuation, conventions, word use • Apply basic formats for documenting sources	• Use context to identify the meaning of words or phrases • Obtain and interpret information using text features • Develop a text that may be limited to one paragraph • Apply simple organizational structures (paragraph, sentence types) in writing	• Apply a concept in a new context • Revise final draft for meaning or progression of ideas • Apply internal consistency of text organization and structure to composing a full composition • Apply word choice, point of view, style to impact readers' or viewers' interpretation of a text	• Illustrate how multiple themes (historical, geographic, social, artistic, literary) may be interrelated • Select or devise an approach among many alternatives to research a novel problem
Analyze Break into constituent parts, determine how parts relate, differentiate between relevant/irrelevant, distinguish, focus, select, organize, outline, find coherence, deconstruct (e.g., for bias or point of view)	• Identify whether specific information is contained in graphic representations (e.g., map, chart, table, graph, T-chart, diagram) or text features (e.g., headings, subheadings, captions) • Decide which text structure is appropriate to audience and purpose	• Categorize or compare literary elements, terms, facts or details, events • Identify use of literary devices • Analyze format, organization, and internal text structure (signal words, transitions, semantic cues) of different texts • Distinguish relevant/irrelevant information, fact/opinion	• Analyze information within data sets or texts • Analyze interrelationships among concepts, issues, problems • Analyze or interpret author's craft (literary devices, viewpoint, or potential bias) to create or critique a text • Use reasoning, planning, and evidence to support inferences	• Analyze multiple sources of evidence, or multiple works by the same author, or across genres, time periods, themes • Analyze complex or abstract themes, perspectives, concepts • Gather, analyze, and organize multiple information sources • Analyze discourse styles

FIGURE 3.8 Cutaway of CBE Tool 3: Self-Evaluation Rubric for Examining or Revising Competency Statements

CBE Tool 3	Self-Evaluation Rubric for Examining or Revising Competency Statements			
To what degree are competency statements . . .	**4**	**3**	**2**	**1**
	← Stronger		Weaker →	
1—Relevant to Big Ideas/ enduring understandings of the content domain (Why is this important to learn?)	Includes essential skills that are transferable (across content domains, applicable to real-world situations, etc.) Requires broader connections between/among theories, principles, or concepts	Includes skills that are transferable across content areas or real-world situations Focuses on key concepts of the content domain, supported by topics and facts, with broader connections possible	Based on topics applicable to a specific course or project Lacks explicit connections to enduring understandings/Big Ideas of the content domain Unlikely to lead to broader learning connections	Limited to scope and sequence of textbooks or specific programs Very specific to facts and skills in content area (more like a skills checklist; skills performed in isolation)
2—Aligned to prioritized outcomes (national/state/ local standards)	Reflects prioritized national/ state standards or local frameworks, bundled for deeper learning (Big Ideas)	Aligns with prioritized national/ state standards or local frameworks	Has alignment with national/ state/local standards Lacks a sense of learning that has been prioritized (too few–too many)	May be either too vague or too specific or detailed in its content area focus to identify clear alignment
3—Designed to assess deeper cognitive demand, complex performances, and products of learning	Requires complex conceptual understanding and applications in unfamiliar/authentic contexts Asks students to investigate, create, solve, and defend their thinking or products	Promotes authentic applications of conceptual knowledge using reasoning, planning, interpreting, problem-solving, or investigation	Requires mental processes/ skills, such as defining, summarizing, constructing, organizing, displaying, etc. Promotes routine applications of conceptual knowledge	Asks students to show what they know using only routine or basic applications Mostly requires recall of facts, information, definitions, terms, procedures
4—Equitable for all students Student-centered, personalized Multiple opportunities Varied assessment formats Fairness, UDL	Promotes varied formats/UDL and multiple opportunities to demonstrate evidence of learning (e.g., interdisciplinary, student-designed, group– individual, scaffolded)	Supports some varied assessment formats applying UDL Multiple opportunities to demonstrate learning (e.g., interdisciplinary, group, or individual, multiple courses)	Supports traditional assessments applying UDL to demonstrate evidence of learning Limited to retaking the same assessment (with more time, read aloud, etc.)	Implies limited opportunities to demonstrate individual or personalized learning Does not support varied assessment formats/UDL
5—Designed with learning pathways/ progressions Within grades	Provides clear continuity for important learning within and across grades (e.g., when to	Articulates what is important in understanding the content and possible pathways to get there	Defines what is to be observed or measured Provides some continuity for	Defines what is to be observed or measured Lacks meaningful connections

STOP AND REFLECT

Think of a current learning outcome (competency statement) used at your school. How does this learning outcome align with the criteria in CBE Tool 3 (relevance, alignment, cognitive demand, equity, a learning pathway, and opportunity to learn)?

_____

_____

_____

_____

Examining Implied Learning Progressions Across Grades

Use CBE Tool 4, Development or Analysis of Competency Statements Across Grades (see Figure 3.9), to determine if competencies articulate a defensible K–12 learning progression. We used this tool while working with New Hampshire educators to develop the state's model competencies. Having a K–12 grade span view helped to ensure that learning at each grade or grade span built the foundation for deeper learning at the next level. During this process, teachers representing grade span groups identified and underlined new learning (skills, concepts, or complexity of application) when it was introduced at the next level. After much discussion and refining of wording, teams then worked to align the competency statements with Big Ideas in each content domain (at the top of the tool) and academic content standards or personal success skills (at the bottom of the tool). Finally, "I can . . ." statements were written at each grade span to indicate in student-friendly language what it would look like when students were making progress in demonstrating mastery.

The full version of CBE Tool 4, Development or Analysis of Competency Statements Across Grades, is included in Appendix A and can be downloaded. Appendix C includes a link to the New Hampshire Model Competencies. (To read more about the development and uses of learning progressions, see Module 4 of *A Local Assessment Toolkit to Promote Deeper Learning*, Hess, 2018. To read more about the development of the NH Model Competencies, see pp. 34–43, *Competency-Based Education*, Colby, 2017.)

FIGURE 3.9 Cutaway of CBE Tool 4: Development or Analysis of Competency Statements Across Grades

CBE Tool 4	Development or Analysis of Competency Statements Across Grades: Is There a Defensible Learning Progression?		
Linked to a Big Idea?			
Grade Levels or Grade Spans*			
Competency Statement (Learning Goal)	Students will . . .	Students will . . .	Students will . . .
Break down competency statement into learning targets** Use kid-friendly language "I can . . ."	I can I can I can I can I can	I can I can I can I can I can	I can I can I can I can I can

Validation Pit Stop 2: Analyze and Align Competencies—Link Learning Goals, Standards, and Assessments With Instruction

If your school's competency statements have undergone a review for clarity and rigor or if you have drafted a small number of competencies that teachers are ready to begin implementing in their classrooms, then **CBE Tool 5**, Analyzing a Competency, can be a useful collaborative planning tool. This tool drills down into one competency statement to uncover what content and skills will be learned and how they might be demonstrated and assessed. A six-step process is used by grade-level or department teams to come to an agreement about how to plan instruction and collect evidence of learning. This agreement about the intended learning and how to assess it supports more consistent implementation among teachers, whether they decide to use common assessments, different (unique) assessments, or a combination of both.

2 Analyze and Align Competencies: Standards or Skills, Intended Rigor, "I Can . . ." Statements

Linking Learning Expectations With Instructional Planning

Use **CBE Tool 5**, Analyzing a Competency, to link learning expectations with instructional planning: content, performance, and possible assessments. These six steps are illustrated in Figure 3.10 using a Grade 3 ELA example in the partially completed **CBE Tool 5**.

← Teacher Clarity: Expectations for Learning (Effect Size = 0.75)

Steps for Analyzing a Competency Using CBE Tool 5

Competency Analysis Step 1: Start your analysis by identifying and underlining key learnings stated in the competency.

Competency Analysis Step 2: Break down what students can "do" to show proficiency for this competency, using "I can . . ." statements at different task complexity (DOK) levels.

Competency Analysis Step 3: List specific content and concepts to be learned. Some content will be precursors or prerequisites to demonstrating proficiency of more complex content.

Competency Analysis Step 4: Identify the intended DOK levels of products or performance (related to "I can . . ." statements). Hess CRM tools (Appendix B) are helpful with this analysis step.

Competency Analysis Step 5: Identify national/state/local standards and personal success skills that will be taught, reinforced, and assessed with this competency. There will be multiple (bundles of) standards addressing all of the "I can . . ." statements.

Competency Analysis Step 6: Generate possible formative, interim, and summative assessment tasks as a means of collecting evidence of learning along a learning progression.

When working with teachers, we have found that providing a partially completed example for **CBE Tool 5**, such as the example shown in Figure 3.10, is an effective way to begin discussing alignment of competencies with standards and personal success skills, reviewing distinctions among DOK levels, and generating a variety of ways to assess "I can . . ." statements. Teams are then ready to analyze and discuss their own local competencies using a similar process. **CBE Tool 5** also helps teachers to develop a deeper understanding about how "bundles" of standards can support each competency and be rebundled for other competencies.

STOP AND REFLECT

How could you use **CBE Tool 5** to develop new competency statements (academic or personal) or validate existing ones?

_____

_____

_____

_____

FIGURE 3.10 Analyzing a Competency (Learning Goal): Language Arts Example

CBE Tool 5	Analyzing a Competency (Learning Goal): What Learning Is Implied?	

Content Area: *ELA (Source: NH Model Competencies)*	Grade Level: *3*

Competency Statement 6

Students will <u>analyze a topic or text</u>(s) using a <u>variety of sources</u> and apply organizational strategies and <u>use evidence</u> to <u>support an opinion</u> for varied audiences.

Step 1: Underline key learnings in competency statement.

Learning Targets

- *I can state an opinion that answers a question about a topic or text.*
- *I can use sources (pictures, primary and secondary sources, discussion) to expand my understanding of the topic/text and locate information to support my point of view.*
- *I can organize my ideas by stating reasons that support my opinion and use facts and details to say more about each reason.*
- *I can add visuals to help elaborate on my reasons.*
- *I can connect reasons and facts with linking words and provide a conclusion that restates my opinion and considers why others might not agree with me.*
- *With support, I can edit and revise my text for clarity, focus, and coherence (e.g., using grade-appropriate mechanics, grammar, language, sentence types, description/elaboration, and relevant visuals).*

Step 2: Create "I can . . ." statements showing proficiency.

Content/Concepts	Performance/ Products/Intended DOK
Step 3: List content, concepts to be learned.	**Step 4: Identify DOK of products, performances.**
Transitional words, language use, sentence types *Text features and uses* *Facts (evidence) versus opinions* *Multiparagraph writing in support of an opinion* *Developing a schema for opinion writing* *Summarizing versus using elaboration strategies* *Close reading strategies (implied)*	**DOK 1**: *State an opinion; edit grammar, language usage, and mechanics (GUM).* **DOK 2**: *Locate information to support; organize my ideas; add visuals to help elaborate on ideas.* **DOK 3**: *Connect reasons and facts with linking words and provide a conclusion; revise my text for clarity, focus, and coherence.* **DOK 4**: *Use a variety of sources.*
Alignment: List Content Standards	**Alignment: Personal Success Skills**
Step 5: Align standards, personal success skills assessed with competency.	
List Possible Common (Formative, Interim, Summative) Assessment Tasks	
Step 6: List possible assessment tasks that will generate "evidence" of learning.	

Validation Pit Stop 3: Create Performance Scales—Using Progressions to Guide Instruction, Learning, and Assessment Design

Developing performance scales is an essential step in the CBE implementation process that many schools either are not aware of or decide to skip because they see little value in taking time to create them. We hope to convince our readers that thoughtfully designed performance scales are one of the best ways to ensure that different teachers using different assessments in different courses or classrooms can still collect evidence of learning for the same competencies. Performance scales help teachers to plan instruction and develop aligned CB assessment tasks and scoring rubrics. Students can also use performance scales to build their body of evidence and for self-reflection and conferencing.

What Is a Performance Scale?

Various terms are used to describe a continuum of distinct levels of demonstrated knowledge and skills relative to a learning outcome or competency-based statement. Scales describe ways to assess content from less to greater complexity. They can be used to plan instruction, develop scoring guides, monitor progress over time, and guide the development of artifacts to be included in a student's body of evidence. We use the term *performance scale* here (rather than *proficiency scale*) so as not to imply this is only for scoring or grading purposes; we recommend creating a performance scale for each competency (not for each standard).

Quality Criteria for Performance Scale Development

1. **A performance scale is written to be "task neutral."** This allows different educators to design both common and different assessments and learning activities to align with (all or parts of) the more generalized (agreed upon) performance scale. Rubrics and scoring guides can also be developed, drawing from the descriptors at some or all levels of the scale. Assessments—especially those used formatively—align with different performance levels of the scale.

2. **Increasing complexity and cognitive demand (DOK) are represented** in how performance indicators (PIs) at each level of the scale are written from foundational (least complex) to the ability to transfer (apply) learning to new contexts at the *Proficient* and *Advanced* performance levels. Scale levels do not necessarily equate with DOK levels, although most descriptions used at the *Proficient* and *Advanced* levels will be at DOK 3 or DOK 4 complexity and depth of

Teacher Clarity:
Expectations
for Learning
(Effect Size = 0.75)

Teachers at the Concord (New Hampshire) Regional Technical Center struggled at first with how to communicate to students what was required to reach proficiency for different career paths and how those learning goals related to different DOK levels. Eventually, they came up with an idea that now hangs in every CTE classroom at the high school. Wall posters (see Figure 3.11) for each CTE course, designed by Tom Mungovan, graphic arts teacher at the school, show stair steps for each career path (health care worker, auto technician, graphic artist, building trades, etc.) to illustrate performance levels from least to more complex skills and knowledge needed for that career. Each step shows the different corresponding depth-of-knowledge levels for skills leading to mastery and related real-world jobs. This approach to communicating "I can . . ." statements to CTE students has clarified why mastering lower-level skills (such as changing a tire or taking a blood pressure) is not adequate for being fully career ready. The visual of stair steps is more relevant to the goals of the CTE students, helping them to understand what evidence of learning will contribute to demonstrating competency, and why more complex tasks are necessary for them to learn.

understanding. A specific PI at the *Proficient* level of a scale could be described as DOK 2, such as demonstrating conceptual understanding.

3. **Use descriptive language** (not subjective or judgmental) when writing PIs for the scale. This results in more focus on quality of work products than on quantity of work completed. This language is repeated in scoring rubrics, strengthening alignment from the competency pathway to performance task to scoring criteria.

During a yearlong professional development series for Illinois educators to learn about designing CB performance assessments, participants followed a similar process to what is described in this chapter: analyze a competency, develop a performance scale for the competency, and then develop an aligned performance task and scoring rubric. Angelique Hamilton (Project Administrator, Curriculum and Instruction, Illinois State Board of Education) created the example described in Table 3.5, linking performance levels in the scale with possible assessment evidence for each level.

This was the *beginning* of Angelique's performance scale for a mathematics competency, using CBE Tool 6. Her next step was to design formative and summative assessment tasks and scoring rubrics, aligned with the performance scale for this competency.

(Continued)

(Continued)

TABLE 3.5 Sample Mathematics Performance Scale

Mathematics Competency: Students can apply (use) function notation in authentic/real-world scenarios to analyze, evaluate, and draw statistical conclusions to solve problems and inform decisions.	
Levels of Scale	*Evidence of Learning Using "I Can" Statements*
Advanced Extends thinking/uses far transfer	**Student demonstrates mastery of *Proficient* level, plus:** • Demonstrates ability to transfer knowledge to other situations to solve problems • Extends thinking beyond course objectives to create and design new applications demonstrating transfer of knowledge in the form of new inquiries (e.g., further inquiries for investigation based on interpretation of data)
Proficient Constructs knowledge, attempts far transfer	**Student demonstrates mastery of *Approaching Proficient* level, plus:** • Can reason, articulate, and inform on mathematical algorithm to explain function • Can interpret graphical representation and explain slope of graph • Makes attempts at extending thinking beyond the function and applying concept to other situations • Demonstrates ability to critique other algorithms and propose alternative solutions
Approaching Proficiency Tasks require (near) transfer and integration of skills and knowledge	**Student demonstrates mastery of *Developing* level, plus:** • Can construct a correct algorithm for the function using algebraic expressions • Can construct an accurate model in the form of a graph to evaluate function • Can develop a logical argument to defend algorithm
Developing Performs or understands the less complex aspects, parts (in isolation) required for more complex tasks	**Student demonstrates mastery of prerequisite skills in *Rookie* level, plus:** • Can reason mathematically through collaboration and construct meaning through discussion • Can connect ideas and express ideas mathematically and/or construct argument based on evidence • Can construct and defend a function algorithm • Can organize facts and construct a graph based on algorithm to display a model of function
Rookie/Emerging Foundational skills developing and building to create comprehension	• Can write an algebraic equation using symbolic representation • Can use arithmetic operations to solve algebraic equations • Can model graphically labeling x and y axis. • Can reason mathematically and think creatively to create comprehension

Source: Created by Angelique Hamilton. Used with permission.

FIGURE 3.11 Sample Classroom Poster

Source: **Created by Tom Mungovan for the Concord Regional and Technical Center. Used with permission.**

Student Self-Reflection (Effect Size = 0.75)

→ 4. **Descriptions in the scale are written in student-friendly language.** All performance levels are stated in the affirmative (I can do, write, organize, analyze, etc.) and in the present tense. Students can use a scale to articulate or reflect on evidence of their own progress during student-led conferences or in written reflections.

> Kirsten Soroko, Curriculum and Instruction Coordinator at Pinkerton Academy in New Hampshire, shared with us that after teachers at her school began to develop and use performance scales for their competencies, they also asked students to use the scales as a conferencing tool for self-reflection on learning. The students had to find evidence within their work samples to "justify" their growth to their peers and teachers. This process helped students to learn how to articulate their progress and sustain inquiry because of their ability to understand DOK and transfer their knowledge and skills to other contexts or personal applications. At Pinkerton, using this type of evaluation helps teachers and students become partners in the learning process, and advance true authenticity in student-centered learning.

5. **The grain size of competency statements matters!** Too many smaller-grained scales can lead to management issues. This is what happens when scales are built for each individual standard. Too small a grain size also means that deeper thinking and reasoning may never be assessed at the higher performance levels of the scale when the competency describes an isolated skill.

6. **The most useful performance scales—in terms of planning instruction and designing assessments—actually describe how students typically learn and develop expertise over time.** Learning progressions are not made-up ideas about what learning *could* look like. Descriptors of learning along a continuum should reflect what empirical research tells us about learning and cognitive development. If you are not using existing research to inform your scales, you can use teacher action research to collect evidence and validate your performance scales.

Here is what we would expect to see in a validated learning progression or performance scale:

- Lower levels of the (learning) performance scale represent **prerequisites** or foundational skills to be built upon. The fewest number of performance indicators (PIs) would be at the lowest performance level, a starting point for learning that can be built upon. Assessments at this level are more like "practice drills" for isolated skills.

- Students are "making progress" when foundational skills and concepts begin to come together. Students are now making connections (near transfer) but may still struggle with increasingly complex content or processes. Assessments are more like "scrimmages" that provide feedback on the application of skills and concepts in shorter problem-solving situations.

- To demonstrate proficiency, students can integrate skills, concepts, and deeper levels of application (far transfer). This implies that multiple PIs are now at play, and demonstration of learning is more complex than any single performance indicator (I can . . .) could ever be when assessed in isolation. Assessments are more like "games" (performance tasks and project-based assessments).

- At the advanced level of the performance, students can apply what they know in ways that have not been directly taught. Work products show true student ownership of the learning. There is no need to specifically describe what this looks like in your scale. However, assessments do need to open the door for individual students to take unique personalized pathways to demonstrate their learning.

Once the performance scale is developed, course and unit assessments (and assessment evidence) can be linked with levels of the scale, providing clarity to students about how their work products indicate where they are in terms of their own progress. Examination of student work after intentional "targeted" instruction may inform the need to "tweak" performance descriptors at different levels of the scale. (To read more about collecting student work to develop and validate learning progressions, see Module 4 of *A Local Assessment Toolkit to Promote Deeper Learning,* Hess, 2018.)

Getting Started With Performance Scale Development

Use **CBE Tool 6,** Developing Performance Scales (and information already generated after completing **Tool 5,** such as the "I can . . ." statements, content/concepts to learned, and performance-based tasks with DOK levels) to complete the following steps:

← Teacher Cognitive Task Analysis (Effect Size = 1.29)

Performance Scale Step 1: Fill in the competency statement at the top of the page.

Performance Scale Step 2: Begin by describing *Proficient* performance. (We suggest starting with using Level 3 of a four-point scale to denote *Proficient* performance.)

The *Proficient* level includes multiple PIs (performance indicators) drawn from "I can . . ." statements.

Describe an integration of skills, concepts, and dispositions at this and the *Advanced* performance levels.

Assessments will be complex with varied processes and products. Proficiency cannot be fully assessed with a single paper-and-pencil test or with a single assessment.

Performance Scale Step 3: Determine what *Getting Started* and *Making Progress* might look like, moving from foundational to conceptual understanding. Draw upon research whenever possible. "I can . . ." statements— stated in the positive at all levels—describe demonstrating skills in isolation or in less complex contexts.

Performance Scale Step 4: Finally, consider what the *Advanced/Expanding* performance *could* look like; don't assume you know what this actually looks like. *Advanced* performance should be about "far" transfer, student choice, and voice. "I can . . ." statements imply where students have choices or are invited to direct the products, processes, and content of their learning.

After getting feedback from colleagues during a validation process and making several revisions to their performance scale, a development team from Proviso East High School in Maywood, Illinois—Megan Delaney (instructional coach), Jennifer Moore (teacher), and Patrick Hardy (principal)—were finally successful in designing a task-neutral performance scale (seen in Figure 3.12) that was later used to develop three different content-specific performance tasks, offering choices to students taking different learning pathways. Their three assessment task options (aligned with this performance scale) are shown in the next section.

☁ STOP AND REFLECT

How could *task-neutral* performance scales guide varied ways to demonstrate learning and contribute evidence (BOE) of competency for each student?

_____

_____

_____

_____

FIGURE 3.12 Example Using CBE Tool 6: Developing a Task-Neutral Performance Scale

CBE Tool 6	Performance Scale Developed by Proviso East High School	

Competency Statement:

The student will analyze how an author's content and rhetorical choices communicate a text's purpose.

Grade Level: *Grade 11*

Unit of Study: *Rhetorical Analysis—Analyze the rhetorical techniques from an author's argumentative work.*

		Evidence From This Unit/Course (List Instructional or Assessment Tasks)
EXPANDING Score 4.0 Construct new knowledge/(far) transfer, extend thinking	**In addition to Score 3.0**, in-depth insights, solutions, and/or applications go beyond what was explicitly taught. **The student:** *Decides how an author uses satire or irony as well as point of view to challenge expectations or common practice.*	• *Write a reflection explaining theme, purpose, use of rhetoric, and effectiveness of each strategy.*
	3.5 | **In addition to score 3.0 performance,** exhibits some in-depth insight or applications **with partial success** = attempts to go beyond what was taught; extends thinking, but was not completely successful.	
PROFICIENT Score 3.0 Integrate skills and knowledge (near and far) transfer with more complex tasks	The student exhibits *no major misconceptions*, no key factual inaccuracies, nor relevant omissions. **The student:** *Analyzes how an author's content and rhetorical choices communicate a text's purpose.*	• *Create an original product incorporating each rhetorical strategy (ethos, logos, and pathos).*
	2.5 | **In addition to score 2.0 performance,** no major errors and partial knowledge of most of the 3.0 content and skills. Evidence of some flawed explanations, thinking/misconceptions.	
DEVELOPING Score 2.0 Perform or understand the less complex aspects (e.g., parts in isolation) required for more complex tasks	There are no major errors or omissions regarding *the basic details, facts, and routine processes.* The student may exhibit some *key misconceptions* regarding the integration of more complex ideas and processes. **The student:** *Describes the purpose of the text.* *Explains the main ideas or themes presented in a text.* *Explains how the main ideas or themes of a text are addressed by the author.* *Explains the impact the rhetorical techniques and content had upon the text purpose.*	• *Complete a rhetorical analysis graphic organizer for two additional examples.* • *Compare and contrast the rhetorical strategies used in each.*
BEGINNING Score 1.0 Demonstrate foundational skills	With extensive scaffolding and added supports, the student demonstrates a partial understanding of some basic details, terms, and routine processes. **The student:** *Recognizes or recalls specific vocabulary (content, entertain, ethos, inform, logos, pathos, persuade, purpose, rhetoric, omit).* *Identifies the purpose of a text.* *Identifies the main ideas or themes in a text.* *Annotates the use of ethos, logos, and pathos in a text.* *Highlights sections of a text where an author poses debatable questions or omits expected information.* *Describes common purposes of a text (such as to inform, persuade, entertain).*	• *Annotate the use of ethos, logos, and pathos in a text.*

Source: Used with permission from Proviso East High School.

Validation Pit Stop 4: Develop and Validate Performance Assessment Tasks and Rubrics

Many schools that we have worked with over the years have wanted to begin this work by developing and using performance assessments to measure student progress demonstrating proficiency on academic and personal success skills competencies. We often have to slow them down by asking teams to analyze and consider how clearly their competencies are written (CBE Tools 3–4), what learning and rigor are implied in each competency (CBE Tool 5), and how they might teach and measure progress along a learning continuum (CBE Tool 6). Once these planning steps have been completed, developing or adapting existing CB assessments is much easier. In this section, we guide you through developing performance tasks (CBE Tools 7–8) and protocols for providing review and peer feedback on draft performance assessments and scoring rubrics using a validation protocol (CBE Tools 9, 10, and 11). These protocols and tools are drawn from Hess (2018, Module 3), with renumbering of the original tools for ease of use here. What we have not included in this chapter from Karin's *Local Assessment Toolkit* are detailed protocols for **piloting** performance tasks using **cognitive labs (think-alouds)** with students, how to develop an administration guide for common assessments, or how to set up schoolwide scoring, annotation, and calibration sessions.

Developing CB Performance Assessment Tasks and Scoring Rubrics

High-quality performance assessments are important to use when asking students to demonstrate a learning stretch (far transfer). Our focus here is on developing course-embedded tasks and extended performance assessments, both of which are not as easy to design as you might think. This is partly because there is not one "right" answer or approach to complete the tasks successfully and because we probably have not seen as many strong models to guide us as we have had for more traditional assessment items and tasks. Your teams might want to start by modifying an existing performance assessment aligned to one of your competencies rather than starting from scratch to develop a new one. The more you do this, the better you'll get. The more you look critically at the assessments of your peers (during task development or task validations), the more confidence you'll have in creating your own.

The more you look critically at the assessments of your peers (during task development or task validations), the more confidence you'll have in creating your own.

Course-embedded tasks and extended performance assessments *for and of deeper learning* are framed by these common characteristics (Hess, 2018, pp. 248–249):

1. *Performance assessments require (far) transfer.* Products and performances embed the use of basic skills and concepts in novel, authentic contexts. Although skills and concepts are being assessed, it is how (and how many) skills and concepts are applied that results in a learning stretch for students.

Students' Ability to → Transfer Learning
(Effect Size = 0.86)

2. *Performance assessments are open-ended.* Prompts or situations posed to (or designed by) students are open-ended. Varied approaches and use of multiple resources are expected. Solutions are not intended to result in only one correct solution path.

3. *Performance assessments are challenging.* Prompts cause students to actively grapple with concepts (e.g., apply strategies and approaches), stretch their thinking, and explore alternative solutions and constraints.

4. *Performance assessments uncover thinking.* Products/performances require students to engage in substantive reasoning related to concepts/theories (e.g., research, justification, explaining thought process). Generating ideas, questions, propositions, alternative strategies, representations, and so on are integral to completion of the task or project.

> ←| Student Strategy Monitoring
>
> (Effect Size = 0.58)

5. *Performance assessments focus on doing authentic tasks.* Products/ performances reflect real-world skills and dispositions for the context presented. A health sciences assessment or arts assessment reflects what health or arts professionals actually do.

6. *Performance assessments require reflection and use of metacognitive skills.* Unlike traditional tests that may ask for recall and near transfer of less- to more-complex skills and concepts, performance assessments require students to reflect on/be informed by what they have done in the past, self-monitor what they are doing and how well it's working now, and articulate what was learned and how they have extended their own knowledge.

> ←| Student Metacognitive Strategies
>
> (Effect Size = 0.55)

Beginning Performance Assessment Design With "The End in Mind"
Assessment design requires that you consider four key questions as you begin to develop a task description. You might want to refer to your earlier analysis of the competency you will be assessing (CBE Tool 5) as you develop your performance task using CBE Tool 7, A Guide to Performance Assessment Development. The full version of CBE Tool 7 is included in Appendix A.

Begin by answering these questions with colleagues:

> ←| Teacher Cognitive Task Analysis
>
> (Effect Size = 1.29)

* What (content, skills, and applications) will this assess?

* Within what (authentic) context?

* Using what assessment format (case study analysis, role playing scenario, research project, performance task, etc.)?

* To what degree will students be given choices or be required to make decisions about the task design, approach, resources used, or presentation of their learning?

TABLE 3.6 Using Rubric Criteria Types to Plan Performance Assessments

Criterion Types	Questions Typically Answered by Each Scoring Criterion
Process	Will the student follow particular processes (e.g., procedures for a science investigation; data collection; validating credibility of sources)? (Usually DOK 2 for more complex tasks)
Form	Are there formats or rules to be applied (e.g., correct citation format; organize parts of lab report; use required camera shots/visuals; edit for grammar and usage)? (Usually DOK 1)
Accuracy of Content	List essential domain-specific terms, calculations, concepts, or principles to be applied. (Usually DOK 1 or 2)
Construction of New Knowledge	How will the student go beyond the accurate solution and correct processes to gain new insights and raise new questions? Are there any personal success skills that might also be employed? (Usually DOK 3 or 4)
Impact	How will the final product achieve its intended purpose (e.g., solve a complex problem; persuade the audience; synthesize information to create a new product/performance)? (Usually DOK 3 or 4)

Before deciding what format the assessment will take or the specifics of what students will "produce" to demonstrate proficiency, we suggest using Table 3.6, which shows types of rubric criteria to identify what the assessment is intended to measure. This is only an initial brainstorm to clarify your assessment purpose and scope; the details will likely change as the design of the performance task evolves. For each criterion, generate a list of the expected processes/skills, concepts, dispositions, and thinking strategies you plan to assess. All criteria do not need to be included in the final assessment, but all *should be considered* during this phase of the planning.

CBE Tool 7, A Guide to Performance Assessment Development, incorporates Table 3.6 into Step 1 of the assessment design process and walks you through a protocol for assessment development.

Suggested Steps for Designing a New Performance Assessment Task or Analyzing an Existing Assessment

Task Development Step 1: Use the rubric criteria types (in Table 3.6) to identify what will be assessed. Hess CRM Tools #1–#5D (Appendix B) will be useful in identifying specific performance indicators and intended DOK levels for different content domains. All rubric criteria do not need to be included for every summative assessment, but they should be considered during the design phase. Only the last two criteria (*Construction of New Knowledge* and *Impact*) will allow you to assess "far transfer" of skills, concepts, and dispositions.

Task Development Step 2: Identify one or more authentic contexts for applying these skills, concepts, and dispositions. Consider how real-world professionals employ these skills (scientists, artists, historians, researchers, choreographers, writers, etc.).

Task Development Step 3: Identify an appropriate assessment format for demonstrating learning. Once you decide on a format, your team might want to explore existing models and use/modify one as a template for your assessment design:

- Case study analysis
- Role-playing scenario
- Research project
- Science investigation
- Performance task, develop a product
- Performance/presentation
- Problem-based projects
- Student Self-Reflection

Task Development Step 4: Determine to what degree students will be given choices or be required to make decisions about the task design, approach to solution, resources used, or presentation (products) of learning.

Task Development Step 5: Use **CBE Tools 5 and 6** to identify and align **success criteria** (competencies, standards, DOK levels).

A Guide to Scoring Rubric Development

A well-written rubric provides direction to both the teacher and student as to what to do next to advance the learning. You may end up creating a teacher- and a student-friendly version of your rubrics. Student-friendly versions encourage student self-assessment and timely feedback.

← **Timely Self-Regulatory Feedback** (Effect Size = 0.66)

Now that you have a draft performance assessment based on your performance scale, you can use **CBE Tool 11** to develop a reliable scoring guide/rubric to measure learning. Scoring criteria for the performance task link back to the "I can . . . " statements in the performance scale, as illustrated in the example in Table 3.7. This research-based protocol for rubric development is based on Hess (2018, pp. 146–147). The full version of **CBE Tool 11** is included in Appendix A.

When developed collaboratively with colleagues, rubrics reflect common understandings of expectations, and the quality and use of rubrics is vastly improved. Teachers can co-develop rubrics with students by showing exemplars of student work (e.g., from a previous school year) and guide them to derive criteria and performance indicators, based on the examples.

TABLE 3.7 Making Connections: From Performance Scale to Performance Task to Scoring Rubric

Performance Scale (I Can . . .)	Sample Performance Task	Criteria for Scoring Rubric
• I can research a topic. • I can analyze events and link past to present. • I can communicate findings in a variety of ways.	Research a "giant of science," explaining the significance of his/her discovery, both past and present. Share in an oral and a written report and reflect on what you've learned.	• Research skills • Accuracy of science content, theories, and concepts • Analyze the impact of the discovery • Reflect on what it means to be a "giant of science"

Reminders for High-Quality Rubric Development

- Be descriptive, not judgmental or vague with language.

- Quantity does not equal quality. Emphasize quality!

- Keep wording positive! Describe what *is* there, not what is missing, if at possible (e.g., "one of the three sections is complete").

- Excellence is not the same as perfection. Describe quality, not perfection.

- Criteria should include both basic (foundational) understandings and deeper thinking.

- Describe a specific progression of development moving from less to more complex understanding and performance.

- Be kid friendly, especially if you use "headings" rather than numbers for each performance level. Students would probably not want to self-assess with a heading like *Below Basic*, which is quite negative. *Beginning* or *Novice* means the same thing but says it in a more positive way. After all, we've all been a novice at everything we've ever learned how to do.

Rubric Development Step 1: Articulate a continuum of increasingly complex learning.

Begin by writing the desired learning outcomes for the *Proficient* level in observable, measurable, and descriptive language. Consider how students will develop understanding and expertise to get to the desired performance. Emphasize skills in lower levels that move from foundational to conceptual to transfer and deeper understanding at the *Advanced/Expert* level. Don't worry if you can't clearly describe advanced performance before seeing student work samples. Your early descriptions may actually limit what students will try to do. It's OK to say "meets all criteria at the *Proficient* level, plus provides a more sophisticated or deeper understanding of the concepts and skills." You can fill in examples to describe advanced work after analyzing what you saw in the

FIGURE 3.13 Cutaway of CBE Tool 11**: Rubric Quality Review Worksheet**

CBE Tool 11	Rubric Quality Review Worksheet	

Assessment Task:	
Date:	Reviewer(s):

Questions for Evaluating Rubric Quality	Comments/Feedback for Each Review Question
1. **Do the number of performance levels and rubric format make sense?** ☐ Format matches purpose and use. ☐ Adjacent performance levels are *qualitatively* different. ☐ Levels reflect how completion of the task might naturally progress with instruction.	
2. **Is descriptive language maximized?** ☐ Little or no judgmental language. ☐ Avoids use of subjective language (poor, neat, ample, etc.) and frequency indicators (rarely, often, etc.).	
3. **Do descriptors emphasize quality over quantity?** (e.g., relevant, descriptive details/sources versus three details/sources)	
4. **Do descriptors state performance in the positive?** (e.g., what *is* happening rather than what is *not* happening) ☐ Lowest levels focus on beginning stages.	

student work. Finally, don't assume every cell in the rubric needs to be filled in. There is not always a way to describe advanced levels of skills such as editing or calculating or citing sources.

Rubric Development Step 2: Focus on the quality of student work at all performance levels.

Although specific products will differ, criteria at *Proficient* and *Advanced* levels should explicitly describe the knowledge, skills, and performance expected. Scoring criteria for levels below *Proficient* will not include all elements encompassed in a competency statement, but should consider what might be completed first, such as drafting a plan and collecting data at the lower performance levels and analyzing data collected at the upper performance levels.

Rubric Development Step 3: Review criteria and performance indicators to see if they can apply to a variety of performances and products.

When scoring criteria can be used to assess multiple artifacts of student work—rather than only one specific task—students have the opportunity to demonstrate their knowledge and skills in a variety of ways and over time. Criteria that are "task neutral" help teachers to meet diverse learning needs of students and to integrate assessment data more meaningfully.

Rubric Development Step 4: Use CBE Tool 11 to get feedback on your draft rubric.

Deciding Where and When to Use Performance Assessments

After your assessment task scoring rubric has been developed, use CBE Tool 8 (see Figure 3.14) to provide an overview of what this task assesses, where and when this will be embedded in curriculum (unit/course), how results will be used (formative vs. summative), and how it relates to other assessments in the unit of study/course (e.g., "relates" might mean that there is a unit preassessment and this is the postassessment for the same unit). The full version of CBE Tool 8 is included in Appendix A.

☁ STOP AND REFLECT

How might these tools and processes ensure the technical quality (alignment, rigor, student engagement, fairness) of your CB performance assessments?

_____

_____

_____

_____

Figure 3.15 illustrates how the team from Proviso East High School answered the questions in CBE Tool 8, using a task-neutral performance scale (shown earlier in Figure 3.12) to design three comparable task options for students in different career academies. This example shows an authentic application of how to assess a competency in different content domains, as well as comparable pathways of learning for the same competency using multiple assessment tasks of increasing complexity.

- Part 1 of this task formatively assesses foundational knowledge of rhetorical strategies, asking students to complete a graphic organizer (DOK 2).

- Part 2 of this task includes several assessment tasks: Students select and complete a rhetorical analysis of two different pieces of persuasive media (DOK 3); use the analyses to compare and contrast the two sources (DOK 4); and then critique the analysis work of a classmate (DOK3).

- Part 3 of this task requires students to use what they have learned to develop an original example of persuasive media (DOK 3) and write a reflection, drawing from multiple sources to critique its effectiveness (DOK 4).

FIGURE 3.14 Cutaway of CBE Tool 8: Performance Assessment Overview: Purpose and Use

CBE Tool 8	Performance Assessment Overview: Purpose and Use	

Use this tool to provide an overview of when the assessment will be used and what it is intended to assess.	
Unit of Study/Course:	**Grade Level:**

Enduring Understandings/Big Ideas
Essential Question(s) to Guide Inquiry/Learning

Performance Assessment /Task Overview

Assessment Alignment to Learning Goals: List . . . Academic or Personal Success Skills Competencies	**Performance Indicators (in Student "Language"):** I can . . .
Students Will Know (key terms, concepts, principles):	**Students Will Do/Apply** (include intended DOK levels):
Assessment Success Criteria (and intended DOK) • Scoring Guide attached?	**Allowable/Possible Accommodations/Supports** • Student choice in topic or product • Choice to work individually or with a group • Teacher consultations (one for launch and work

Getting Peer Feedback on Draft Assessment Tasks and Rubrics

Once your team has designed task prompts, scoring rubrics, and administration guides for an assessment, we recommend getting peer feedback to help refine it before implementing the assessment widely. We've included three tools and protocols from *A Local Assessment Toolkit* (Hess, 2018, Module 3) to guide this work.

- **CBE Tool 9**, Task Quality Validation Protocol, is a protocol that guides teams to answer questions about assessment task clarity, alignment, rigor, student engagement, and fairness (equity). (This is also Tool #9 from *A Local Assessment Toolkit.*)

- **CBE Tool 10**, Task Validation Summary (Streamlined Version), is a worksheet teams can use to give feedback to their peers after a task review and validation session. (This is Tool #16A from *A Local Assessment Toolkit.*)

- **CBE Tool 11**, Rubric Quality Review Worksheet, is both a development and review tool teams can use for rubric design. (This is also Tool #11 from *A Local Assessment Toolkit.*)

FIGURE 3.15 Three Comparable Task Options to Assess Progress on the Same Competency

Rhetorical Analysis and Rhetorical Writing:

Competency-Based Performance Assessment Tasks

© Delaney, Moore, & Hardy (2019)

It is time to show what you have learned about conducting rhetorical analysis and using rhetorical strategies in communication!

Below are three sets of performance tasks. Each one has been created for your personal pathway according to your career academy. If you are in ACA, please do the ACA Pathway task. If you are in BHA, please do the BHA Pathway task, and if you are in STEM, please do the STEM Pathway task. **You only need to do the task that relates to your academy.**

Each part will receive a separate score that contributes to your overall score for the summative performance tasks. Please consult the attached rubrics to see how you will be scored.

Competency:

The student will analyze how an author's content and rhetorical choices communicate a text's purpose.

Learning Targets:

I can determine the author's theme and purpose when viewing a piece of persuasive media.

I can view a piece of persuasive media and identify the rhetorical strategies used by the author.

I can evaluate the impact of an author's use of rhetorical strategies in a piece of persuasive media.

I can compare and contrast the use of rhetorical strategies between authors on a particular topic.

I can effectively use rhetorical strategies in my communication with others that best fit my audience to prove my point of view.

	ACA Pathway (Arts and Communications Focus)	BHA Pathway (Business and Human Services Focus)	STEM Pathway (Science, Technology, Engineering, and Math Focus)
Part 1	Rhetorical Analysis and Rhetorical Writing: Formative Assessment Rhetorical Strategies Identification		
(DOK 1 and DOK 2) Identify author's rhetorical strategies.	• Choose a product that carries one or more brand (e.g., shoes, clothing, hamburgers). • Select a brand and view an advertisement (may be print, video, or audio commercial) and identify which rhetorical strategies are used in the advertisement. • Complete a graphic organizer detailing the rhetorical strategies you have identified.	• Choose a highly debatable political issue (e.g., immigration, tax reform, gun laws). • Select an election promise speech (may be via website, print, or video, etc.) that deals with the issue you chose and identify which rhetorical strategies are used in the article. • Complete a graphic organizer detailing the rhetorical strategies you have identified.	• Choose a highly debatable scientific issue (e.g., climate change, vaccination, stem cell research). • Select a scholarly article or video that deals with the scientific issue you chose and identify which rhetorical strategies are used in the article. • Complete a graphic organizer detailing the rhetorical strategies you have identified.

Rhetorical Analysis and Rhetorical Writing: Summative Assessment Tasks

Complete a rhetorical analysis of two different pieces of persuasive media. Compare and contrast the two sources using Flip Grid. Review and critique classmate posts.

Part 2		

(DOK 3 and DOK 4)
 	
Compare, contrast, and evaluate rhetorical strategies used, the theme and purpose of each piece of persuasive media, and evaluate their overall impact.
	• Select **two different brands or companies** from the product you selected in Part 1 and evaluate their advertisements. (For example, if you chose an advertisement for Geico Auto Insurance, then you would want to choose an advertisement for State Farm and Progressive Auto Insurance.)
	
	• Complete a rhetorical analysis graphic organizer for the two additional advertisements.
	
	• Compare and contrast the rhetorical strategies used in each advertisement and present your findings via video on the class Flip Grid, "ACA." Your video should be no more than 10 minutes and should include
	
	  ○ A brief summary of your ads, including the theme and purpose with evidence from the ad
	
	  ○ Which rhetorical strategies were used and whether you believe they had an impact on the viewer of the advertisement and why
	
	• Log into the class Flip Grid and select the topic "ACA" and view one classmate's video and record a video responding to your classmate's analysis of their ads' purpose, theme, and rhetorical strategies.
		• Select **two different political speeches** from the previous election promise speech you selected in Part 1 and evaluate their speeches. (For example, if you chose former President Obama speaking about immigration reform, you would then select President Trump or former President George H. W. Bush's speeches concerning immigration.)
		
		• Complete a rhetorical analysis graphic organizer for the two additional speeches.
		
		• Compare and contrast the rhetorical strategies used in each speech and present your findings via video on the class Flip Grid, "BHA." Your video should be no more than 10 minutes and should include
		
		  ○ A brief summary of your speeches, including the theme and purpose with evidence from the speeches
		
		  ○ Which rhetorical strategies were used and whether you believe they had an impact on the viewer of the speech and why
		
		• Log into the class Flip Grid and select the topic "BHA" and view one classmate's video and record a video responding to your classmate's analysis of her or his ads' purpose, theme, and rhetorical strategies.
			• Select **two different scholarly articles** from the previous article you selected in Part 1 and evaluate their messages. (For example, if you chose an article about the killed vaccines, you could then select an article about the live, attenuated vaccines or oral vaccines.)
			
			• Complete a rhetorical analysis graphic organizer for the two additional articles.
			
			• Compare and contrast the rhetorical strategies used in each article and present your findings via video on the class Flip Grid, "STEM." Your video should be no more than 10 minutes and should include
			
			  ○ A brief summary of your articles, including the theme and purpose with evidence from the articles
			
			  ○ Which rhetorical strategies were used and whether you believe they had an impact on the viewer of the article and why
			
			• Log into the class Flip Grid and select the topic "STEM" and view one classmate's video and record a video responding to your classmate's analysis of her of his ads' purpose, theme, and rhetorical strategies.

(Continued)

FIGURE 3.15 (Continued)

Part 3	Rhetorical Analysis and Rhetorical Writing: Summative Assessment Tasks Create an original persuasive communication using rhetorical strategies. Write a reflection evaluating its effectiveness.		
(DOK 3 and DOK 4)	**Advertisement**	**Campaign Promise**	**Scientific Treatise**

Effectively communicate using rhetorical strategies appropriate for a particular audience.	• Create an original advertisement for the product you selected in Part 1 (this may be a commercial, a flyer, window poster, etc.).
	
	• Your advertisement should incorporate each of the rhetorical strategies (ethos, logos, and pathos).
	
	• You should write a reflection explaining your advertisement:
	  ○ The theme and purpose of your advertisement
	  ○ The use of rhetoric and explanation of how you demonstrated each strategy
	  ○ Your intended audience and why you think your advertisement rhetoric addresses them specifically
		• Create an original political campaign promise for the debatable political topic you selected in Part 1 (this may be a commercial, a pamphlet, speech, etc.).
		
		• Your promise should incorporate each of the rhetorical strategies (ethos, logos, and pathos).
		
		• You should write a reflection explaining your campaign promise:
		  ○ The theme and purpose of your promise
		  ○ The use of rhetoric and explanation of how you demonstrated each strategy
		  ○ Your intended audience and why you think your promise and rhetoric address them specifically
			• Create an original scientific treatise for the debatable scientific topic you selected in Part 1 (this may be framed as a journal article, infographic, speech, etc.).
			
			• Your treatise should incorporate each of the rhetorical strategies (ethos, logos, and pathos).
			
			• You should write a reflection explaining your treatise:
			  ○ The theme and purpose of your treatise
			  ○ The use of rhetoric and explanation of how you demonstrated each strategy
			  ○ Your intended audience and why you think your treatise and rhetoric address them specifically

Source: Used with permission from Proviso East High School.

STOP AND REFLECT

Review the three optional assessment examples in Figure 3.15. How do these examples support the idea of a "task-neutral" performance scale (same competency, different evidence)?

_____

_____

_____

_____

_____

_____

_____

_____

_____

_____

_____

_____

_____

_____

_____

_____

_____

_____

_____

_____

_____

Analyzing the Technical Quality of Local Assessments

Even if your school district purchases its assessments, many protocols in this chapter can and should be used to ensure that all assessments are of high quality and administered with fidelity. Over the years, we have found that high-priority **summative assessments** (e.g., final exams, unit tests, **exhibitions**, project-based assessments) and performance assessments used as common formative, interim, or summative assessments improve greatly when there is a formal review of their technical quality. A review of this kind answers several questions: Is the assessment valid (aligned to both the intended content and rigor); do scoring guides and support materials, such as annotated student work, ensure that the assessment will be scored reliably (the same) by different teachers; will it engage students in authentic applications of skills and concepts (transfer); and is it free of bias and designed to be flexible enough for all students to show what they have learned? Our term for conducting a formal, collaborative review is *task validation*.

- Task validations are part of an ongoing development and refinement process, not one-time events.

- Task validations are not necessary for all assessments, so start with the ones used for making high-stakes decisions, such as determining whether a student has met a district proficiency requirement.

- A *validated assessment* is one that has gone through a critical review and revision process and has been determined to measure what it was intended to measure. Therefore, users of the assessment can make valid interpretations about student learning based on scores given.

During a task validation, a school- or district-based team meets to analyze assessments developed by their peers. The overall goals of task validation are

| Teacher Cognitive Task Analysis (Effect Size = 1.29) | $\longrightarrow$ |

developing a common language for assessment quality/calibration and providing constructive advice for improving both assessment and instructional practice across all content areas. Teams often review the same assessment more than once using a validation process guided by criteria and questions in **CBE Tool 9** (see Figure 3.16).

Two things we can say for sure about using this task validation process over more than two decades in many states: No assessment ever gets by with "flying colors" on the first review, and the resulting quality of the revised assessment always improves. Collaboration works!

Validation criteria—clarity, alignment to content and rigor, scoring reliability, student engagement, and fairness—are systematically reviewed, discussed, and documented. Validation team members then give their peers feedback in the form of descriptive comments and questions, using **CBE Tool 10**. Teacher teams who developed the assessment reflect on the feedback, decide what should be revised, and at some point, may resubmit their assessment for a second review. Two things we can say for sure about using this task validation process over more than two decades in many states:

FIGURE 3.16 Cutaway of CBE Tool 9: Task Quality Validation Protocol

CBE Tool 9	Task Quality Validation Protocol: Purpose, Alignment, Engagement, and Fairness | Use for Assessment *Development* or *Analysis of Performance Tasks*

Title of Assessment/Task:	Grade Level/Dept/Course/Subject:
Author(s):	or Reviewer(s):

How will the assessment results be used?

(e.g., screening for placement; diagnostic to inform instruction or to provide targeted additional support; formative or interim for progress monitoring; summative for grading/report card; or other?)

Analyze and discuss each of the assessment components. Check the box if there is evidence of each indicator of high-quality assessment listed. Then add any additional notes.

Clarity and Focus

☐ 1. Addresses an **essential issue, big idea, or key concept or skill** of the unit, course, or discipline:

☐ 2. Directions or prompts clearly indicate what the student is being asked to do or produce:

☐ 3. If parts are completed within a group: Specifies what will be assessed **individually** (e.g., projects, multimedia presentations)

☐ 4. **Assesses what is intended to be assessed**—will elicit what the student knows and can do related to the chosen standards and benchmarks.

   Any scaffolding provided (e.g., task broken into smaller steps; graphic organizer to preplan) does not change what is actually being assessed.

☐ 5. Is clearly linked to **ongoing instruction or opportunity to learn** (e.g., assessed within or at the end of a unit of study or course)

Clarity and Focus Notes

Content Alignment

☐ 6. Items or tasks are clearly **aligned with specific or identified content standards** (or intended parts or combinations of content standards)

☐ 7. Appropriate **rubric(s) or scoring guide(s)** assess all intended parts of content standards assessed. Scoring

No assessment ever gets by with "flying colors" on the first review, and the resulting quality of the revised assessment always improves. Collaboration works!

Preparing to Have an Assessment Formally Reviewed

Several important things need to happen before conducting a task validation. Decisions must be made about which teachers will make up each validation team and when time will be allowed for guided practice/calibration and for the actual validation meetings. Most schools try to use existing structures, such as their scheduled professional development days or during grade-level team time, to conduct the validations. Once time structures are determined, the assessments to be reviewed are put on a schedule and prepared for review. Don't be overambitious with scheduling; completing one round each month is a good way to begin. Estimate at least 60 to 90 minutes for a task validation to be completed. We have typically organized several different teams to work simultaneously so that several assessments can be reviewed on the same day. For example, if a middle school has three instructional teams, each team might validate an assessment developed by another team so that three assessments go through the process at the same time. Then, allow at least two to three more weeks for task revisions before scheduling your next session.

Determining the Makeup of Validation Teams

Working over many years with school faculties, we have learned that *every* staff member needs to be involved in the assessment development and validation process. This includes all special subject teachers (fine arts, health/PE, world languages, etc.) as well as all classroom teachers. Special education teachers and instructional coaches can join a grade level or content team to work on task design and validation teams. All building principals should also be members of a validation team.

Each school district will need to consider the best configurations for creating validation teams that involve every staff member at each school. Often, elementary teams are structured differently than middle and high school teams. Here are some ideas to guide your thinking about team makeup.

Validation Principle 1: Each local validation team represents the diversity of the school/district.

- Involve everyone on a team, including administrators, curriculum leaders, instructional coaches, and teachers.

- All content areas and grade levels/grade spans are represented (decisions may differ depending on school configurations and staffing, but diversity in teams is critical, especially including special educators on every team).

- Elementary teams may configure by grade spans, middle schools by instructional teams (e.g., each team with an ELA, math, science, and social studies teacher), and high schools with one department member on *each* team. We do not recommend content-based teams for validations. Content teams develop the assessments; cross-content teams validate the assessments.

- In addition, have representation from special subjects (fine arts, HPE, CTE, foreign language, ELL, etc.) on each validation team (dividing member of this group across teams in the most meaningful ways you can).

- Consider team size. Teams with more than six to eight members are generally too large and become unproductive. Consider having one member to represent each of the core content areas (ELA, math, science, social studies), plus one special subject teacher, plus one special educator/resource teacher/ ELL teacher, plus an administrator or instructional coach on each team.

Validation Principle 2: Provide guided practice in task design and task validation. It's important to educate and engage all staff in processes for developing, validating, and eventually scoring common assessments and analyzing student work products. Yes, this takes time at the start, but it will increase the consistency of schoolwide expectations and build a common language for describing the quality of student work. The first rounds are for calibrating these understandings and processes. Later rounds are for improving assessment quality and interpreting assessment results. We begin each new validation process first by modeling a validation with a sample assessment (not an assessment developed by the staff). Older performance tasks that teachers have been using or new ones that have been purchased work well as a starting point for looking at characteristics of technical quality. We provide guided practice with the assessment review and debriefing. Teams are soon ready to take the lead with their own assessments.

Validation Principle 3: Frequency and involvement will vary/be determined by the intended uses of the assessment task validation tools and protocols. **First, identify** your short- and long-term purpose(s) for validation. Your goals will guide how to structure the size of groups.

- Develop new assessments—smaller content-based or grade-level teams work on new assessments.

- Analyze existing assessments—larger, more-representative teams review and provide feedback on draft assessments.

- Validate a revised assessment or new assessments prior to broader administration or purchase (e.g., tasks available from existing task banks)—smaller, content-based teams who have participated in validation.

- Provide *objective* feedback to assessment developers—involve the whole school/district on a regular basis.

- Promote collaboration and a shared understanding of high-quality assessment—involve the whole school/district on a regular basis.

Assemble (or update) a "collection" (task bank) of validated common performance assessments. As common performance assessments achieve validation with analysis of student work, the whole school/district, working in smaller teams, is responsible for creating electronic files of agreed-upon proficient work samples. Determine the frequency and staff involvement in assessment validation:

- Initially learning and debriefing the process together serves as calibration—so everyone is on the same page—"developing a shared understanding" of what high-quality assessment looks like.

- School teams set up their schedules—once each month or every other month, as needed, identified by highest priority (time/semester to be given, for making high-stakes decisions, etc.).

- Team members may eventually rotate on/off so more (all) staff are regularly involved over time, but *not* before all staff have been engaged with the process.

Preparing Assessments for Validation Panels

- Grade level or department teams develop the assessments using (a) the Hess CRM Tools #1–#5D for the content area; (b) CBE Tool 7, A Guide to Performance Assessment Development; and (c) a scoring rubric/ guide using CBE Tool 11 (e.g., a Grade 2 team might develop a common mathematics assessment for all Grade 2 classes/schools). The team might also decide to pilot the task with one or two classrooms or conduct a cognitive lab with a small number of students prior to bringing the task to the validation panel. This will help to streamline what might need more revision later and allow developers to collect some student work samples. (You can read more about protocols for piloting assessments using cognitive labs in Module 3 of *A Local Assessment Toolkit*.)

- Developers create brief administration guidelines (CBE Tool 8) for the task, providing general instructions to any teacher who might want to use the assessment in his or her classes. This is very important for all commonly administered CB assessments.

- Developers put the assessment on the local (school/district) validation calendar.

- Developers complete a task cover sheet describing the assessment parts/ what will be reviewed by the panel. When we began to run validation panels, we did not require a cover sheet from developers, but we soon found that panels were spending too much time searching for parts that were not included or assessments that were not well organized. The cover page simply lets the validation panel know what to look for (e.g., rubric, texts used, student work samples with indicators of scores given).

- Developers make multiple copies of the assessment or provide a link to where it can be downloaded. Support materials, such as texts/text passages or student work do not need to be copied, but *at least one set* should be available to the validation team.

- Developers also provide scoring rubrics and answer keys, if appropriate.

- Validation panels prioritize the order of validations; for example, common summative CB assessments given early in the school year are reviewed first; second-round reviews are done after giving feedback to developers or after piloting.

A Protocol for Validation Sessions

An assessment task validation session takes about 75 to 90 minutes. The process helps the panel of four to six people ascertain whether the assessment presented has achieved technical quality for each criterion. It may help to have one of the task developers briefly (5 minutes) provide an overview of the assessment submitted for review and answer any clarifying questions right at the start of the session. We have not found it helpful for developers to remain as observers to the panel discussions, at least when you are just starting out with task reviews.

Validation Step 1: Start by determining who on the panel will act in the roles of the facilitator and recorder. Two key jobs of the facilitator are to be sure everyone on the panel has a chance to speak/provide input and to keep the group moving along. Sometimes, a timekeeper can also be helpful (5 minutes).

Validation Step 2: Next, quickly review and update the group's norms. It's helpful to get agreement on norms and to add/delete/revise some before beginning. Agreed-upon norms allow members to hold each other accountable while working (5 minutes).

Validation Step 3: One of the developers briefly walks the panel through the materials and explains the context of the assessment. Then, panel members skim the assessment materials silently and ask a limited number of *clarifying* questions about the materials. If the developer is not there to present the assessment, the panel does a quick skimming of the assessment materials to clarify what they should review. This time is not for depth of understanding the assessment or for analysis (5–10 minutes).

Validation Step 4: Individuals now silently review each part of the assessment and make their own notes on CBE Tool 9. Facilitators may need to remind panels this is for initial impressions/questions (15–20 minutes).

Validation Step 5: After each member has had time to look more closely at the assessment, the facilitator leads the group through each section of the Task Quality Validation Checklist Protocol (CBE Tool 9). Decide on a process to reach consensus (fist 5, thumbs up, etc.). Be sure to *involve each person*! Once there is consensus on each section, the recorder documents key points—including positive points—to be used for summarizing feedback on CBE Tool 10 (30–50 minutes).

Validation Step 6: Summarize final recommendations and choose two panel members to share feedback with the developers. It may sound silly, but they should "rehearse" what they plan to say. Why have two panel members deliver feedback? It's easy to forget what to say and to feel uncomfortable saying it. A second person provides moral support and makes scheduling the brief feedback meeting easier. More than two panel members can make developers feel a bit overwhelmed. We suggest starting with two and meeting in person (10 minutes).

Validation Step 7: Don't skip this team debriefing! (5 minutes)

Did the validation team honor group norms at all times?

Does the team need to modify or revise norms?

What went well?

What could have gone better?

What will the team do differently next time?

Who will meet with task developers to give feedback?

Validation Step 8: You may be tempted to slip your feedback into a school mailbox or to email it. We suggest meeting in person with developers to share feedback—it's the "friendly" part of being a critical friend. It is the developers' job to review feedback and determine their next steps.

Remember that being a "critical friend" means not being too critical (harsh and negative) but also not being too friendly (afraid to be honest with your feedback).

An ongoing validation process helps the school/district maintain a consistent high level of instructional and assessment practice. Validation helps us to build consistency across content areas and make learning expectations described in competencies clear.

Suggestions for Giving Peer Feedback

- Use *descriptive language*, **not** judgmental language.

- While you may wonder about instructional pieces, comments/suggestions about instruction are probably *not appropriate*.

- Your job is *not* to redo/rewrite the assessment! Keep feedback crisp and to the point (e.g., pose a question: We are wondering if students can work with a partner on this step?). It is the developers' job to decide what to do next to strengthen the assessment tasks.

- Well-written, clear feedback guides assessment developers to make a stronger assessment in the end (e.g., we were not able to locate . . .; we were unclear about . . .; we think this might be a DOK 2, not a DOK 3 because . . .).

- Place your most positive (and descriptive) comments under the feedback section at the bottom of **CBE Tool 10**: *What makes this an HQ (high-quality) assessment?* (For example—Students have many opportunities to make decisions about resources and how they will develop their final product.) See feedback example in Appendix A.

STOP AND REFLECT

How might a validation process be used in your school to examine and ensure the quality of your performance assessments and instructional practices?

_____

_____

_____

Validation Pit Stop 5: Collecting Evidence and Verifying Methods and Guidelines for BOE, Grading, and Reporting

This last pit stop comes later in the CBE implementation process and will be revisited many times as the system adds more assessments and updates new grading and reporting policies. **Verification** of the overall system involves a variety of stakeholders, including student representatives, depending on the focus of investigation at the time. The only thing we can tell you for certain is that your system will get better over time only if you pay attention to the learning needs of school leaders, teachers, students, and the larger community. We cannot fix or improve upon what we do not yet fully understand.

5
Collect Evidence and Verify Methods: Guidelines for BOE, Grading, and Reporting

Verification questions that we know will come up over and over again will be about grading and assessment practices, managing instruction and the pacing of learning (students moving on "when ready"), and determining whether a student is or is not "proficient" at any given point in time. Making decisions about whether a student is proficient is not about one test, one task, one observation, or one rubric score. Just as we began this journey with developing a profile of the graduate, we can think about developing typical profiles of the body of evidence for students who are meeting the intended learning goals and what that evidence represents (see Figure 3.17).

← **Collective Teacher Efficacy (Effect Size = 1.39)**

We've included some critical questions that schools might consider exploring as they work to refine and improve the overall CBE system. First, we consider questions regarding the stated goals for learning (competency statements):

- To what degree do our competencies still match the academic and the personal success skills identified in the district's profile of the graduate (POG)?

- How well are we supporting individual students along their learning pathways? What evidence will help us to answer this question?

FIGURE 3.17 Considering What to Include in a Student's Body of Evidence

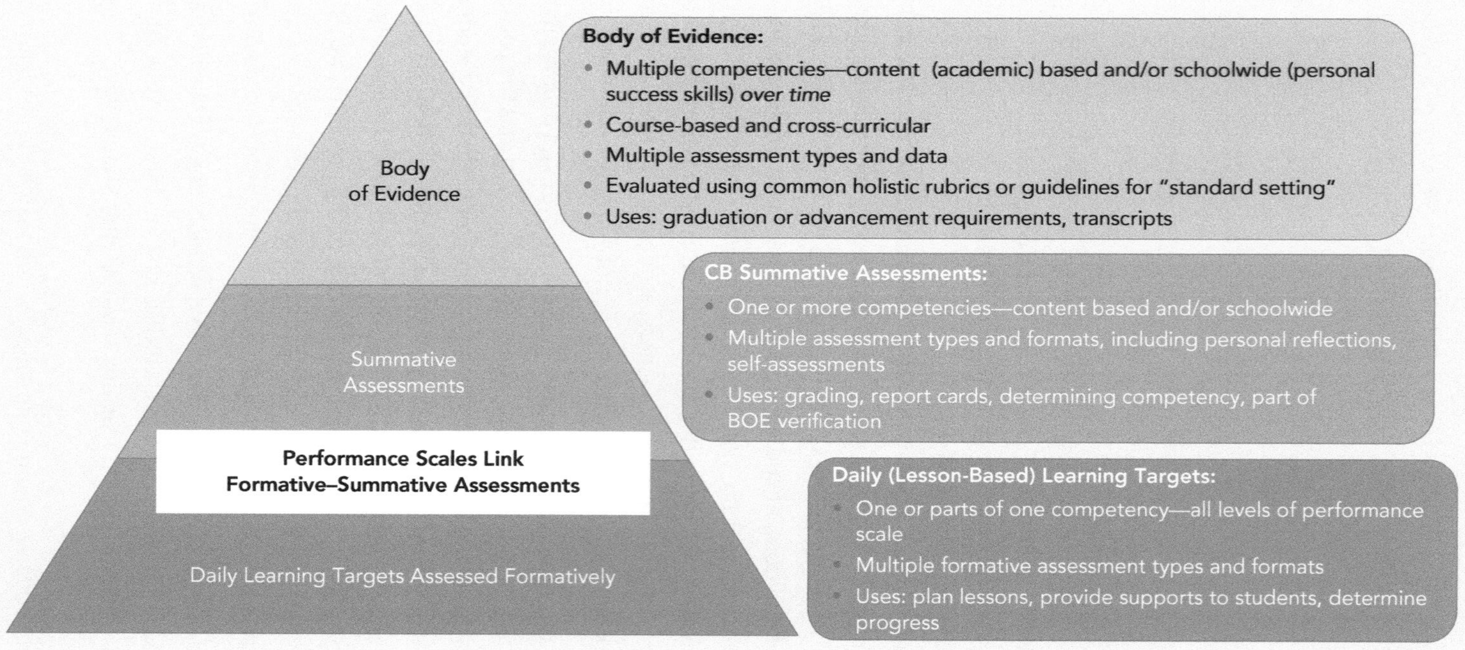

Body of Evidence:
- Multiple competencies—content (academic) based and/or schoolwide (personal success skills) over time
- Course-based and cross-curricular
- Multiple assessment types and data
- Evaluated using common holistic rubrics or guidelines for "standard setting"
- Uses: graduation or advancement requirements, transcripts

CB Summative Assessments:
- One or more competencies—content based and/or schoolwide
- Multiple assessment types and formats, including personal reflections, self-assessments
- Uses: grading, report cards, determining competency, part of BOE verification

Daily (Lesson-Based) Learning Targets:
- One or parts of one competency—all levels of performance scale
- Multiple formative assessment types and formats
- Uses: plan lessons, provide supports to students, determine progress

Body of Evidence

Summative Assessments

Performance Scales Link Formative—Summative Assessments

Daily Learning Targets Assessed Formatively

- Do our common CB assessments align with competencies, and are they being implemented with fidelity?

- Do the performance scales we created help us in designing performance tasks? Why or why not?

- Are our validation protocols working to regularly examine and improve upon quality?

- Do our assessment, grading, and reporting policies need updating? What are we still struggling with?

- What evidence is telling us things are working well?

> ### 💭 STOP AND REFLECT
>
> Review the questions regarding the stated goals for learning (competency statements). Which question resonates most with you now and why?
>
> _____
>
> _____
>
> _____

Next, we offer questions about what types of evidence to collect and how much evidence will be considered enough:

- What evidence should we collect? Do we include student reflections on learning, peer and student self-assessments, and student-designed assessments?

- How often do we collect and contribute evidence to the BOE? Can students contribute evidence from different courses to demonstrate learning for the same competency? Can new (more recent) evidence replace "earlier" evidence?

- How much is sufficient evidence? School teams need to consider the collection of assessment data the way we might analyze an athlete's overall performance. Showing up for practice every day and becoming competent in demonstrating isolated skills (passing, dribbling, shooting, etc.) does not mean the player is proficient in soccer. Likewise, playing well in one or two soccer games is not sufficient evidence to tell us that a player will consistently play well. Rules for sufficiency need to look at patterns of performance over time (consistency) and the rigor of those performances (assessment types).

- Will this be a **conjunctive** CBE system—meaning must a student meet all expectations for each competency (e.g., in each content area)? Does the soccer player need to be competent playing all positions on the field in all types of games?

- Will this be a **compensatory** CBE system—meaning that if a student meets expectations for most competencies (e.g., in a content area), that performance can compensate for not meeting all expectations at the highest levels? Is the soccer player competent when playing most positions on the field in all types of games?

- Is there agreement (among different teachers evaluating different samples of student work) in making judgments about a student's overall performance? Are teachers consistent in how they interpret and evaluate student evidence (scoring reliability)?

- Is a student's overall performance consistent with *comparable* measures on (other) external measures, such as state assessments or other district measures (validity)?

- Is our methodology *practical*, and are the results *reasonable*? Is there a legitimate reason for having widely varying percentages of students classified as proficient across content areas or schools in the district?

STOP AND REFLECT

Review the questions regarding the types and sufficiency of evidence that will be used in the BOE. Which question resonates most with you now and why?

_____

_____

_____

_____

These processes—competency development, assessment design and validation, evidence-based grading, and competency-based reporting—create a very different orientation to what teachers have traditionally been doing for many years. These shifts must be aligned systemically for them to be truly transformational for students.

When MST (Manchester School of Technology) was moving forward, the pain points emerged—this work can be difficult, given that every educator is working every day with their groups of learners. What happens when, all of a sudden, folks have realized that so much has changed and moved from their past experiences? Here again are Jillian and Joe capturing those moments at their school.

A Work in Progress

Everything changed. Every second, every minute, every block, every day—everything changed. And sometimes, that was awesome. In almost every case, students exceeded our planned pace and expectations. But these changes weren't without mistakes and failures. Student engagement in the learning process shone a glaring light on places where we fell short as educators.

Where adequate scaffolding and direction had not been provided in our excitement to give them voice and choice, students did not have the necessary skills to demonstrate proficiency in assessments. We had not anticipated the sometimes lengthy feedback loop process when students did fall short of performance indicators. We had changed our mindset and some critical components, but we had not changed our entire classroom system. With that in mind, we created additional opportunities for intentional targeted instruction, new assessment tools were developed, and an adaptable feedback loop process was embedded in all projects. We still aren't sure who learned more in those early years, but everyone in Room B110 was learning.

—Jillian and Joe

 STOP AND REFLECT

We invite you to doodle on the page with Figure 3.18 to map how you see your CBE journey unfolding. Where are the potential speed bumps? Where are the smooth roads ahead? Who is your "pit crew" to support the work at each pit stop?

FIGURE 3.18 The "Big Picture" of CBE: Use Sketch Notes to Describe the Pit Stops for Your Journey

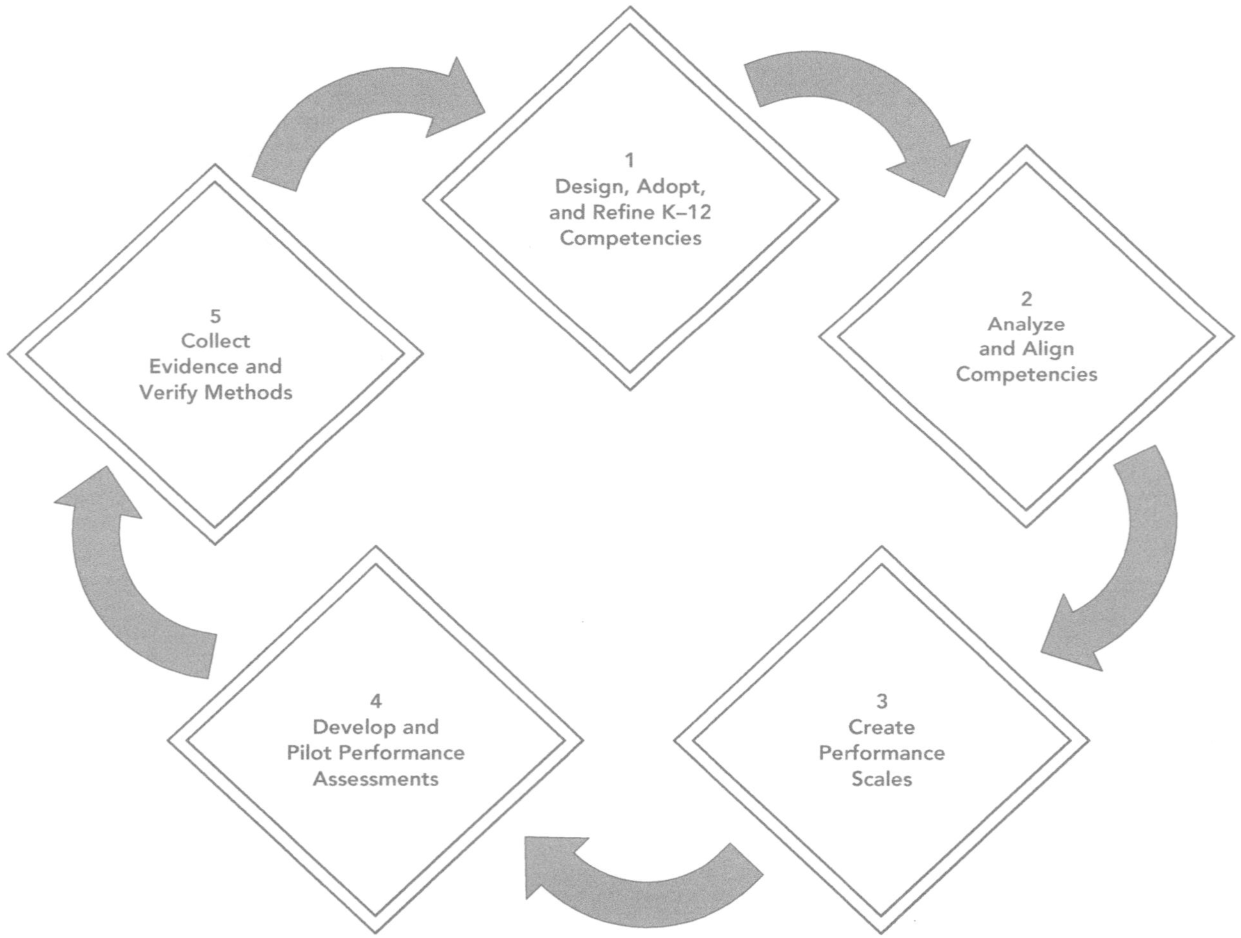

Making the Shift to Student-Centered Classrooms

4

//

What matters is not what we teach; it's what they learn, and the probability of real learning is far higher when the students have a lot to say about both the content and the process.

—Alfie Kohn (2011)

As districts move toward building a more personalized, competency-based system of learning, there are a number of shifts that will occur within classrooms—shifts related to instructional planning, delivery, and pacing, as well as the purposes and uses of assessments *for learning* along a **competency-based (CB) learning pathway**. Shifting these core instructional components would not be possible without also shifting the roles and responsibilities of those within the system of learning—roles of both teachers *and* students. The role of the students must be addressed in a manner that enables them to be engaged as designers of their learning, as well as enabling teachers to support this ownership through intentional assessment practices and flexible pacing of learning. Figure 4.1 illustrates the many moving parts of the shifts that occur in the CB classroom, listed here:

- **Core instruction:** Instruction is responsive to where each student is along a transparent learning progression, with the overarching goal of deeper learning.

CBE Requires Four Major Shifts When Moving to Student-Centered Classrooms

1. Changing Mindsets: Roles, Responsibilities, and Classroom Culture

2. Integrating Personalized Core Instruction With Competencies of Deeper Learning

3. Applying Instructional Practices to CBE Learning Cycles

4. Promoting Intrinsic Motivation and Engagement Through Assessment and Timely Feedback

FIGURE 4.1 Student-Centered Classroom Shifts: From Traditional to Competency-Based Education

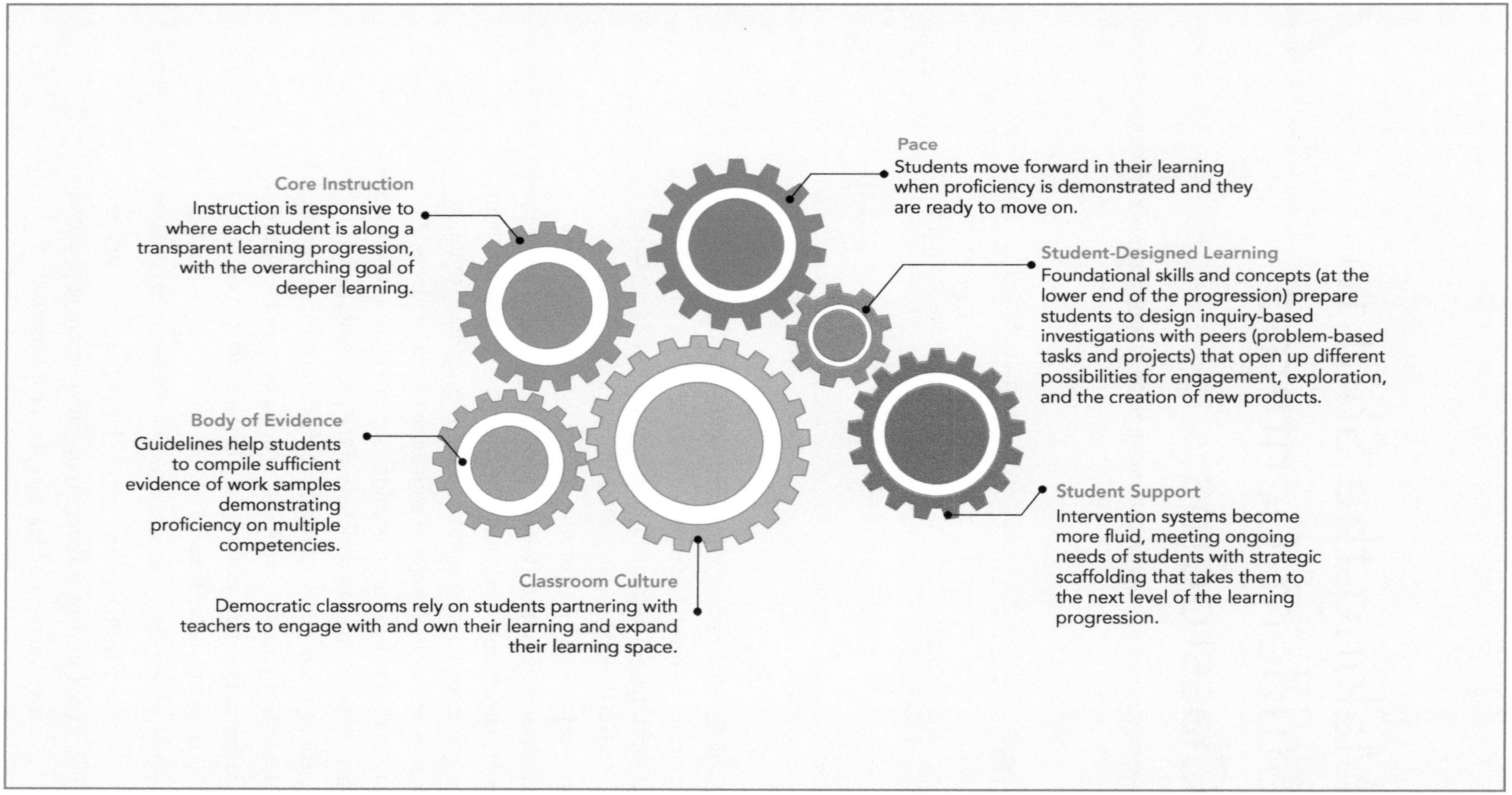

Pace

Students move forward in their learning when proficiency is demonstrated and they are ready to move on.

Student-Designed Learning

Foundational skills and concepts (at the lower end of the progression) prepare students to design inquiry-based investigations with peers (problem-based tasks and projects) that open up different possibilities for engagement, exploration, and the creation of new products.

Student Support

Intervention systems become more fluid, meeting ongoing needs of students with strategic scaffolding that takes them to the next level of the learning progression.

Core Instruction

Instruction is responsive to where each student is along a transparent learning progression, with the overarching goal of deeper learning.

Body of Evidence

Guidelines help students to compile sufficient evidence of work samples demonstrating proficiency on multiple competencies.

Classroom Culture

Democratic classrooms rely on students partnering with teachers to engage with and own their learning and expand their learning space.

- **Pace:** Students move forward in their learning when proficiency is demonstrated and they are ready to move on.

- **Student-designed learning:** Foundational skills and concepts (at the lower end of the progression) prepare students to design inquiry-based investigations with peers (problem-based tasks and projects) that open up different possibilities for engagement, exploration, and the creation of new products.

- **Student support:** Intervention systems become more fluid, meeting ongoing needs of students with strategic scaffolding to take them to the next level of the learning progression.

- **Classroom culture:** Democratic classrooms rely on students partnering with teachers to engage with and own their learning and expand their learning space.

- **Body of evidence:** Guidelines help students to compile sufficient evidence of work, samples demonstrating proficiency on multiple competencies.

STOP AND REFLECT

What does a student-centered classroom look like and feel like? Which features are most like your classrooms right now?

_____

_____

_____

_____

What if educators understood and championed their role as developing future leaders, problem-solvers, and critical thinkers? For students to see the importance of the work they are being asked to do each day, they must be willing to commit time and energy to advance their own learning. This level of student ownership and engagement goes far beyond compliance and redefines the role of learner, as well as the role of teachers. How can we prepare students for a future that we cannot predict? While the Information Age has created a world that is everchanging, it has also created educational opportunities and the necessity for personalized learning. In their book *Pathways to Personalization: A Framework for School Change*, Rubin and Sanford state that classrooms that shift to support increased student voice, choice, and agency empower students as individuals with unique strengths, interests, and identities. Efforts to personalize learning seek to improve engagement and motivation, infusing the curriculum with relevance and purpose for each learner. Practices such as student goal setting, individualized feedback loops, multiple assessment options, and student-driven project-based learning increase student choice and ownership (Rubin & Sanford, 2018).

4.1 CHANGING MINDSETS: ROLES, RESPONSIBILITIES, AND CLASSROOM CULTURE

The transformation from existing teaching and learning models to models of personalized student learning requires a shift in how we prepare students to do more than simply acquire knowledge. The focus is now on knowing how and when to apply skills and dispositions in order to construct new knowledge. Schools can no longer be driven by a "completer mindset," where our measures of impact are determined solely by the percentage of students attaining a high school diploma. Future-focused schools need to provide authentic learning experiences aligned to the needs of the learner, respecting their background experiences, talents, personal challenges, and interests. We are preparing students for their lives, not just for the next project, the next course, or the next grade level. How often do we hear students asking, Why do I have to learn this? or When will I ever use this? Students are telling us that they also need to find their WHY.

As districts engage in the transformation of teacher–student roles, attention should be given to how we develop students' academic and personal skills (competencies), measure and give feedback on their progress (assessments and learning pathways), and evaluate student work products (evidence-based grading). Figure 4.2 captures more detail about five dimensions of classroom culture that will shift when CBE implementation moves into high gear.

Teacher–Student Roles and Responsibilities

Teachers' roles, as well as the role of students in developing learning experiences (curriculum) and using assessments, will be in a state of transformation for quite

FIGURE 4.2 Dimensions of Classroom Culture in Competency-Based Education

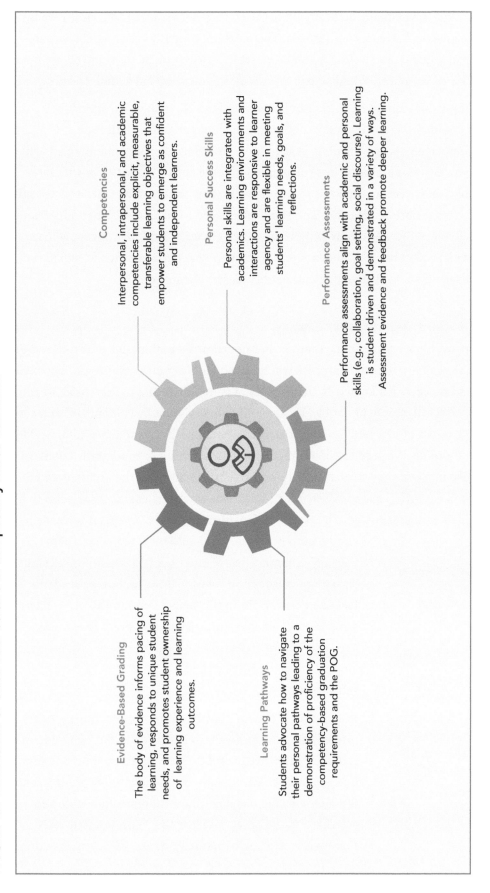

a while as you find your best path to CBE (competency-based education). These changes will stretch your teams' collective thinking and force you to reevaluate instructional practices based on how best to infuse student voice and choice into a new classroom culture that expects students to own and guide their learning.

In previous chapters, we focused on systemic shifts (policies, leadership, assessment, reporting, etc.) that supported and personalized deeper competency-based learning. Many times, our efforts for implementing educational reform are approached in a fragmented manner that does not align with new roles and learning expectations at all levels. This results in an "incomplete" shift from a traditional teacher- and standards-based focus to a student and learning outcomes-driven system. With this learner-centered shift, the impact will be evidenced in the role students play when applying their knowledge, skills, and dispositions in challenging authentic, real-world contexts.

Student Agency and Equity

As we work with schools, there is an important mental model shift that requires a view of learning as a process whereby students acquire meaningful knowledge and transfer that knowledge to a variety of authentic settings. This student-centric model is dynamic in nature. Design and delivery must be customized to meet the needs of learners. As we construct learning pathways that are informed by the profile of a graduate and prepare students for life beyond graduation, we also must employ strategies that "activate" the learner as the architect of his or her future. That goes beyond a traditional view of a learner as a vessel to be filled with knowledge. The concept of **student agency** is central to ensuring equity, empowerment, and authenticity in classroom learning communities. VanderArk (2017) emphasizes that classroom culture and relationships that make students feel like they matter in the school community, as well as authenticity—purposeful work that matters to students, such as high-quality project-based learning—will result in students developing personal qualities of persistence and self-direction.

In building a student-centered classroom culture, we are providing opportunities for equity and authenticity in not only rethinking the design and delivery of instruction but also in how we collect and evaluate the evidence of student learning. Student learning deepens when students find value and relevance in the process of learning. This is a new relationship that we are creating with our students. We are asking them to

Through the tenets of "agency," we help students see effort and practice in a new light and associate both as growth paths, and ultimately, success. We can provide students with the skills to rebound from setbacks and build confidence as they welcome new challenges. Instilling the principles of "agency" helps students find personal relevance in their work and motivates them to participate actively, build relationships, and understand how they impact themselves and their communities.
(New Tech Network, 2017)

STOP AND REFLECT

How do you think your students—as learners—view their roles, responsibilities, and classroom culture in your classroom? Try conducting your own survey and then reflect on how students actually respond.

_____

_____

_____

_____

_____

become partners with us where they are given both support and increasingly more opportunities to direct their own learning.

Many learner dispositions are the skills and habits that support growth and development of student agency. For students to advocate for themselves, they need to understand and apply the skills and habits associated with a particular social or academic situation or problem. The opportunity and the challenge is to concurrently integrate learning mindsets with strategies and subject matter instruction (academic competencies) so that they are supporting each other.

At Kettle Moraine School District in Wales, Wisconsin, they have developed descriptions of "Personalized Learning Look Fors" (Kettle Moraine, 2018) based on the shifting level of teacher or learner control. As shown in Figure 4.3, the school district recognizes the importance of "learner dispositions" as well as the need for students to not only be aware but also to employ the habits and skills necessary to drive their own learning. Note that all of the learner-centered look fors are also linked with Hattie influencers and effect sizes. (Some of the 2009 effect sizes in the table were updated in 2019.) Under the column _Learner-Centered_, one of the district look fors is "Learner mindset is centered around a partnership between student and teacher to meet learning needs."

(Continued)

(Continued)

FIGURE 4.3 Kettle Moraine Personalized Learning "Look Fors": Learner Dispositions

PERSONALIZED LEARNING "LOOK FORS"

PURPOSE: This document was created to build understanding and goals as the district continues to move toward the vision of "personalized learning for all". This is not an evaluative document but rather one that recognizes the many small moves required to provide a personalized learning experience for all students

KM PL Team Revision, March 2018

LEARNER-DRIVEN	LEARNER-CENTERED	TEACHER-DRIVEN	CURRICULUM-CENTERED
LEARNER DISPOSITION All learners follow a customized path that considers skills and habits that impact all areas of life. The dispositions in each area are what will be DEVELOPED in the learner. They are not prerequisites to work within that strand.			
➢ Learner commitment is to reflect on purpose of learning and to pursue mastery with growth focus *(Hattie- Mastery- .58)* ➢ Learner monitors own progress and collaborates with others to build ownership of learning, generate success criteria and create next steps based on reflection and feedback from sources inside and outside the classroom *(Hattie - Self-reported- 1.44)* ➢ Learner tracks own growth and evidence of growing in Habits of Mind and meeting the Profile of a Kettle Moraine Graduate *(Hattie - Self-monitoring- .45)* ➢ Learner mindset is that they are their own best teachers and seeks connections based on own intrinsic needs *(Hattie -Self-instruction- .62)*	➢ Learner commitment is towards competency with continuous progress *(Hattie- Mastery- .58)* ➢ Learner is monitoring their own progress, seeks feedback from teacher or others in classroom, and acts on it. *(Hattie - Feedback -.75)* ➢ Learner tracks growth with teacher to co-create goals aligned to Habits of Mind and the Profile of a Kettle Moraine Graduate. *(Hattie - Self-monitoring- .45)* ➢ Learner mindset is centered around a partnership between student and teacher to meet learning needs *(Hattie - Teacher student relationships- .72)*	➢ Learner commitment is toward earning desired grade ➢ Learner seeks feedback and may not act on it ➢ Learner responds to teacher direction and intermittently demonstrates Habits of Mind and works towards behaviors/goals of the Profile of a Kettle Moraine Graduate ➢ Learner mindset is to complete teacher-designated learning to meet goals outlined	➢ Learner commitment is to following directions when given ➢ Learner doesn't actively seek feedback, rather feedback is given through teacher or resource ➢ Learner is directed to Habits of Mind/Profile of a Kettle Moraine Graduate, though does not yet see the connection to goals and goal setting ➢ Learner mindset is to be encouraged to learn by teacher and comply with teacher-inspired products and directions

Hattie, J. Visible Learning: A synthesis of over 800 meta-analyses relating to achievement (2009)   *- Learning Without Boundaries -*

Kettle Moraine School District • 563 A.J. Allen Circle, Wales, WI 53183 • 262-968-6300 • www.kmsd.edu

Source: **Created by Kettle Morraine School District. Used with permission.**

💭 STOP AND REFLECT

Use the guide in Figure 4.3 to examine the continuum of learner dispositions (moving from curriculum-driven to learner-centered characteristics). How does this reflect possible transitions in your school or classroom?

_____

_____

_____

There is so much to consider when thinking about student roles and learning culture within classrooms. Certainly, the supports that each student needs to be successful (ensuring equity) are first and foremost in any design for learning. These become part of the learning culture. This really speaks to the responsiveness that educators have in creating safe, positive learning environments for students. Teachers also need to be sensitive to the effects of trauma, homelessness, poverty, social and emotional factors, and whatever may impact learning within a classroom. Getting a handle on school culture—especially across classrooms in a school—can sometimes seem elusive and overwhelming. Yet the democracy of students exercising their ability to shape how they learn and where they learn (learning environments within and outside of school) as they mature aligns with the profile of a high school graduate who is best prepared to tackle future endeavors.

As students are given the practice, timely feedback, and support in these personal success skill areas, their level of agency will increase. When students develop a deeper awareness of their strengths, self-confidence increases, and they are better prepared to advocate for themselves as learners. It is in this moment that the words *voice* and *choice* have authentic meaning for both students and teachers.

← | **Student Self-Reflection** (Effect Size = 0.75)

4.2 INTEGRATING PERSONALIZED CORE INSTRUCTION WITH COMPETENCIES OF DEEPER LEARNING

The challenge and promise of **student-centered learning** is not in simply changing our approach to instructional delivery, but to take a new view of how we use assessment data to inform our instructional decisions, and thus how these shifts impact student learning. This is an important conversation for districts to grapple with as they try to balance the demands of standards and high-stakes tests, as well as local- and state-mandated policies and programs. These external forces have unintentionally pushed schools to build systems driven more by the need to manage and report data than how to use data to support student learning. Grading, scoring, homework, credit recovery, and other traditional practices must be transformed to fully allow the creation of a student-centric design and delivery for deeper learning. Suddenly, there will be new awareness of the importance of formative uses of assessment data.

Student-centered learning is different than teacher-centric instruction since it focuses on the individual student and the instructional processes to support a student-centric learning cycle. The core functions and processes that the student-centered learning integrated system must support are learner-centric instead of teacher- or group-centric. In anchoring this system design, one must consider: the individual learner's learning experiences, resources and interactions with peers, educators and others involved in the education; how these experiences and interactions are supported and assessed; and the ways in which these data and reports are used. (Glowa & Goodell, 2016, p. 4)

Walking the hallways of schools, you begin to notice what phase of transformation they are currently working through, if you know what to look for. We may see a district that has a "personalized learning" block that is part of each student's schedule. This approach could be related to a variety of factors that might limit or slow down the overall system's transformation. In other schools, we might see more flexible schedules and course offerings that integrate personalized approaches with academic learning.

At the Manchester School of Technology (MST), two of the teacher leaders working to implement personalized competency-based teaching discuss the shifting practices and mindsets related to a high school attempting to bring CBE into its core instruction. The concepts of self-assessing work quality and developing persistence on the part of the learners during the learning process are yet to be developed. You can see in their reflections that teachers—as well as students—need support in making a transition from a system of lingering external motivations (grades and testing) to one of intrinsic motivation (learning).

Changing Viewpoints and Old Patterns

Intentional correlations between competency statements (and their performance indicators) and assessments provided students with a better understanding of where they were and where they needed to get to. New patterns of learning and transparency (of expectations) ensured that students understood what they were working for and why, as opposed to being told what to do and how to do it. Assessments were being designed with purpose and to authentically engage students as they demonstrated competency.

But old habits die hard—a D is not a thing. The continuum of learning is not always a fun or easy process for the vast majority of humans on this earth, never mind teenagers and public servants. At the beginning of every year, we continue to face students submitting work they believe to be "good enough." Good enough for the D—or the A, for that matter—is an old paradigm concept not in play in CBE. Demonstrating competency is a process of engagement, and as such, our students know no grade is given but that they must earn every level of achievement.

—Jillian and Joe

STOP AND REFLECT

What have you learned from Jillian's and Joe's reflections so far? How does their journey compare with your journey?

_____

_____

_____

_____

Organizations need to be mindful of what supports teachers need in order to become competent in the design and delivery of CBE. Educators must ask: Do our current instructional and assessment systems activate or enable a learner-centric, student-facing system of learning? How do we support each learner as we shift from teacher-centered to student-centric systems of teaching and learning? What do we need to learn in order to do this effectively?

The struggle with shifting mental models and teacher–student roles is evident when we work with school districts moving from a traditional to a more personalized system of learning. Most teachers are willing to engage in a process to reorganize learning goals into a pathway to guide instruction and manage the pace of learning when they can conceptualize their own learning pathway to get there.

An example that captures a continuum of focus and control as it shifts from being teacher-centered to student-centered was developed by Bray (2019). This transfer of focus begins with recognizing our core beliefs about students and learning and how they impact our delivery of instruction. It is then that we can begin to consider how to shift to a more student-centric design and delivery of instruction. Figure 4.4 captures this gradual transformation of culture, and the release of control required of a teacher as student agency is increased.

As we work with schools that are on the path to personalized learning, we help teachers to identify how they might gradually release control as they seek to have students take more ownership of their learning pathway. Instructional practices such as **individualized** and **differentiated** instruction still have teachers making

FIGURE 4.4 Bray's Teaching and Learning Continuum Chart

Teaching and Learning Continuum Moving Toward Personalized Competency-Based Education and Learner Agency				
Criteria	**Traditional**	**Emerging**	**Invested**	**Innovative**
Build the Foundation				
Philosophy	My kids in my classroom	All kids in our school	All learners in our community	All learners as global citizens
Professional learning	Faculty meetings/PD	Professional learning communities	Focus groups/job embedded	Personal professional learning
How students learn	Compared to average	Student variability identified	Know how they learn best	Self-advocate for learning
Learning environment	Desks or tables in rows	Individual and group work	Flexible learning spaces	Anywhere, anytime, any way
Classroom culture	Teacher in control	Voice and choice encouraged	Trust-based relationships	Positive, compassionate culture
Design the Teaching				
Scheduling	Assigned to age/grade levels	Varied opportunities for learning	Flexible scheduling/options	Multiple pathways/challenges
Instructional design	Directed instruction	Facilitated learning	Co-design learning activities	Self-directed learning
Goal setting	Goals/objectives described	Feedback provided for goals	Co-develop/co-monitor goals	Set own goals/seek feedback
Technology	Used for direct instruction	Integrated in lessons or projects	Choose appropriate tools for task	Responsible global digital citizens
Assessment	Graded required assessments	Adapted assessment strategies	Co-design assessment for learning	Self-assessment as learning
Own the Learning				
Ownership	Rules and compliance	Build relationships and voice	Develop skills to want to learn	Responsible for learning
Focus	Content, tests, and grades	Access appropriate content	Acquire skills and dispositions	Develop passions and purpose
Mindset	Little or no focus on effort	Learn mindset strategies	Intrinsically motivated	Demonstrate self-regulation
Collaboration	Little or no collaboration	Collaboration with other classes	Seek out collaborations	Connect to authentic learning

Source: Bray (2019).

most of the instructional decisions on behalf of their students, so they are only a first step to personalized learning. In individualized instruction, the teacher customizes instruction for each student and uses accommodations that help the student meet the same learning objectives expected for all students. We might think of this as one-on-one teaching and support. Differentiation choices are designed by the teacher, based on the learning needs of a whole class or small groups of students. Often, teachers will begin a move to personalization by designing performance tasks that differentiate—and offer students choices—about the content they use, the processes they employ, or the products they develop to demonstrate their learning.

STOP AND REFLECT

What—in your opinion—is the difference between students *doing* the learning (compliance) and *owning* the learning?

_____

_____

_____

_____

_____

Personalized learning offers each student a clear and transparent learning pathway aligned with competency-based performance scales of deeper learning. Students understand which social and academic behaviors are expected and that they will receive timely feedback related to their choices and progress made. If personalization is the goal, then teachers must intentionally build the foundation to help students learn the skills necessary to take greater ownership of their learning. It is not enough to hope that they will magically do this. Many teachable moments related to stages of learning along the performance scales—such as what it means to set and monitor their own goals for learning or how to work with peers to develop an investigation— become part of the instructional planning and co-design of inquiry-based projects.

Developing Capacity for Implementation of Personalized Learning: Educator Competencies

Often, districts have identified their WHY and are willing to begin this work but may not fully understand how to support teachers in meeting the challenges of implementing learner-centered classrooms. Jobs for the Future and the Council of Chief State School Officers have developed a useful set of "Educator Competencies for Personalized, Learner-Centered Teaching" (Wolfe & Poon, 2015, p. 10). They outline four core educator competency domains: cognitive, intrapersonal, interpersonal, and instructional competencies. This comprehensive approach outlines the knowledge, skills, and dispositions educators need in order to design and deliver personalized instruction. Each section of the document offers standards and indicators that promote reflection, collaborative discussions, and direction for educators as they move toward a student-centered system of teaching and learning.

A close reading of these educator competencies and indicators illustrates that the competencies are based not only in day-to-day practice but also in teacher dispositions and belief systems about learning. Table 4.1 shows an excerpt from the "Educator Competencies for Personalized, Learner-Centered Teaching" for intrapersonal skills.

TABLE 4.1 Educator Competencies for Personalized, Learner-Centered Teaching: Intrapersonal Skills

Intrapersonal Competencies	Indicators
Successful educators in a personalized, learner-centered setting will: Convey a dedication to all learners—especially those historically marginalized and/or least served by public higher education—reaching college, career, and civic readiness.	a. Recognize, make transparent, discuss, and adapt as necessary to the cultural biases and inequitable distribution of resources that may challenge learners from attaining postsecondary credentials and career advancement while remaining culturally sensitive and aware of celebrating students' diversity. b. Create structured opportunities in professional development and instruction to reflect on equity, civic participation, and their intersections. c. Demonstrate ability to reflect on personal social location and privilege, and awareness of systemic and intrapersonal forms of oppression.

Source: Wolfe and Poon (2015).

As you reflect on the Manchester School of Technology vignettes, it is a reminder that we are all humans trying to make sense of how to do something that we may never have experienced for ourselves. Therefore, it is every educator's professional responsibility to adopt a growth mindset and perseverance in this work as a deeper understanding of CBE evolves.

STOP AND REFLECT

As you reflect on your own intrapersonal skills, what are your strengths? Where could you benefit from new learning or a deeper understanding of personalization?

_____

_____

_____

_____

Sometimes, educators can enhance their understanding of personalization by observing how students can be guided in making decisions for their learning.

While working with a high school in Maine, Dan helped the staff create a student leadership team made up of students from all social groups found in that school. We referred to the group as our "Breakfast Club." During a whole-day strategic planning session, we asked the students to lead themselves and each other through a series of processes and protocols to foster deep collaborative thinking around core school-based values, beliefs, and practices in their school. There were some administrators and teachers in the room as facilitators, who were instructed not to engage unless they were invited by students to do so. The adults were not given any responsibilities other than to allow the students to create the space for learning. The students were given the opportunity to reflect and offer feedback on several schoolwide personalized learning practices and policies that were currently employed in their school. With students, we developed norms, a clear process, and a set of outcomes for the students. During this session, we witnessed at-risk students engaging in constructive discourse with National Honor Society students about the role of homework and grading. In the end, students performed beyond most expectations the adults had for them. We observed that when given clear expectations, protocols for discourse, and feedback, students were able to engage in these important life skills, such as collaboration, problem-solving, and communication. Students gained a voice and a sense of ownership around their learning as it related to the school's practices and policies. The adults left with a renewed sense of purpose related to students as engaged learners and the importance of developing the personal success skills they needed to teach, monitor, and measure with students. The staff members in the room that day needed to witness this exchange, as it enabled them to cast aside some broad assumptions around school and learning.

Personalization and Competencies of Deeper Learning

In earlier chapters, we introduced the concepts of rigorous academic and personal skills competencies and described ways to develop competencies and assess deeper learning. We want to remind readers that in addition to academic competencies, personal success skills are sometimes further broken down into interpersonal skills and intrapersonal skills. Different CBE models describe the scope of each type of competency in similar ways, with some overlap but often with a differing focus. With such a broad scope of possibilities, schools need to determine what to focus on first in order to teach and assess them effectively. We suggest that your school consider the best starting point for your school, your students, and your teachers with a goal of integrating some academic competencies with some personal success skills. HOW you integrate the

Deeper learning is supported through rich instructional and assessment practices that create a positive, collaborative learning environment in which students gain content knowledge while developing their intrapersonal and interpersonal skills. For example, developing metacognitive skills— the ability to reflect on one's own thinking and make strategic adjustments accordingly—deepens academic content learning as well. (Hess, 2018, p. 3) competencies for meaningful learning is more important than which specific competencies you begin with. As a reminder,

- **Academic competencies** include domain-specific content and ways to interact deeply with content, such as through problem-solving, critical thinking, and investigation (e.g., problem-based learning).

- **Intrapersonal skills** generally include skills such as goal setting, metacognition and self-reflection, and managing social and emotional skills (e.g., self-awareness, responsible decision-making).

- **Interpersonal skills** include the ability to work with others (collaboration and communication) and other social and emotional skills (e.g., relationship skills, social awareness).

💭 STOP AND REFLECT

How have your thinking and mindset changed about ways to integrate academic, interpersonal, and intrapersonal competencies (e.g., POG, career readiness)?

_____

_____

_____

_____

_____

While we do not recommend any specific program or set of competencies for your school to adopt, we feel it is important to point you in the right direction to find high-quality CB resources—those that demonstrate integration of academic and personal skills. The Collaborative for Academic, Social, and Emotional Learning (CASEL; 2017) has developed a comprehensive SEL (social-emotional learning) competencies model that describes both learning goals and supports to students. CASEL's framework is designed for the integration of skills, attitudes, and behaviors at the student level. Each SEL competency has a number of specific skills, attitudes, or behaviors that can be demonstrated by learners as they develop interpersonal, intrapersonal, and cognitive competence. For example, in the CASEL model, "self-awareness" is described as the ability to accurately recognize one's own emotions, thoughts, and values and how they influence personal behavior. The CASEL model, illustrated in Figure 4.5, reminds educators that supports to students go well beyond the classroom. (For a deeper exploration into the CASEL resources for social and emotional learning, a link is provided in Appendix C.)

Another model, CareerOneStop, is a CBE model frequently used in career and technical education centers that focuses on professionalism and workplace skills (Competency Model Clearinghouse, 2020). In this model, students use goal setting and a reflection scale to determine where they are in relation to where they need to be in demonstrating particular skills within work-related tasks. This approach engages students in the intentional use of some interpersonal and intrapersonal skills required during the learning task. Deeper learning is fostered through conferencing and reflecting on the ability to integrate personal success skills with content knowledge. Think of a carpentry student or a student

FIGURE 4.5 CASEL Core Competencies Model for Social-Emotional Learning

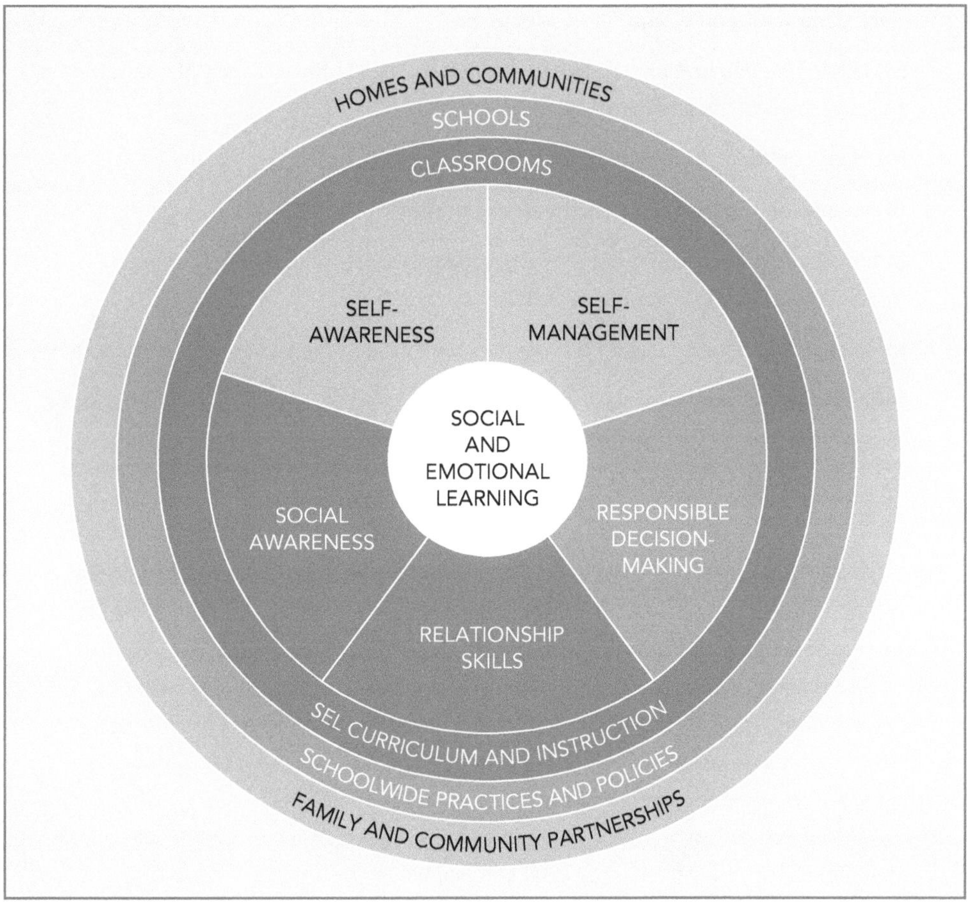

Source: Published with permission from © 2017 CASEL. Available at https//casel.org/

in a science lab. Both of those students must perform tasks that could require collaboration and teamwork—skills that are required of students in their daily lives and future careers. A CBE model such as this would be relevant to students engaged in a work-based learning experience or a collaborative learning activity with a teamwork goal. As students progress through each learning activity, they monitor and measure their progress using a "student-friendly" performance scale for teamwork. (To locate more information on the CareerOneStop model, see Appendix C.)

Student Self-Reflection

(Effect Size = 0.75)

$\rightarrow$

During a yearlong professional development series for Illinois educators to learn about designing CB performance assessments, participants followed a similar process to what is described in Chapter 3: analyze a competency, develop a performance scale for the competency, and then develop an aligned performance task and scoring rubric. Karin worked with a school team from Chicago Public Schools (CPS), led by Damarr Smith (Project Manager of Competency-Based Education) and Roshaun Bowen (SEL Instructional Specialist), to develop an SEL competency, performance scale, and performance task for goal setting. Students were working on several "mindsets" throughout the school and could choose one of them as the focus of their goal-setting plans:

Is there a mindset you would like to focus on?

M1. Belief in development of whole self, including a healthy balance of mental, social/emotional, and physical well-being

M2. Self-confidence in ability to succeed

M3. Sense of belonging in the school environment

M4. Understanding that postsecondary education and life-long learning are necessary for long-term career success

M5. Belief in using abilities to their fullest to achieve high-quality results and outcomes

M6. Positive attitude toward work and learning

Source: ASCA Mindsets & Behaviors for Student Success Standards, American School Counselor Association: https://www.schoolcounselor.org/school-counselors/standards.

There were three stages of learning identified in the performance scale developed by the team for this competency: PLAN (develop a goal setting plan); ACTUALIZE (implement the plan and collect evidence); and REFLECT (use evidence to reflect on implementation; and revise or set new goals). The CPS team decided that the performance assessment for this SEL competency really needed to be a self-reflection—not a "teacher-scored" assessment—Karin showed the team how to adapt a self-assessment rubric template (Hess, 2018, p. 427) to create a "What I Need to Do" self-assessment for goal setting. Figure 4.6 shows a rubric that could be developed for self-reflection or goal setting, using the stages of development in the performance scale as criteria for self-assessment.

FIGURE 4.6 Example of a Rubric Designed for Self-Reflection Using the Performance Scale Indicators as Scoring Criteria

Scoring Criteria	Goal Setting and Self-Reflection: "What I Need to Do" Rubric (This area is provided for you to indicate that you understand the requirements and success criteria of the assessment task.)	Evidence of What I Did (This is for your final self-assessment. You can color code or provide a key to show where evidence is found in your reflection or plan.)
PLAN **Develop a Goal-Setting Plan** Make a plan to improve upon performance in a chosen subject area or skill.	I completed my **Goal-Setting Worksheet** on _____ (date). My greatest personal strengths are: My greatest academic strengths are: A challenge I'll try to overcome is: _____ has reviewed my Goal-Setting Worksheet and agrees that my plan is clear, complete, and feasible. (Requires peer or adult sign off—read this like a critical friend!)	Ideas I got from my peers: Ideas I got from other sources (teacher, mentor, adviser, etc.):
ACTUALIZE **Implement, Collect Evidence, and Make Connections**	My reflection . . . _____ restates my goal. _____ examines which strategies worked best for reflecting on progress and explains why some did not help. _____ uses my analysis to discuss a connection. My analysis used evidence or examples to shape my interpretation and assumptions. (List evidence in the column to the right.) My conclusion . . . _____ summarizes my analysis. _____ reflects upon my progress. _____ considers what I might do next time:	Evidence I documented:
REFLECT **Update Plan** Revise or update to improve my performance based on new evidence.	My Goal-Setting Plan was updated on (date) _____. To do this . . . I discussed and got feedback on my reflections from: I've added these strategies: I've modified or deleted these strategies:	My key learning(s):

Self-Systems: Metacognition, Reflection, and Goal Setting

Student Metacognitive Strategies

(Effect Size = 0.55)

Metacognition is a student's ability to plan, monitor, and regulate him- or herself during the process of learning. Metacognition skills, combined with ongoing self-reflection, are essential elements of student engagement in a student-centered classroom. A learner's metacognitive system is responsible for monitoring, evaluating, and regulating the functioning of all other types of thought. Marzano and Kendall (2008) state that these processes working together form what they refer to as "executive control." Therefore, metacognition, self-reflection, and goal setting are essential if students are expected to "own their learning."

A classroom that has made the shift to personalized learning not only has students working at their "just-right" level for acquiring content, but it also defines, monitors, and measures student dispositions (interpersonal, intrapersonal) as they apply critical and creative thinking skills. Teachers need to consider these questions as they leverage learning: Can students access learning strategies independently or collaboratively? Can they engage in tasks, problem solve, and develop quality products that demonstrate learning outcomes? Can they identify a goal and advocate

Student Self-Reflection

(Effect Size = 0.75)

for support to achieve the goal? Strategies and techniques that have students engaged in self-reflection and feedback are the engines that drive students to take ownership of their learning.

Frey, Hattie, and Fisher (2018) describe a set of characteristics that all assessment-capable learners must develop. Each characteristic that follows also includes references to Hattie's influencers that positively impact learning. As you are reading these characteristics and their descriptions, reflect on how your own instructional and formative assessment practices can support students in acquiring them.

- **I know where I am going.** Students understand their current performance and how it relates to the learning intention and success criteria. (Transparency, Clarity, Feedback)

- **I have the tools for the journey.** Students understand that they can select from a range of strategies to move their learning forward, especially when progress is interrupted. (Intentionality, Perseverance, Learner Inventory, and Choice)

- **I monitor my progress.** Students seek and respond to feedback from others, including peers and teachers, as they assess their performance. Students know that making mistakes is expected in learning and indicates an opportunity for further learning. (Feedback, Growth Mindset, Appropriate Challenge)

- **I recognize when I'm ready for what's next.** Students interpret their data in light of the learning intention and success criteria of the lessons, as well as the overall learning progression to identify when they are ready to move on. (Transparency, Self-Reflection)

- **I know what to do next.** Knowing what to do when you do not know what to do is surely the mark of the educated person. It is the difference between knowing how to persist and simply giving up when faced with the early challenge. It is the essence of being a lifelong learner, one who knows how to research, organize information, and continue his or her own learning. (Engagement, Agency)

STOP AND REFLECT

How often do you or teachers in your school use metacognitive (during learning) and reflective (after learning) practices? Where can you begin to collect examples? How might your school begin to regularly integrate these practices?

_____

_____

_____

_____

_____

4.3 APPLYING INSTRUCTIONAL PRACTICES TO CBE LEARNING CYCLES

When thinking about an instructional system designed to meet the needs of all learners with respect to learning anytime and anyplace, managing use of time is a challenge, given our traditional structures in education. The concept "Learning is the constant and time is the variable" presents a systemic challenge for districts as they rethink systems and structures based on individual students' needs and instructional pacing.

In most curricular models, students move through the fixed curriculum as a whole class, using the teacher's pacing. The learning outcomes defined by content standards are stretched out across the school year and delivered through planned learning activities in a series of units of study. A variety of assessments are used to determine acquisition of standards and grades; but there are few opportunities for assessments to be used to find students' "entry points" for learning or to determine when a student is ready to move on. Figure 4.7 illustrates a typical "fixed-pace" curriculum plan with units of study based on grade-level standards. Admittedly, as former teachers and administrators, the authors of this book designed standards-based curriculum maps just like this in the past!

Teacher Cognitive
Task Analysis
(Effect Size = 1.29) $\longrightarrow$ In CBE, the idea is that core instruction meets students where they are along their learning pathways. This implies a new role for assessment and assessment data, as teachers use ongoing and varied assessments to determine where students are in their learning, what they need next, and at what point they can say that students have demonstrated mastery. If we thought of curriculum mapping as a means of connecting learning along a progression, it might look more like the visual in Figure 4.8.

In this illustration, you can see (hypothetically) how each learner might have a different entry point along a progression of learning, based on the interpretation of formative assessment results. Preassessments that focus on prerequisite skills for a unit of study or competency would indicate which students have already acquired skills from earlier

FIGURE 4.7 A Typical Standards-Based Curriculum Plan With Units of Study

FIGURE 4.8 Mapping CB Curriculum Along a Learning Progression

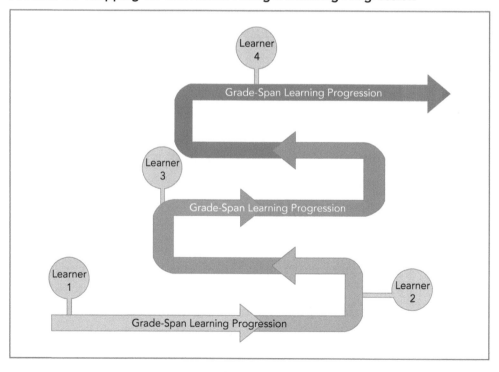

lessons and are ready to move on and which students will need to build a more solid foundation. Additional formative assessment strategies, aligned with levels of the CB performance scales, help teachers to monitor progress and **strategically scaffold** learning for individual learners or groups of students. Therefore, the pace of learning is not solely directed by the teacher or the pace of the class, but by the use of short-cycle assessments to ensure that learning has taken place and a learner is ready to move on. This requires flexible (as needed) grouping and intentional use of feedback to drive learning. Depending upon the complexity of the content and scope of the learning targets within a unit of study, some students may progress more slowly through one level of the progression and move faster through other levels.

← Timely Self-Regulatory Feedback (Effect Size = 0.66)

> ## 💭 STOP AND REFLECT
>
> What role can strategic scaffolding play in bringing all students to competency?
>
> _____
>
> _____
>
> _____
>
> _____

The cold hard fact is that a fixed-paced curriculum creates learning gaps while moving students along whether or not they have learned the current material. The ever-widening gaps must then be addressed later on when new learning needs to build upon prior learning. These "relearning" interventions usually happen after the class has moved on and is now learning new content. When students move at their own pace with teacher support (strategic scaffolding, differentiation, etc.) to close the gaps, traditional interventions may not be completely replaced, but they are minimized to a large degree. Intentionally building in ways to support learners along each level of the performance scale allows some students to independently move on, freeing up teacher time to support other students. Strategies such as **flipped classrooms**, **blended learning**, **station rotations**, **differentiated learning/assignment menus**, and **team-learning** activities are only some of the ways that teachers can use flexible groupings and vary the pace of learning.

Competency-based planning teams may want to examine their school's readiness to establish and map learning pathways (Figure 4.9) with competencies, using **CBE Tool 1D**. The full version of **CBE Tool 1D** is in Appendix A.

← Collective Teacher Efficacy (Effect Size = 1.39)

FIGURE 4.9 Cutaway of CBE Tool 1D: **Learning Pathways**

CBE Tool 1D	Core Components of Competency-Based Education: CBE Readiness Tool			
Component 4: Learning Pathways Competencies drive a rigorous, transparent, flexible system of learning in which students are empowered by opportunities to choose what and how they learn.				
Focus	**Phase 1: Initiating**	**Phase 2: Emerging**	**Phase 3: Implementing**	**Where is your school now? What are possible next steps?**
Leadership	Policies aspire to prepare students for college and careers, but practices support a single learning pathway to promotion or graduation for all students.	Policies and practices become more flexible in determining how and where learning can occur. The development of multiple, rigorous pathways ensures each student's learning is possible within the school-based accountability system.	Policies and practices support multiple pathways for authentic, rigorous student learning, which is appropriately credentialed within and outside learning agencies (e.g., college-course taking for graduation credit).	
Instruction and Assessment	Course-level standards and learning outcomes are taught and scaffolded by teachers and made transparent to parents and learners using course syllabi.	Competency-based learning outcomes are scaffolded and begin to be integrated across content areas and grade levels. Students have some options for learning (e.g., online, blended, face-to-face, community-based learning).	Competencies and learning outcomes are scaffolded and integrated across content areas as well as grade levels. Personalized learning plans guide students in their learning choices, pathways, and learning support.	
Learner Culture	Limited pathways and choice are offered to students in meeting grade-level or graduation requirements.	Multiple course and content pathways are aligned to competencies. Students have some options in how to demonstrate their learning across courses or content disciplines.	Students advocate how to navigate their personal pathways, leading to a demonstration of proficiency of the competency-based graduation requirements and the POG.	
Organizational Structures	A single system of teaching and learning is organized in the same way for all students, with provisions for remediation.	Equitable pathways articulate the alignment to academic or personal success skill competencies and are mapped to curricular programs or course offerings.	Equitable pathways clearly articulate the alignment to academic and personal success skill competencies and are mapped to learning opportunities anytime and anywhere.	

STOP AND REFLECT

Take some time to review CBE Tool 1D. How will the perspective of *learning along a pathway* drive changes to planning and delivery of instruction for teachers?

_____

_____

_____

_____

_____

_____

Pace of Learning: The Elephant in the CBE Classroom

We get it. The two biggest challenges for teachers implementing CBE are figuring out how to manage pacing of instruction and shifting to evidence-based grading. In a traditional classroom, students move lockstep through a sequence of learning that is primarily based on content standards, differentiation, and programs that attempt to address variations in learning pace and depth of learning for different students. Sometimes, schools have addressed varied pace of learning by creating tracks, as well as levels (e.g., different math courses), within their systems. While some pacing "solutions" may solve one problem, they also can raise concern for equity and access if all learners are not offered adequate opportunities to learn complex content. In a personalized competency-based system of learning, individualized pacing can be achieved through intentional instruction and process feedback along a transparent learning progression. Students can set goals, co-design their learning activities, and make informed choices only when they know where they are going (success criteria) and where they are on the path to get there (the learning pathway). Assessment and instructional practices that flow from performance scales are designed to support learners using learning progressions that are flexible, equitable, and accessible.

Student-Friendly Progressions: Pacing Instruction at the Elementary Level

Transparent learning progressions help students to navigate not only the general sequence of their learning but also to recognize what evidence of learning they need to collect along the way to build their body of evidence. Students understand that the learning activities in the progression will increase in complexity, depth, and scope as they get closer to demonstrating competency. The concept of "just-right work," meaning work that is appropriately challenging and has relevance to a larger picture of learning, is the primary driver of a student-friendly self-monitoring progression. At different grade levels, teachers can "zoom in" on one or two levels of the full performance scale to create smaller-grained, miniprogressions that help students see their progress day-to-day or week-to-week. "When a student can see (and track) her own progress over time, it validates that she can learn deeply" (Hess, 2018, p. 5). Seeing individual progress, in turn, motivates each student to put forth effort in future learning.

We found one example of how student-friendly pacing looks in an elementary school in New Hampshire where teachers created visual pathways that students use to navigate their math learning goals for the year. The icons in the pathway (progression) also guide students in where to access learning resources in the classroom as they engage with their "just-right" learning goals. The design of these visual progressions (Figure 4.10) is based on a progression of *prioritized* standards that students need to build upon as they work through the

When a student can see (and track) her own progress over time, it validates that she can learn deeply. (Hess, 2018)

→ Grade 2 Math Standards across the school year. Each icon graphically represents an essential standard that is measured to mastery prior to students moving on to the next level of learning. Standards in the progression provide foundational knowledge and skills for subsequent content (standards) that follow.

FIGURE 4.10 Sample Grade 2 Student-Friendly Math Progression

2.OA.4 I can write an equation to match an array.			
2.G.3 I can partition circles and rectangles into equal shares and can identify ½, ⅓, and ¼ of the shapes.			
2.MD.10 I can draw a picture graph and bar graph to represent data and read, interpret, and compare the data.	2.MD.1 I can measure length by selecting and using appropriate tools.	2.MD.5 I can use addition and subtraction within 100 to solve word problems involving length.	2.NBT.9 I can explain addition and subtraction strategies using place value and properties of operation.
			2.OA.1 I can solve addition and subtraction story problems within 100.
2.NBT.4 I can compare three-digit numbers.	2.MD.8 I can solve money word problems using dollars, quarters, dimes, nickels, and pennies.	2.NBT.8 I can mentally add and subtract 10 or 100 to a number.	2.NBT.6 27 + 33 + 41 = ? Ones: 7 + 3 = 10 + 1 = 11 Tens: 20 + 30 + 40 = 90 90 + 11 = 101 I can add up to 4 two-digit numbers based on place value.
2.MD.7 I can tell time to the nearest 5 minutes. I can identify a.m. or p.m. (2.MD.7)			

Source: Images from istock.com/TopVectors, istock.com/nezezon2, istock.com/naulicreative, istock.com/fjmoura, istock.com/rambo182, istock.com/Armation74, istock.com/FARBAI, istock.com/DStarky, istock.com/LysenkoAlexander, istock.com/kraphix.

To encourage even greater student engagement, teachers at this school also developed what they called a "Math Matrix" tool for each essential standard in the progression to use as a student self-assessment guide while they work on a particular standard or cluster of standards related to a broader competency statement. These incremental, short-term learning goals—which can be developed in the same way we suggest developing a performance scale—are documented as student-friendly "evidences" of learning.

← Timely Self-Regulatory Feedback (Effect Size = 0.66)

Figure 4.11 shows our adapted version of this school's weekly self-monitoring tool. This is designed as both an assessment and a learning tool for the student, helping learners to articulate and navigate their process of learning as related to the essential standard. In this math example, students are proficient when they reach the Level 3 indicator: "I can tell time to the nearest 5 minutes. I can identify a.m. or p.m." The tracking tool supports a student's pace of learning as it provides transparency of the learning process and provides for feedback along the way. Students document their evidence and receive feedback related to what level they are on compared to the proficiency level (Level 3) for that given learning target.

FIGURE 4.11 Sample Student Self-Assessment: Tracking My Learning Pathway

Name		Unit/Project: Measurement	
Tracking My Learning Pathway **NH Math Competency #5:** Use measurement tools, units, and attributes to describe and compare objects, situations, or events, and to solve authentic applied measurement problems.		**2.MD.7**  **I can tell time to the nearest 5 minutes.**	**2.NBT.A.2**  **I can count within 1000 by 5s, 10s, and 100s.**
Performance Level	**Learning Target**	**My Evidence (and Dates)**	
Extending My Learning **4**	I can tell time to the nearest minute in a variety of problem-solving situations.		
Demonstrating Proficiency **3**	I can tell time to the nearest 5 minutes. I can identify a.m. or p.m.		
Making Progress **2**	I can tell time to the nearest hour, half-hour, and quarter-hour and share my answer in minutes (e.g., 3 = 15, 6 = 30, 9 = 45).		
Working on the Basics **1**	I can count by 5s, 10s, and 100s to 1,000. I can identify the hour and minute hand.		

Source: Images from istock.com/kraphix and istock.com/bombuscreative

As students "level up" (complete a level), they know what learning step is next. This approach to pacing and documenting learning provides instructional feedback that the teacher can use to plan targeted small-group instruction and to share at student-led parent conferences. (A generic template for creating self-monitoring performance scales in any content area or grade level [Figure 4.12] is available in Appendix A and online.)

FIGURE 4.12 Student Self-Assessment Template: Tracking My Learning Pathway

CBE Tool 12	Student Self-Assessment Template: Tracking My Learning Pathway	
Name:		**Unit/Project:**
Tracking My Learning Pathway Competency Statement:		**Standard(s) I Am Working On:**
Performance Levels	*My Learning Targets*	*My Evidence (and Dates)*
Extending My Learning **4**	I can . . .	
Demonstrating Proficiency **3**	I can . . .	
Making Progress **2**	I can . . .	
Working on the Basics **1**	I can . . .	

Every week, teachers at this school have a goals conference with students to offer feedback on their math goals in the learning progression. Teachers have told us that the students are excited to share their learning progress with them and will cheer each other on because they understand that everyone is working on and achieving her or his own learning goals. These classrooms still employ whole-group instruction at times, such as when a new concept or skill is introduced or when providing guided practice for everyone. The primary difference is that now the students know what their learning goal is and what evidence is required for them to move on to the next level. Students are not asking or relying on the teachers to direct them. Instead, students are working at their pace, which is supported by evidence and growth feedback on their learning.

Student-Friendly Progressions: Pacing Instruction at the Middle and High School Levels

Student-friendly learning progressions can look very similar at the middle and high school levels, sometimes encompassing additional levels of the CB performance scale and connecting daily lesson learning targets. Figure 4.13 illustrates an example of a self-monitoring tool based on a high school science competency in chemistry, developed at Biddeford High School in Maine. Science topics are highlighted at each performance level with the intended rigor (in capital letters).

⟵ Student Strategy Monitoring

(Effect Size = 0.58)

Teachers can use each performance level in the progression to plan and deliver whole-class instruction, as seen in Figure 4.14, an adapted version of Biddeford's Learning Plan Progression (LPP). The teacher's pace and science content for instruction is indicated (by the number of estimated instructional days) in LPPs.

FIGURE 4.13 Sample High School Science CB Self-Monitoring Tool

UNIT 1: Universe and Stars		
Competency Statement: (HS-ESS1-1) **DEVELOP A MODEL BASED ON EVIDENCE** to illustrate the life span of the sun and the role of nuclear fusion in the sun's core to release energy that eventually reaches Earth in the form of radiation.		
Science Concepts: life span of the sun, nuclear fusion, form of radiation, anatomy of the sun		
Score	**Performance Level**	**Criteria for Evidence of Learning**
4.0 Advanced	Analyzing knowledge (Analyzing perspectives)	I can **EXPLAIN THE REASONS BEHIND THE EVIDENCE** of the life span of the sun and the role of nuclear fusion in the sun's core to release energy that eventually reaches Earth in the form of radiation.
3.0 Proficient	Comprehending knowledge (Symbolize)	I can **DEVELOP** a model based on evidence to illustrate the life span of the sun and the role of nuclear fusion in the sun's core to release energy that eventually reaches Earth in the form of radiation.
2.0 Developing	Retrieving knowledge (Recall)	I can **EXPLAIN** • The life span of the sun • Nuclear fusion • The forms of radiation • The anatomy of the Sun (internal and atmospheric layers, features)
1.0 Beginning	Retrieving knowledge (Recognize)	I can **RECOGNIZE** explanations of • The life span of the sun • Nuclear fusion • The forms of radiation • The anatomy of the Sun (internal and atmospheric layers, features)

Source: Developed by Biddeford High School. Used with permission.

FIGURE 4.14 Sample High School Science Learning Plan Progression

Unit Title: Conservation of Momentum (Unit 3)	Essential Question(s): What happens to the total momentum of two objects when they collide with one another?
DESIRED RESULTS	

Performance Indicator(s):	Rigor:
(HS-PS2-2) Use mathematical representations to **SUPPORT THE CLAIM** that the total momentum of a system of objects is conserved when there is no net force on the system.	• Solving—Decipher more complex problems involving the impulse/change in momentum equation ($p = m \times v$) and/or the conservation equations for either elastic or inelastic collisions. • Analyzing Knowledge—Using basic math, demonstrate the ability to use conservation of momentum to solve exit conditions for either elastic or inelastic collisions. • Comprehending Knowledge—Nonmathematically, describe relationships between force, time, and change in momentum; describe the concept of conservation of momentum regarding collisions. • Recognizing—Identify variables involved with impulse, momentum, collisions, and conservation of momentum.

Formative Assessments (Performance Levels):

- Pretest
- Posttest (4)
- Conservation of Momentum Collision Worksheet (3)
- Exit Ticket (2)
- Matching or True/False Vocab Worksheet (1)

Summative Assessment(s):

- Physics Classroom "Collision Carts" Simulator
- Vernier Momentum Lab
- Momentum Quiz

Unpacked Concepts—What Students Will KNOW:	Unpacked Skills (With Performance Levels)— What Students Will Be Able to DO:

(HS-PS2-2)
 	
    Types of Collisions
 	
    Conservation of Momentum
	(HS-PS2-2)
	
	• Solve (4)
	
	• Calculate (3)
	
	• Describe Relationships (2)
	
	• Recognize (1)

Unit Title: Conservation of Momentum (Unit 3)		Essential Question(s): What happens to the total momentum of two objects when they collide with one another?	
LEARNING PLAN PROGRESSION (LPP)			
Duration	Learning Objective	Instructional Strategy	Formative Assessment
1 class period	Students will be able to define *momentum* and *impulse*, identify *elastic* vs. *inelastic collisions*.	Momentum demonstration with dynamics carts and discussion Impulse: Applying brakes gently for a long time vs. sharply for a short time to stop at a red light	Momentum discussion, demonstration with "Happy Balls" Vocab worksheet: Std 3 FA Level 1 Vocab Note helper sheet: Std 3 Note Sheet
1 class period	Students will understand relationship between impact force and time of collision (impulse); that objects must be moving to have momentum (mass x velocity); that collisions do *not* change the amount of momentum (conservation of momentum)	NO BRAKES! (the oak tree vs. the cornfield discussion); NO WALLET! (borrowing money at a store/cons of momentum discussion)	Worksheet for understanding impulse and momentum: Std 3 FA Level 2 Relationships
1 class period	Collision activity	pHET simulation for momentum or "Collision Carts" interactive (Collision Carts	Activity sheet for pHET activity Activity sheet for "Collision Carts" Collision Carts Worksheet
1 class period	Analyzing collisions: before vs. after using conservation of momentum	Examples on the whiteboard	Formative assessment worksheet: Std 3 FA Level 3 Analyzing
2 class periods	Egg drop activity: Crumple Zone Design (lengthen time of collision) or Parachute Design (introduce counterforce to decrease impact force)?	Examine both design objectives; design protection method for an egg dropped one flight of stairs; create from provided materials; test and evaluate	Egg Drop Materials and Rules Egg Drop Wrap-up Notes Egg Drop Sample Write-up
1 class period	Review and practice summative assessment	Review	Std 3 Practice Summative Assessment
1 class period	Summative assessment		Std 3 Summative Assessment

Source: **Developed by Biddeford High School. Used with permission.**

Plans like these are shared with students in the class, reminding them of the general pacing of learning and including weblinks to instructional supports and resources along the performance levels of the progression. Sharing the plan with students makes the learning goals clear and promotes more learner independence, with students knowing where to access instructional supports and instructional information at each step.

Students are provided with ongoing feedback regarding where they are relative to the pace of whole-group instruction. It is here that teachers and students can have one-on-one conversations based on a student's personal success skills (e.g., habit of work or engagement) or gaps in content knowledge if the student "falls off" pace. It is important to note, small-group or individualized targeted instruction is offered to students who need added support and time to learn. Targeted personalized instruction can take many forms beyond direct instruction from teachers, such as using technology and access to learning resources within and beyond the classroom (e.g., Kahn Academy lessons).

Teacher Clarity: Expectations for Learning (Effect Size = 0.75)

Pacing With Technology-Enabled Strategies

Pacing at the classroom level is a challenge often met using technology-enabled strategies, such as a flipped classroom approach where a teacher videotapes short lesson segments for students to access and view individually. Viewing these teacher-created segments can be done prior to the whole-class instruction, as an option for students to move ahead at their own pace, or as a review.

> When Karin was working with a high school math teacher in Delaware, she suggested that in order to free up more class time for students to delve deeply into math content with performance tasks and math investigations, the teacher videotape 8- to 10-minute teaching segments that would normally be delivered as whole-class instruction. These were assigned as homework, so when students arrived at class, they were already prepared to dive into the problem-solving activities. After about a month, Karin returned to the school and asked the teacher, "So how did this flipped approach work?"
>
> "The students love learning this way," the teacher told her. "My only problem is that I had to figure out what my new role was going to be if I am not standing in front of the room teaching. I have now become more of a facilitator and coach."

Another popular approach using technology to personalize and vary the pace of learning is blended learning. Blended learning combines the use of online resources and technology tools with team-learning activities and traditional teacher-directed instruction. Blended learning takes more advanced planning and technology expertise on the part of teachers, but like the flipped classroom approach, it shifts the teacher's role during class to more of a facilitator to guide and personalize learning. According to Tucker, Wycoff, and Green (2017, p. 6), the hallmarks of blended learning are personalization, student agency, authentic audiences, connectivity, and creativity.

With any of these technology-enabled approaches, we remind educators that technology needs to be viewed as a tool to support learning, not as a replacement for core or targeted instruction. Putting students in front of computers to work on their own is *not* personalization! Technology—when it is accessible to every student and used appropriately—can provide clear learning targets, timely feedback to students, and generate assessment evidence collected along the progression of learning. The combination of competency-based learning progressions and flipped classrooms or blended learning environments need to make sure that there are still teacher-to-student partnerships and engaging student-to-student relationships that promote learning.

STOP AND REFLECT

We've shared several examples in this chapter showing how we have seen teachers address pacing. What are some flexible pacing strategies that are currently being used or that might work in your school or PLC group?

_____

_____

_____

_____

_____

_____

_____

4.4 PROMOTING INTRINSIC MOTIVATION AND ENGAGEMENT THROUGH ASSESSMENTS AND TIMELY FEEDBACK

Students in CB classrooms are partners in monitoring their academic and personal success skills growth. They actively engage in goal setting, reflection, and feedback as part of a continuous improvement model. *Mindset* author Dr. Carol Dweck (2006) found that students with a growth mindset tend to generate other new ideas and problems to solve, whereas students with fixed mindsets will consistently quit after one route doesn't work. Learners with a growth mindset want to be engaged in self-monitoring and strategizing because growth mindset feedback encourages the effort rather than praises the ability. If this all sounds like formative uses of assessment to you, then you are right on target.

Examine Current Assessment Uses and Effectiveness

Hess (2018, pp. 235–236) describes five key ideas related to high-quality formative assessment that we can apply to CB learning and instructional planning.

High-Quality Formative Assessment

Key Idea #1: Authentic assessment is continuous. Formative assessment is both integral to the cycle of learning and part of a balanced assessment system.

Key Idea #2: Formative assessment may take different forms, but should always inform instruction and learning—and be *actionable*.

Key Idea #3: Feedback is multifaceted and used to gauge how close a student is to the intended learning target.

Key Idea #4: Students are actively involved in formative assessment.

Key Idea #5: All high-quality assessment uses three key components: understanding how one learns, how one demonstrates what was learned, and how we interpret/measure the evidence observed.

Source: Hess, 2018.

Collective
Teacher Efficacy

(Effect Size = 1.39)

→ When considering *to what degree* classroom assessment practices are supporting and motivating student learning, your teams might want to revisit local assessment policies and practices outlined in **CBE Tool 2** (described in greater detail in Chapter 2). This tool provides discussion questions for five indicators of a comprehensive **local assessment system**. Local assessment system (LAS) indicator

3 asks: Do we communicate how learning expectations for all students relate to assessment types, purpose, and uses?

With a focus on formative uses of classroom assessments that align with different levels of CB performance scales, teachers should collaboratively examine the types of assessments currently being used to measure progress and proficiency and their effectiveness in capturing actionable assessment evidence. We suggest that teams focus discussions on which specific classroom assessment practices address the following key ideas:

- **Formative Assessment Key Idea #2:** Formative assessment may take different forms, but it should always inform instruction and learning—and be *actionable.* Actionable evidence means that student thinking and reasoning have been uncovered (made visible) by **systematically observing** measurable indicators or asking students to use words, visuals, and physical models to represent what they know and can transfer to new situations.

  Teacher Clarity: Expectations for Learning (Effect Size = 0.75)

- **Formative Assessment Key Idea #3:** Feedback is multifaceted and used to gauge how close a student is to the intended learning target. Are assessments aligned with each level of a performance scale? Do assessments at the lower end of performance scales and learning progressions measure foundational skills? Do units of study have preassessments measuring prerequisite skills and knowledge? Do assessments measure increasingly more complex content learning (at DOK 3 and DOK 4) at the upper end of performance scales? Do assessments include open-ended constructed response questions and performance-based tasks? For example, in **project-based learning**, students engage in meaningful, self-designed projects to demonstrate authentic integration of essential skills and concepts. Not only do these assessments require students to apply personal success skills, but they also provide teachers with opportunities to directly observe processes used (e.g., investigation, research) and conference with students at different stages during the project's development.

  Teacher Cognitive Task Analysis (Effect Size = 1.29)

- **Formative Assessment Key Idea #4:** Students are actively involved in formative assessment. How are metacognition and reflection *regularly* built into completing performance-based tasks and investigations? When and how are peer and self-assessment most useful in driving student learning and construction of new knowledge? Is classroom discourse designed to elicit student choice, voice, and self-monitoring strategies? Are there mechanisms for students to track their own progress, such as using performance scales to conference with teachers about evidence they are including in their body of evidence?

  Student Self-Reflection (Effect Size = 0.75)

> ### 💭 STOP AND REFLECT
>
> To what degree do your current formative assessment practices engage students and give them a voice? In what ways could you increase student engagement with assessment?
>
> _____
>
> _____
>
> _____
>
> _____
>
> _____

A Final Note About Feedback on Student Performance

Feedback on a student's performance—not generic praise (great job!) or advice (what you need to do is . . .)—is essential in moving learning forward. Motivation to continue to learn and put forth effort is fostered when feedback includes concrete examples (evidence) of progress measured or compared against indicators for mastering a learning goal. Teaching students how to develop the criteria by which their work will be judged (e.g., by examining high-quality exemplars) and providing practice with clear models and examples for them to learn how to evaluate the quality of products are just as important as teaching content.

As the students become familiar with the process and take more ownership of their learning, teachers need to allow them to take leadership. (Jones, 2018)

When students can tell you what they are learning, why they are learning it, and what they'll be able to do next as a result of that learning . . . you have fully engaged learners!

Teaching and empowering students to become leaders in their own education can take many forms. In fact, many traditional "best practices" may find new life in a personalized competency-based learning classroom. Student-led conferences are bolstered by a level of understanding and articulation of learning that students acquire through transparent and intentional design.

As an example, in our work with a school district in South Carolina a kindergarten teacher took on the challenge of having students set and achieve learning goals. This teacher developed transparent learning pathways for reading, writing, and mathematics.

Her students worked independently or collaboratively on their personal learning goals and determined their "just-right" work choices throughout the day. When asking her students about their learning, they could articulate their learning goals and strategies as well as what they needed to do to move on to the next level or target. The design for transparency and rigorous progressions with feedback was only a part of this amazing story. The instructional practice that engaged and ignited these students as leaders of their learning was their weekly goal conferences with their teacher who wrote this reflection:

> According to John Hattie, "The aim is to get the students actively involved in seeking this evidence: their role is not simply to do tasks as decided by teachers, but to actively manage and understand their learning gains." This quote speaks to me, as it reinforced something that I intuitively knew and that my students craved. They loved talking about and demonstrating their learning to me. As the teacher, I found these conversations to be some of the best instructional feedback I could ever ask for. I don't want to downplay technology, but I do believe learning needs to sanctify the connections between the student, teacher, and the learning. I had weekly goals conferences with each of my students. It allowed them to take ownership of their learning and to show me where they are on their own personal progression of learning. To promote ownership of learning, the students used the visual progression and matrices to articulate their learning goal, and the steps needed to master their current essential standard. As the students become familiar with the process and take more ownership of their learning, teachers need to allow them to take leadership. (Jones, 2018)

Revisiting the Profile of the Graduate

The ability for districts to design a system of learning that prepares all students for college, careers, and life has created a huge challenge, as postsecondary metrics are generally not indicating anticipated levels of student achievement. This leaves many districts and communities asking, Why are only some of our students prepared for life after high school? and Are we missing something?

We began our discussion of CBE suggesting that schools take time to collaboratively develop a profile of the high school graduate (POG). Now might be the time to revisit your system in light of how you originally framed your learning goals and expectations. How much progress have you and your students made? What have you learned along the way? What does learning for life after high school really mean?

We end with a reflection from Young Whan Choi, manager of performance assessments for the Oakland Unified School District:

> As the graduate profile becomes more widely adopted in our district, we will align ourselves toward a vision for public education where career readiness and community readiness are as important as college readiness.

By taking a more holistic approach, we will better be able to serve more of the students who are homeless, healing from the trauma of violence, and on the verge of dropping out. Students might no longer experience school as a solitary building where they are talked at, disciplined, and tested. Instead, school would function more like a grand transit station where students, teachers, and mentors come together to learn from one another and where they regularly leave to study real-world problems and work collaboratively to implement solutions. (Young Whan Choi, 2019)

The Road Ahead

We have centered this work by looking carefully at the structures of traditional education that have held many of us back as educators while setting forward new ways for you to think about shifting into a higher gear with learner-centered competency-based education. We have raised and answered many questions and put forward strategies and tools that we have used in many schools as educational designers. As much as these strategies will help you to move your learning system toward the future readiness of your learners, we know the work ahead of you will raise more questions and challenge you in many ways as never before. The work you will do is important for your learners and for your community. Share it to inspire others and take pride in shaping the future of education!

Appendix A

CBE Tools 1–12

SUMMARY OF CBE TOOLS AND THEIR USES

CBE Tool	Title	Use This CBE Tool To . . .
1A–1E	CBE Readiness	Examine and reflect on the current status of your CBE system and collaboratively engage in action planning for each core component.
2	Discussion Questions—Examining Local Assessment Systems	Examine the current local assessment philosophy and system components, as well as to determine next steps. (This is Tool #28 in *A Local Assessment Toolkit.*)
3	Self-Evaluation Rubric for Examining or Revising Competency Statements	Examine or revise the quality and intended rigor of your competency statements.
4	Development or Analysis of Competencies Statements Across Grades	Develop or analyze the potential learning progressions described in competency statements across grades or grade spans.
5	Analyzing a Competency (Learning Goal): What Learning Is Implied?	Collaboratively examine each competency statement to uncover what content and skills will be learned and how they might be demonstrated and assessed.
6	Performance Scale Development Template	Use information generated from CBE Tool 5 (I can . . . statements, intended DOK levels, content to be taught) to create a scale from least to most complex skills to be demonstrated by the competency.
7	A Guide to Performance Assessment Development	Analyze or design new performance assessment tasks. Use the content-specific Hess CRMs with this tool when analyzing cognitive demands described in the assessment. (This is Tool #20 in *A Local Assessment Toolkit.*)
8	Performance Assessment Overview: Purpose and Use	Provide an overview of when the assessment will be given (unit of study, project, etc.), what it is intended to assess, and how results will be used (as formative, interim, or summative). (This is Tool #21 in *A Local Assessment Toolkit.*)
9	Task Quality Validation Protocol	Develop, provide peer feedback, or validate performance assessment tasks. Use the content-specific Hess CRMs with this tool when analyzing cognitive demands described in the assessment. (This is Tool #9 in *A Local Assessment Toolkit.*)
10	Task Validation Summary (Streamlined Version)	Summarize peer feedback from validation panel to development team; use with CBE Tool 9 (Task Quality Validation Protocol). (This is Tool #16A in *A Local Assessment Toolkit.*)
11	Rubric Quality Review Worksheet	Develop, provide peer feedback, or validate new scoring guides and rubrics based on seven key indicators of high-quality rubrics. (This is Tool #11 in *A Local Assessment Toolkit.*)
12	Student Self-Assessment Template: Tracking My Learning Pathway Template	Use the template version of Figure 4.12 to develop a learning pathway plan for each student to track progress over a short period of time, such as a unit of study.

CBE Tool 1A — Core Components of Competency-Based Education: CBE Readiness Tool

Component 1: Competencies

Develop a K–12 continuum of rigorous competencies describing how students will apply or transfer essential knowledge, skills, and dispositions across the grades leading to graduation.

Focus	Phase 1: Initiating	Phase 2: Emerging	Phase 3: Implementing	Where is your school now? What are possible next steps?
Leadership	Graduation requirements are policy driven. Curriculum and course offerings are used to develop scope and sequences by course or content area.	Articulated profile of a graduate (POG) is developed with input from staff and shared with community stakeholders. Graduation requirements, curriculum, college and career pathways are not yet aligned to POG.	Articulated profile of a graduate (POG) is developed with input from staff and community stakeholders. Graduation requirements are clearly articulated and integrated into curriculum and college and career pathways.	
Instruction and Assessment	Learning outcomes are clear and articulated by course or grade level. Instructional design emphasizes application of knowledge and skills described in state-adopted standards.	Learning outcomes are clear and articulated by course and standards-based curriculum. K–12 academic competencies are adopted but not incorporated into instruction or assessment design.	Learning outcomes emphasize competencies that include application and creation of knowledge, along with the development of important personal skills and dispositions. Instruction and assessments support and measure competencies.	
Learner Culture	Interpersonal skills are expressed as personal behaviors. Students are aware of these skills and monitored by teachers.	Interpersonal and intrapersonal competencies are developing and evidenced by students when they monitor and reflect on these skills.	Interpersonal, intrapersonal, and learning competencies include explicit, measurable, transferable learning objectives that empower students to have input into their learning path.	
Organizational Structures	The system is driven by "seat time" and whole-class instruction with some differentiation and remediation. Departments and grade-level teams with content expertise guide the delivery of instruction.	The structure and schedule allow for teacher collaboration and flexible grouping of students. School structures and systems are developing new pathways for students to advance to the next level of learning.	Structures and scheduling support collaboration in creating multiple pathways and academies that integrate standards and skills into core competencies aligned to career readiness standards and postsecondary expectations.	

- **Initiating:** District has begun to examine its existing system and identify where shifts in teaching and learning are needed.
- **Emerging:** District is beginning to develop and deploy competency-based systems and structures and is monitoring shifts in teaching and learning to measure impact.
- **Implementing:** District uses an ongoing feedback cycle to design, evaluate, and revise all core components of CBE for equitable and deeper learning.

Available for download at http://resources.corwin.com/DeeperCompetencyBasedLearning.

© Karin Hess (2009, updated 2017). A local assessment toolkit to support deeper learning: Guiding school leaders in linking research with classroom practice. Permission to reproduce is given only when authorship is fully cited [karinhessvt@gmail.com].

CBE Tool 1B — Core Components of Competency-Based Education: CBE Readiness Tool

Component 2: Personal Success Skills

Dispositions, soft skills, and 21st century skills (critical thinking, problem-solving, collaboration, goal setting, etc.) articulate qualities that are essential for success in life and are integrated with academic learning.

Focus	Phase 1: Initiating	Phase 2: Emerging	Phase 3: Implementing	Where is your school now? What are possible next steps?
Leadership	Current policies and practices (grading, discipline, etc.) lack an awareness of the importance of personal success skills in promoting academic success and overall well-being.	Policies and practices are aligned to the POG and revised to promote equity and personal learning skills in supporting students and staff.	Policies and practices reflect the POG and integrate personal success skills as indicators of competence for graduation.	
Instruction and Assessment	Student engagement and reflection opportunities are evidenced in some learning areas and situations.	Student engagement and reflection opportunities are being aligned to learning experiences and targeted personal success skills, leading to student goal setting and self-reflection.	Student engagement measures and reflection opportunities consistently monitor the learning experience, learning outcomes, and personal success skills.	
Learner Culture	Learning culture is teacher-centered and content-driven, where students are mostly compliant and passive learners. Personal success skills are not directly taught by teachers or consistently practiced by students.	Learning environments and interactions promote independent and collaborative learning opportunities for students to exercise voice and choice. Personal success skills are integrated with academics.	Learning environments and interactions are responsive to learner agency and are flexible in meeting students' learning needs, as articulated by the learner's goals and self-reflections. Learners emerge as confident and independent learners.	
Organizational Structures	Individual teacher grading practices sometimes emphasize different personal success skills (e.g., collaboration, study skills) when reporting on academic grades.	Personal success skills are aligned to the POG and identified school wide to promote learning for all students. School structures (team planning) are used to clarify a developmental continuum and disseminate common expectations.	School/district instructional delivery methods support the integration of personal success skills with academic learning. Educators co-design personalized learning activities and assessments consistent with the POG.	

- **Initiating:** District has begun to examine its existing system and identify where shifts in teaching and learning are needed.
- **Emerging:** District is beginning to develop and deploy competency-based systems and structures and is monitoring shifts in teaching and learning to measure impact.
- **Implementing:** District uses an ongoing feedback cycle to design, evaluate, and revise all core components of CBE for equitable and deeper learning.

CBE Tool 1C — Core Components of Competency-Based Education: CBE Readiness Tool

Component 3: Performance Assessments

To determine a student's college and career readiness, the continuum of assessments rely on varied formats and multiple opportunities for students to demonstrate learning in authentic (real-world) tasks.

Focus	Phase 1: Initiating	Phase 2: Emerging	Phase 3: Implementing	Where is your school now? What are possible next steps?
Leadership	Assessments of student learning are evidenced within courses and content areas and guided by policies (grading, graduation, etc.) and curriculum.	Policies support multiple and varied assessments, including rigorous assessments that capture student learning and mastery within a standards-based curriculum.	Timely, rigorous, and competency-based assessments capture student learning and mastery within and beyond the school-based environment.	
Instruction and Assessment	Standards are expressed as learning outcomes and are assessed in all content areas. Assessments are given to all students on the same day. Performance assessments are rarely used to capture evidence of deeper learning.	Rigorous competencies with learning outcomes are identified. Performance tasks are introduced as a part of a balanced assessment system used both formatively and summatively in most courses and content areas.	Rigorous competencies and learning outcomes are scaffolded and integrated across content areas. Performance assessments provide meaningful feedback and measure both academic and personal success skills to promote deeper learning.	
Learner Culture	Students are aware of the knowledge and skills that will be assessed. Students do not view most assessments as relevant to their learning because there is only one way to demonstrate what they know.	Performance assessments begin to align with the knowledge, skills, and dispositions that all students should acquire within and across content areas or courses. Learning can be demonstrated in a variety of ways.	Performance assessments align with academic and personal skills (e.g. collaboration, goal setting, social discourse). Learning is student driven and demonstrated in a variety of ways. Assessment evidence and feedback promote deeper learning.	
Organizational Structures	Grading methods are often limited by the student information systems (SIS). Grades are reported by traditional assessment types (e.g., exams, state assessments), methods (averaging), and timelines.	Teachers are given the time and tools to co-plan and co-develop common rigorous assessments, including performance tasks and projects.	District protocols guide consistent design and use of assessments and review of student evidence from competency-based performance assessments. Evidence informs instruction and student learning.	

- **Initiating:** District has begun to examine its existing system and identify where shifts in teaching and learning are needed.
- **Emerging:** District is beginning to develop and deploy competency-based systems and structures and is monitoring shifts in teaching and learning to measure impact.
- **Implementing:** District uses an ongoing feedback cycle to design, evaluate, and revise all core components of CBE for equitable and deeper learning.

CBE Tool 1D — Core Components of Competency-Based Education: CBE Readiness Tool

Component 4: Learning Pathways
Competencies drive a rigorous, transparent, flexible system of learning in which students are empowered by opportunities to choose what and how they learn.

Focus	Phase 1: Initiating	Phase 2: Emerging	Phase 3: Implementing	Where is your school now? What are possible next steps?
Leadership	Policies aspire to prepare students for college and careers, but practices support a single learning pathway to promotion or graduation for all students.	Policies and practices become more flexible in determining how and where learning can occur. The development of multiple, rigorous pathways ensures each student's learning is possible within the school-based accountability system.	Policies and practices support multiple pathways for authentic, rigorous student learning, which is appropriately credentialed within and outside learning agencies (e.g., college-course taking for graduation credit).	
Instruction and Assessment	Course-level standards and learning outcomes are taught and scaffolded by teachers and made transparent to parents and learners using course syllabi.	Competency-based learning outcomes are scaffolded and begin to be integrated across content areas and grade levels. Students have some options for learning (e.g., online, blended, face-to-face, community-based learning).	Competencies and learning outcomes are scaffolded and integrated across content areas as well as grade levels. Personalized learning plans guide students in their learning choices, pathways, and learning support.	
Learner Culture	Limited pathways and choice are offered to students in meeting grade-level or graduation requirements.	Multiple course and content pathways are aligned to competencies. Students have some options in how to demonstrate their learning across courses or content disciplines.	Students advocate how to navigate their personal pathways, leading to a demonstration of proficiency of the competency-based graduation requirements and the POG.	
Organizational Structures	A single system of teaching and learning is organized in the same way for all students, with provisions for remediation.	Equitable pathways articulate the alignment to academic or personal competencies and are mapped to curricular programs or course offerings.	Equitable pathways clearly articulate the alignment to academic and personal success skill competencies and are mapped to learning opportunities anytime and anywhere.	

- **Initiating:** District has begun to examine its existing system and identify where shifts in teaching and learning are needed.
- **Emerging:** District is beginning to develop and deploy competency-based systems and structures and is monitoring shifts in teaching and learning to measure impact.
- **Implementing:** District uses an ongoing feedback cycle to design, evaluate, and revise all core components of CBE for equitable and deeper learning.

 Available for download at **http://resources.corwin.com/DeeperCompetencyBasedLearning.**

CBE Tool 1E — Core Components of Competency-Based Education: CBE Readiness Tool

Component 5: Evidence-Based Grading

Scoring, grading, and reporting reflect students' progress toward unit, course, and graduation competencies.

Focus	Phase 1: Initiating	Phase 2: Emerging	Phase 3: Implementing	Where is your school now? What are possible next steps?
Leadership	Grading and reporting policies and practices are different at the elementary, middle, and high school levels.	Grading and reporting policies support practices in standards-based grading. Competency-based assessments are graded but are not part of a larger body of evidence (BOE) for meeting graduation requirements.	Policies define the body of evidence (BOE) needed to demonstrate proficiency in relation to academic and personal skills competencies. CB reporting indicates student progress toward mastery of competencies.	
Instruction and Assessment	Grading and reporting are done within the context of a course or content area. Mathematical calculations and averaging generally determine grades.	Formative assessments provide a level of transparency to inform where a student is in relation to a particular learning outcome for a course or content area. Learning outcomes are tracked and measured relative to standards.	Formative assessment data provide the body of evidence used for instructional and learner feedback. Evidence informs where a student is in relation to a competency and whether the student is ready for a summative assessment.	
Learner Culture	Grading practices affect both positive and negative student attitudes toward learning and self-image.	Grading practices are more transparent to the learner, relative to progress in demonstrating skills described in standards.	The body of evidence informs pacing of learning, is responsive to addressing student needs, and promotes student reflection and ownership of learning experience and learning outcomes.	
Organizational Structures	Systems of scoring and reporting are aligned to course expectations, reporting policies, and school year timelines.	Systems of scoring and reporting are aligned to course and graduation requirements, standards-based reporting, and school year timelines.	Competency-based systems of building a student's BOE, scoring work samples, and reporting results informs graduation readiness relative to the POG.	

- **Initiating:** District has begun to examine its existing system and identify where shifts in teaching and learning are needed.
- **Emerging:** District is beginning to develop and deploy competency-based systems and structures and is monitoring shifts in teaching and learning to measure impact.
- **Implementing:** District uses an ongoing feedback cycle to design, evaluate, and revise all core components of CBE for equitable and deeper learning.

Available for download at http://resources.corwin.com/DeeperCompetencyBasedLearning.

Karin Hess (2009, updated 2017). A local assessment toolkit to support deeper learning: Guiding school leaders in linking research with classroom practice. Permission to reproduce is given only when authorship is fully cited (karinhessvt@gmail.com).

CBE Tool 2

Discussion Questions
Examining Our Local Assessment System (LAS)

LAS Indicator 1: *Do we include these key components in our local assessment system? How comprehensive is our system?*

To what degree does our system . . .

- include technically sound assessments of academic achievement and explicit or shared district-based goals for learning (e.g., proficiencies/competencies, transferable skills, community service);
- illustrate how assessments and assessment data interact;
- provide adequate protocols, professional development, and leadership regarding implementation of assessment principles and practices; and
- establish explicit and well-coordinated mechanisms (feedback loops) for managing use of assessments, assessment data or results, and using data to address individual student needs?

Aces (what's useful and relevant right now):

Spaces (where do we need work; what are the gaps):

LAS Indicator 2: *Is our (proficiency-based) assessment philosophy supported by coherent policy and practices?*

Do we have a clear statement of purpose? What is the focus (e.g., "common" learning targets, learning environments and pathways, student-centered or personalized learning)?

Does the (proficiency-based) assessment system . . .

- establish a common language and perspective about assessing content, skills, and deeper understanding and the interpretation and use of data?
- improve curriculum, instruction, and student engagement?
- elevate expectations and learning opportunities for all students?
- strengthen communication about student performance with students, their families, and within the educational community?
- Other?

Aces (what's useful and relevant right now):

Spaces (where do we need work; what are the gaps):

LAS Indicator 3: *Do we communicate how learning expectations for all students relate to assessment types, purposes, and uses?*

Start by ranking these components as follows: *Fully* in place, *Partly* in place, or *Limited*, needing updating or revision or replacement. Then, decide what's working well and potential gaps.

How comprehensive is our assessment system? Does it include . . .

- A range of assessment types and formats—observation, short answer, constructed response, unit assessments, performance tasks, or extended projects, for example?
- Guidelines for assessment purposes and users (audience)—Formative, Interim, Summative?
- Alignment with opportunity to learn or curriculum and instruction (e.g., use of common or interim assessments with administration guidelines and student work samples; progress monitoring)?
- Considerations for assessing young children, special populations?
- A **communication plan**—communicating expectations and results to students, parents, and the community?

Discussion Questions
Examining Our Local Assessment System (LAS)

Aces (what's useful and relevant right now):

Spaces (where do we need work; what are the gaps):

LAS Indicator 4: *Do our assessment processes ensure that assessments and bodies of evidence are of high quality?*

Are there common protocols and structures in place for . . .

- providing clear, agreed-upon learning expectations (proficiencies/competencies) and performance scales that guide assessment development, evidence-based grading, and interpreting and reporting results?
- establishing validity: content + performance or cognitive rigor alignment (standards, proficiencies)?
- checking reliability: consistency of scoring and interpretations?
- ensuring fairness and engagement: all students are able to access and demonstrate authentic learning?
- combining multiple measures: a process for combining results from different assessments, comparability?
- developing and using common tools: assessment system is articulated by content area and assessment blueprints (alignment), useful in determining proficiency (e.g., standard setting, student work analysis, body of evidence), validation protocols (e.g., cognitive labs, performance task review), classroom observations?
- creating verification methods for evaluating a student's "body of assessment evidence" (body of evidence = each student's assessment evidence collected over time, such in a portfolio)?

Aces (what's useful and relevant right now):

Spaces (where do we need work; what are the gaps):

Identify tools, protocols, and activities that will help you accomplish these:

LAS Indicator 5: *Do we have a comprehensive district implementation plan?*

Does the district assessment plan . . .

- lay out multiyear implementation for each content area K–12: developing, piloting, refining assessments and curriculum that are proficiency based and responsive to established learning progressions?
- describe and provide for feedback loops and leadership (e.g., to document and support implementation)?
- identify supports to teachers: professional development, curriculum, PLCs, student work analysis?
- systematically collect accreditation evidence?

Aces (what's useful and relevant right now):

Spaces (where do we need work; what are the gaps):

Possible Action Steps				
Steps to be taken	Why is it important to us?	Supports or resources needed	Lead people?	Start by when?

CBE Tool 3 — Self-Evaluation Rubric for Examining or Revising Competency Statements

To what degree are competency statements . . .	4 (Stronger)	3 (Stronger)	2 (Weaker)	1 (Weaker)
1—Relevant to Big Ideas/ enduring understandings of the content domain (**Why is this important to learn?**)	Includes essential skills that are transferable (across content domains, applicable to real-world situations, etc.) Requires broader connections between/among theories, principles, or concepts	Includes skills that are transferable across content areas or real-world situations. Focuses on key concepts of the content domain, supported by topics and facts, with broader connections possible	Based on topics applicable to a specific course or project. Lacks explicit connections to enduring understandings/Big Ideas of the content domain. Unlikely to lead to broader learning connections	Limited to scope and sequence of textbooks or specific programs. Very specific to facts and skills in content area (more like a skills checklist; skills performed in isolation)
2—Aligned to prioritized outcomes (national/state/ local standards)	Reflects prioritized national/ state standards or local frameworks, bundled for deeper learning (Big Ideas)	Aligns with prioritized national/ state content standards and local frameworks (personal skills/ practices)	Has alignment with national/ state/local standards. Lacks a sense of learning that has been prioritized (too few–too many)	May be either too vague or too specific or detailed in its content area focus to identify clear alignment
3—Designed to assess deeper cognitive demand, complex performances, and products of learning	Requires complex conceptual understanding and applications in unfamiliar/authentic contexts. Asks students to investigate, create, solve, and defend their thinking or products	Promotes authentic applications of conceptual knowledge using reasoning, planning, interpreting, problem-solving, or investigation. Integrates personal skills	Requires mental processes/skills, such as defining, summarizing, constructing, organizing, displaying, etc. Promotes routine applications of conceptual knowledge	Asks students to show what they know using only routine or basic applications. Mostly requires recall of facts, information, definitions, terms, procedures
4—Equitable for all students. Student-centered, personalized. Multiple opportunities. Varied assessment formats. Fairness, UDL	Promotes varied formats/UDL and multiple opportunities to demonstrate evidence of learning (e.g., interdisciplinary, student-designed, group—individual, scaffolded)	Supports some varied assessment formats applying UDL. Multiple opportunities to demonstrate learning (e.g., interdisciplinary, group, or individual, multiple courses)	Supports traditional assessments applying UDL to demonstrate evidence of learning. Limited to retaking the same assessment (with more time, read aloud, etc.)	Implies limited opportunities to demonstrate individual or personalized learning. Does not support varied assessment formats/UDL
5—Designed with learning pathways/ progressions. Within grades. Across grades. Extends to real-world/CCR (college and career readiness)	Provides clear continuity for important learning within and across grades (e.g., when to advance upon mastery). Learning pathways not limited to mastering the content; students can go "beyond"	Articulates what is important in understanding the content and possible pathways to get there (courses, projects, etc.). Provides clear continuity for learning within and across grades	Defines what is to be observed or measured. Provides some continuity for learning from one grade to the next (prior learning clearly builds to later learning)	Defines what is to be observed or measured. Lacks meaningful connections for possible learning pathways from one grade level to the next (more like new learning each year)
6—Embedded in ongoing instruction and opportunities to learn	Promotes opportunities for learners to co-design some of the assignments/assessments. Learners expected to set goals and self-monitor progress within and across courses	Expectations may be applied across courses with varying types of supports and resources	Expectations are course-specific. Instruction and materials may be differentiated for subgroups or individuals	Expectations are course-specific, but may differ for some individual students. Pacing and materials are same for whole class

CBE Tool 4

Development or Analysis of Competency Statements Across Grades: Is There a Defensible Learning Progression?

Linked to a Big Idea?			
Grade Levels or Grade Spans*			
Competency Statement (Learning Goal)	Students will . . .	Students will . . .	Students will . . .
Break down competency statement into learning targets** **Use kid-friendly language** "I can . . . "	I can I can I can I can I can	I can I can I can I can I can	I can I can I can I can I can
Identify alignment to content standards?			
Identify alignment to personal success skills? (SEL, work habits, etc.)			

*Listing competencies for adjacent grade levels or grade spans allows for a review of potential learning progressions across grades.

**Creating learning targets (I can . . .) helps in the development of scales that describe performance (and learning) from *Beginning* to *Proficient* +.

Available for download at **http://resources.corwin.com/DeeperCompetencyBasedLearning.**

| CBE Tool 5 | Analyzing a Competency (Learning Goal): What Learning Is Implied? | |

Content Area:	Grade Level:

Competency Statement # _____

Students will . . .

Learning targets (guide instruction and assessment)

- I can
- I can
- I can
- I can
- I can
- I can

Content/Concepts	⟷	Performance/ Products/Intended DOK
		DOK 1:
		DOK 2:
		DOK 3:
		DOK 4:

Alignment: List Content Standards	Alignment: Personal Success Skills

List Possible Common (Formative, Interim, Summative) Assessment Tasks:

CBE Tool 6	Performance Scale Development Template	

Competency Statement:		
Grade Level, Course, or Unit of Study:		
EXPANDING **Score 4.0** Construct new knowledge/(far) transfer, extend thinking	In addition to score 3.0 performance, in-depth insights, solutions, and/or applications go beyond what was explicitly taught. **The student:**	**Evidence From This Unit or Course** **(List Instructional or Assessment Tasks)**
	3.5 In addition to score 3.0 performance, exhibits some in-depth insight or applications **with partial success** = attempts to go beyond what was taught; extends thinking, but was not completely successful.	
PROFICIENT **Score 3.0** Integrate skills and knowledge (near and far) transfer with more complex tasks	The student exhibits *no major misconceptions*, no key factual inaccuracies, nor relevant omissions. **The student:**	
	2.5 In addition to score 2.0 performance, no major errors and partial knowledge of most of the 3.0 content and skills. Evidence of some flawed explanations, thinking/misconceptions.	
DEVELOPING **Score 2.0** Perform or understand the less complex aspects (e.g., parts in isolation) required for more complex tasks	There are no major errors or omissions regarding *the basic details, facts, and routine processes.* The student may exhibit some *key misconceptions* regarding the integration of more complex ideas and processes. **The student:**	
BEGINNING **Score 1.0** Demonstrate foundational skills	With extensive scaffolding and added supports, demonstrates a partial understanding of some basic details, terms, and routine processes. **The student:**	

CBE Tool 6	Performance Scale Development Template With Sample Wording	

Competency Statement:		
Grade Level, Course, or Unit of Study:		
EXPANDING **Score 4.0** Construct new knowledge/(far) transfer, extend thinking	**In addition to score 3.0 performance**, in-depth insights, solutions, and/or applications go beyond what was explicitly taught. Tasks offer opportunities for extended thinking (e.g., drawing upon cross-curricular knowledge; expanding personal or world perspectives; using elaborated communication). **The student:** *Constructs knowledge and extends thinking by . . .*	**Evidence From This Unit or Course** **(List Instructional or Assessment Tasks)** *Self-design an individual or group project* *Extend an investigation using additional sources*
	3.5 | **In addition to score 3.0 performance,** exhibits some in-depth insight or applications **with partial success** = attempts to go beyond what was taught; extends thinking, but was not completely successful.	
PROFICIENT **Score 3.0** Integrate skills and knowledge (near and far) transfer with more complex tasks	The student exhibits *no major misconceptions*, no key factual inaccuracies, nor relevant omissions. **The student:** • *Uses . . .* • *Analyzes . . .* • *Supports conclusion about . . .* • *Makes deep connections . . .* • *Creates . . .*	*Develop and deliver an oral presentation* *Prepare for and participate in a debate* *Develop a model to . . .*
	2.5 | **In addition to score 2.0 performance,** no major errors and partial knowledge of most of the 3.0 content and skills. Evidence of some flawed explanations, thinking/misconceptions.	
DEVELOPING **Score 2.0** Perform or understand the less complex aspects (e.g., parts in isolation) required for more complex tasks	There are no major errors or omissions regarding *the basic details, facts, and routine processes.* The student may exhibit some *key misconceptions* regarding the integration of more complex ideas and processes. **The student:** • *Recalls terminology or basic concepts . . .* • *Performs basic processes . . .* • *Constructs or interprets . . .* • *Connects . . .* • *Organizes . . .*	*Complete a graphic organizer to compare/contrast key ideas* *Develop research or survey questions related to an issue*
BEGINNING **Score 1.0** Demonstrate foundational skills	With extensive scaffolding and added supports, demonstrates a partial understanding of some basic details, terms, and routine processes. **The student:**	*Identify definitions for basic vocabulary terms* *Practice _____ with a peer*

Available for download at **http://resources.corwin.com/DeeperCompetencyBasedLearning**.

CBE Tool 7 — A Guide to Performance Assessment Development

Performance assessment design requires that you consider four key questions prior to actually developing an assessment task or scoring rubric:

- What (content, skills, dispositions) will this assess?
- Within what (authentic) context?
- Using what assessment format (case study analysis, role-playing scenario, research project, performance task, etc.)?
- To what degree will students be given choices or be required to make decisions about the task design, approach, resources used, or presentation of their learning?

Before deciding what format the assessment will take or the specifics of what students will "produce" or demonstrate, identify what the assessment is intended to measure. This is only an initial brainstorm to clarify your assessment purpose and scope; the details will likely change as the task evolves. For each criterion, generate a list of the expected processes/skills, concepts, dispositions, and thinking strategies you plan to assess. All criteria do not need to be included in the final assessment, but all *should be* considered during this phase of the planning. CBE Tool 7 can be used to examine existing assessments or to develop new ones. It is designed to walk you through a process to unpack the assessment purpose and to clarify the context, format, and task expectations.

Step 1:

Use the five rubric criteria types (in the following table) to identify what will be assessed. Hess CRM Tools #1–#5D will be useful in identifying specific performance indicators and intended DOK levels. All criteria do not need to be included, but they should be considered in the design phase. Only the last two criteria will allow you to assess far transfer of skills or concepts, so one of them *should* be included.

Criterion	Questions Typically Answered by Each Criterion
Process	Will the student follow particular processes (e.g., procedures for a science investigation; data collection; validating credibility of sources)? (Usually DOK 2 for more complex tasks)
Form	Are there formats or rules to be applied (e.g., correct citation format; organize parts of lab report; use required camera shots/visuals; edit for grammar and usage)? (Usually DOK 1)

(Continued)

(Continued)

CBE Tool 7	A Guide to Performance Assessment Development

Accuracy of Content	List essential domain-specific terms, calculations, concepts, etc., to be applied. (Usually DOK 1 or 2)
Construction of New Knowledge	How will the student go beyond the accurate solution and correct processes to gain new insights and raise new questions? (Usually DOK 3 or 4)
Impact	How will the final product achieve its intended purpose (e.g., solve a complex problem; persuade the audience; synthesize information to create a new product/performance)? (Usually DOK 3 or 4)

Step 2:

Identify one or more authentic contexts for applying these skills, concepts, and dispositions. Consider how real-world professionals employ these skills and concepts (scientists, artists, historians, researchers, choreographers, etc.).

Step 3:

Identify an appropriate assessment format for demonstrating learning:

- Case study analysis
- Role-playing scenario
- Research project—gather and organize information
- Science investigation
- Performance task (e.g., using a task shell)
- Performance/presentation
- Develop a product—oral and written
- Engineering design task
- Personal reflection, goal setting plan

Once you decide on the design format, explore existing models and use one as a template for your assessment design.

CBE Tool 7	A Guide to Performance Assessment Development	

Step 4:

To what degree will students be **given choices or be required to make decisions** about the task design, approach to solution, resources used, or presentation or products of learning? Use this "Shifting Roles" table to consider and make notes about the student's role in assessment and what is emphasized.

Shifting Roles: Moving From Teacher-Directed to Student-Directed Learning		
DOK Levels	**Teacher Roles**	**Student Roles**
1 **Acquires a Foundation**	Asks basic questions *(Who? What? Where? How? When?)* Scaffolds for access and focus	Recalls vocabulary, facts, rules Retrieves information Practices and self-monitors basic skills
	In this assessment:	**In this assessment:**
2 **Uses, Connects, Conceptualizes**	Asks questions to build schema: differentiate parts/whole, classify, draw out inferences Assesses conceptual understanding *(Why does this work? Under what conditions?)* Asks for examples/nonexamples	Explains relationships; sorts, classifies, compares, organizes information Makes predictions based on estimates, observations, prior knowledge Proposes problems, issues, or questions to investigate Raises conceptual or strategy questions
	In this assessment:	**In this assessment:**

(Continued)

(Continued)

CBE Tool 7	A Guide to Performance Assessment Development	

3 **Develops and Constructs Meaning**	Asks questions to probe reasoning and thinking and to promote peer discourse/self-reflection Links Big Ideas Requires proof, justification, analysis of evidence quality and accuracy	Uncovers relevant, accurate, credible information; flaws in a design; or proposed solution and links with Big Ideas Plans how to develop supporting (hard) evidence for conclusions or claims Researches or tests ideas, solves nonroutine problems, perseveres
	In this assessment:	**In this assessment:**
4 **Extends, Transfers, Broadens Meaning**	Asks questions to extend thinking, explore sources, broaden perspectives/Big Ideas *(Are there potential biases? Can you propose an alternative model?)* Encourages use of relevant and valid resources, peer-to-peer discourse, or self-reflection	Initiates, transfers, and constructs new knowledge or insights linked to Big Ideas Modifies, creates, elaborates based on analysis and interpretation of multiple sources Investigates real-world problems and issues, perseveres, manages time–task
	In this assessment:	**In this assessment:**

Step 5: Use CBE Tools 5–6 to identify and align success criteria (competencies, standards, DOK levels).

Step 6: Use CBE Tool 11 to develop a reliable scoring guide/rubric.

CBE Tool 8	Performance Assessment Overview: Purpose and Use	

Use this tool to provide an overview of when the assessment will be used and what it is intended to assess.

Unit of Study/Course:	Grade Level:

Enduring Understandings/Big Ideas

Essential Question(s) to Guide Inquiry/Learning

Performance Assessment/Task Overview

Assessment Alignment to Learning Goals: List . . . Academic or Personal Success Skills Competencies	**Performance Indicators (in Student "Language"):** I can . . .
Students Will Know (key terms, concepts, principles):	**Students Will Do/Apply** (include intended DOK levels):
Assessment Success Criteria (and intended DOK) • Scoring Guide attached?	**Allowable/Possible Accommodations/Supports** • Student choice in topic or product • Choice to work individually or with a group • Teacher consultations (one for launch and work plan and others for progress monitoring)

How will results be used? Formative/Preassess _____ Interim/Progress Monitoring _____ Summative/Post _____

List other *related* performance assessments in this unit of study/course:

Formative/Preassessment:

Interim/Progress Monitoring:

Summative/Postassessment:

(Continued)

(Continued)

| CBE Tool 8 | Performance Assessment Overview: Purpose and Use | |

Describe Student's Role/Decisions/Engagement/Input Into Task Expectations or Task Design

- Choices/decisions to be made *during* the assessment:
- Group collaborations (*prior to* or *during* the assessment):
- Student input into task design or presentation/product format:
- Self-assessment, reflections:
- Other:

Develop an Administration Guide

A common assessment requires a short administration guide to ensure fidelity of implementation across teachers and schools. The following are four essential things to include in the administration guide. Most schools create and store this information with each assessment in a digital task bank for easy access.

1. **Student Prompt/Stimulus: What directions will the student see?** (Make this short, clear, and visually interesting)
   - Student directions attached?

2. **Teacher Instructions: What directions will help the teacher prepare for and use the assessment?**

These are more detailed than what is given to students, including any important considerations, such as special setup requirements, equipment/materials, or scribing guidelines. At minimum, include . . .

Name of Assessment Task: **Grade:**

Purpose:

Suggested Time to Administer:

(For example, time of year, part of a unit of study or course, after students have learned particular content or completed a specific activity, such as an investigation in science or viewing a play or video.)

Suggested Use: Formative _____ Interim _____ Summative _____

Estimated Time Needed:

Resources Needed to Complete the Assessment (equipment, texts, digital tools, data, case study, etc.):

Specific Skills, Concepts, or Practices *Emphasized* in Task:

Additional Allowable Accommodations:

3. **Attach Scoring Guide or Rubric**

4. **If possible, include a sample of annotated student work at the *Proficient* level.**
   - This is a new assessment that we have yet to administer.

Annotated student work samples available for these performance levels:
   - Excelling/Advanced
   - Proficient
   - Progressing
   - Beginning

CBE Tool 9 — Task Quality Validation Protocol: Purpose, Alignment, Engagement, and Fairness | Use for Assessment *Development* or *Analysis of Performance Tasks*

Title of Assessment/Task:	Grade Level/Dept/Course/Subject:
Author(s):	or Reviewer(s):

How will the assessment results be used?

Analyze and discuss each of the assessment components. Check the box if there is evidence of each indicator of high-quality assessment listed.
Then add any additional notes.

Clarity and Focus

☐ 1. Addresses an **essential issue, big idea, or key concept or skill** of the unit, course, or discipline:

☐ 2. Directions or prompts clearly indicate what the student is being asked to do or produce:

☐ 3. If parts are completed within a group: Specifies what will be assessed **individually** (e.g., projects, multimedia presentations)

☐ 4. **Assesses what is intended to be assessed**—will elicit what the student knows and can do related to the chosen standards and **benchmarks**.

 Any scaffolding provided (e.g., task broken into smaller steps; graphic organizer to preplan) does not change what is actually being assessed.

☐ 5. Is clearly linked to **ongoing instruction or opportunity to learn** (e.g., assessed within or at the end of a unit of study or course)

Clarity and Focus Notes

Content Alignment

☐ 6. Items or tasks are clearly **aligned with specific or identified content standards** (or intended parts or combinations of content standards)

☐ 7. Appropriate **rubric(s) or scoring guide(s)** assess all intended parts of content standards assessed. Scoring guides are useful in determining what the student knows or does not know, not simply yield a score (e.g., What does a score of 25 really mean? What additional or next steps in instruction does the student need? Are some rubric criteria "weighted" reflecting greater instructional emphasis for this time of year?).

☐ 8. **Exemplars or anchor papers** illustrate expectations aligned to standards at proficient level and performance levels above or below proficient.

 Qualitative distinctions between performance levels are evident.

Content Alignment Notes

(Continued)

(Continued)

CBE Tool 9	Task Quality Validation Protocol: Purpose, Alignment, Engagement, and Fairness | Use for Assessment *Development* or *Analysis of Performance Tasks*

Rigor Alignment or Cognitive Demand

☐ 9. Identify Depth-of-Knowledge/DOK levels assessed or emphasized (e.g., number of score points given, weighting in the rubric). For example, an essay would mostly assess DOK 3 (full multiparagraph composition), but also have some DOK 2 items or parts (text organization, structure) and DOK 1 (grammar, conventions) also assessed. You would check "most of the test/task" for DOK 3 and "some of the test/task" for DOK 2 and DOK 1. (See Hess Cognitive Rigor Matrix /CRM Tools for content-specific descriptors of each DOK level.)

DOK 1: Students recall, locate, and reproduce: words, terms, facts; basic application of rules, procedures, which may be routine and multistep

(☐ most of the test/task   ☐ some of the test/task   ☐ none of the test/task)

DOK 2: Students apply level 1 within the ability to paraphrase, summarize, interpret, infer, classify, organize, compare; determine fact from fiction; solve, as in routine word problems; determine meanings in context. There is a correct answer, but may involve multiple concepts or decision points.

(☐ most of the test/task   ☐ some of the test/task   ☐ none of the test/task)

DOK 3: Students must support their thinking by citing evidence (e.g., text, data, calculations, models). Students are asked to go beyond the text or data collection to analyze, generalize, or connect to bigger ideas. Requires "uncovering" and interpreting less explicit knowledge. Items may require abstract reasoning, alternate approaches, inferences that connect information, application of prior knowledge, or text support for an analytical judgment.

(☐ most of the test/task   ☐ some of the test/task   ☐ none of the test/task)

DOK 4: Students use deeper knowledge of content, and evidence of complex reasoning, planning, and developing new ideas, insights, or products **from multiple sources**. Usually applies to an extended task or project. Examples: evaluate works by the same author; critique an issue across time periods or research topic or issue from different perspectives; longer science, math, or arts investigations or research projects involving all phases of design, testing, and refining.

(☐ most of the test/task   ☐ some of the test/task   ☐ none of the test/task)

☐ 10. Has alignment with the **intended rigor** of the content standards (or parts or combinations of the content standards). Scaffolding does not significantly reduce cognitive demand.

Rigor Alignment Notes

Student Engagement

☐ 11. The situation or scenario or application is **authentic.** Reflects a meaningful, real-world problem, issue, or theme worth exploring.

☐ 12. Provides for student ownership, **choice, and/or decision making**; requires the student to be actively engaged in solution finding.

☐ 13. Is administered after students have had adequate time to learn, practice, and expand their understanding of skills or concepts assessed.

Student Engagement Notes

| CBE Tool 9 | Task Quality Validation Protocol: Purpose, Alignment, Engagement, and Fairness \| Use for Assessment *Development* or *Analysis of Performance Tasks* | |

Fairness: Universal Access and Design Features

☐ 14. Is fair and unbiased in language and design.

- ☐ Material is familiar to students from identifiable cultural, gender, linguistic, and other groups
- ☐ The task stimulus or prompt and materials (context/texts used) are free of stereotypes
- ☐ All students (e.g., all ability levels) are on a level playing field and have had opportunity to learn
- ☐ All students have access to necessary resources (e.g., Internet, calculators, spellcheck)
- ☐ Assessment conditions are the same for all students or flexible enough not to change what's actually being assessed (e.g., reading a passage aloud may be fine for interpreting overall meaning, but not for assessing ability to decode words)
- ☐ The task can be reasonably completed under the specified conditions; extended time is allowable
- ☐ The rubric or scoring guide allows for different response modes (oral, written, etc.)

☐ 15. Adheres to the principles of **Universal Design for Learning (UDL).**

- ☐ Instructions are free of excessive wordiness or irrelevant (unnecessary) information
- ☐ Instructions are free of unusual words (unusual spellings or unfamiliar word use) that the student may not understand or have been exposed to
- ☐ Low frequency words (words not used in other content areas, such as technical terms) are only used when explicitly needed or when the assessment is explicitly testing understanding of terms
- ☐ Instructions are free of ambiguous words
- ☐ Irregularly spelled words have been avoided whenever possible
- ☐ There are no proper names that students may not understand (e.g., students have never seen them before in instruction)
- ☐ Multiple words, symbols, or pronouns intended to mean the same thing are NOT used in the same sentence or stimulus or prompt (e.g., inches and the double prime symbol (") for inches; phrases such as the boys, they, the friends)
- ☐ The format or layout conveys the focus of the expected tasks and products and allows adequate space for responding
- ☐ The format clearly indicates what the actual questions to answer or prompts are (e.g., each question or prompt is clearly separated from the introductory stimulus or problem context)
- ☐ Questions or prompts are consistently marked with graphic or visual cues (bullets, numbers, in a text box, etc.)
- ☐ The test format (spacing, presentation, etc.) is familiar, consistent, and predictable as to what students will be expected to do

☐ 16. Allows for accommodations for students with IEPs or 504 Plans.

- ☐ **Presentation**—Students may access information in ways that do not require them to visually read standard print (auditory, multisensory, tactile, and visual).
- ☐ **Response**—Students may complete activities in different ways or use some type of assistive device or organizer to assist them in responding.
- ☐ **Setting**—Location in which a test is given or the conditions of the assessment setting are flexible.
- ☐ **Timing or Scheduling**—The length of time to complete an assessment may be increased and/or the way the time is organized may be changed.

Fairness: Universal Access and Design Notes

| CBE Tool 10 | Task Validation Summary (Streamlined Version) | |

(Use your notes from CBE Tool 9 to develop your team summary.)

Assessment: Date of Review:	Validation Team:	
Feedback Summary: Comments and Questions From Validation Team		
Clarity and Focus		
Validity: Content Alignment (Competency)		
Validity: Rigor Alignment		
Scoring Reliability		
Student Engagement		
Fairness and UDL		
What makes this a HQ assessment?		

Validation Team Recommendation:

_____ Validation pending—please review feedback, make revisions, and schedule another review.

_____ Validation complete—please submit final edited version to team leader.

First submission (date) _____   Resubmission (date) _____

CBE Tool 10	**Task Validation Summary: An Example**

(Use your notes from **CBE Tool 9** to develop your team summary.)

Assessment: *"Picking Up the Pieces"—Students explore, contextualize, and analyze the perspectives of major groups involved in and impacted by global 20th century conflict and its aftermath. Then, draw connections to a current conflict you care about with the goal of analyzing the impact on those involved in order to develop a proposed resolution.*

© Aquino, CPS

Feedback Summary: Comments and Questions From Validation Team

Clarity and Focus	*Suggestion: Throughout, regarding academic versus SEL competencies, you seem to have parallel expectations, so you need to be clear that both strands are addressed in task directions and rubric criteria. We were unclear.*
Validity: Content Alignment (Competency)	*Clarify "contextualize" in the task statement for students—does this mean that students provide personal or historical context or both in their response? It was not clear from the task directions or rubric how students will do this. Is the student contextualizing? Or is the analysis done within a specific context?* *If so, revise student directions (e.g., identify, explore, and analyze perspectives of major groups involved). Your analysis should include a discussion of how the context contributes to the impact/outcome.*
Validity: Rigor Alignment	*We could not locate your intended DOK levels on Tool 8 (assessment overview). These should be added.*
Scoring Reliability	*Suggestion: Clarify rubric—What evidence will students use and where does the evidence come from? Are sources cited? Clarify—Are you looking for personal insights, as well as accurate information?* *Suggestion: You could add a self-reflection related to how personal bias or perspective has changed.*
Student Engagement	*You offer many opportunities for choices for students—choosing sources, individual/peer work, and final products.*
Fairness and UDL	*Suggestion: You could also include—"Provide documents/sources at different access/complexity levels. Students can access texts through read-alouds or viewing."*
What makes this a HQ assessment?	*Integration of academic and SEL competencies makes authentic connections for each student to personally reflect upon.* *Clearly stated Big Ideas—Rubric articulates a progression, stated in the positive.* *Accommodations listed.* *Multiple options or choices for students to make.*

Validation Team Recommendation:

__X__ Validation pending—please review feedback, make revisions, and schedule another review.

_____Validation complete—please submit final edited version to team leader.

First submission (date)_____   Resubmission (date) _____

 Available for download at **http://resources.corwin.com/DeeperCompetencyBasedLearning**.

| CBE Tool 11 | Rubric Quality Review Worksheet | |

Assessment Task:	
Date:	Reviewer(s):

Questions for Evaluating Rubric Quality	Comments/Feedback for Each Review Question
1. Do the number of performance levels and rubric format make sense? ☐ Format matches purpose and use. ☐ Adjacent performance levels are *qualitatively* different. ☐ Levels reflect how completion of the task might naturally progress with instruction.	
2. Is descriptive language maximized? ☐ Little or no judgmental language. ☐ Avoids use of subjective language (poor, neat, ample, etc.) and frequency indicators (rarely, often, etc.).	
3. Do descriptors emphasize quality over quantity? (e.g., relevant, descriptive details/sources versus three details/sources)	
4. Do descriptors state performance in the positive? (e.g., what *is* happening rather than what is *not* happening) ☐ Lowest levels focus on beginning stages. ☐ Describes a (real) progression of learning. ☐ Have student work samples or piloting informed performance descriptions?	
5. Do descriptors describe excellent rather than perfect performance? ☐ Describes a progression from *Novice* to *Expert* performance. ☐ Performance descriptors increase with depth, complexity, and/or breadth of knowledge. ☐ Minor errors not weighted more than quality of ideas or thinking.	
6. Do rubric language and criteria match rigor expectations of task? ☐ Range of criteria aligns with task expectations (form, accuracy, process, impact, construction of knowledge). ☐ Not limited to basic skills and concepts or only routine tasks. ☐ At least one criterion builds to transfer and construction of knowledge/deeper understanding.	
7. Is the language kid-friendly? ☐ Could this be used for peer and self-assessment? ☐ Have students had input into the writing or refinement of performance level descriptions?	
Additional Notes:	

CBE Tool 12	Student Self-Assessment: Tracking My Learning Pathway	

Name:	Unit/Project:
Tracking My Learning Pathway Competency Statement:	**Standard(s) I Am Working On:**

Performance Levels	My Learning Targets	My Evidence (and Dates)
Extending My Learning 4	I can . . .	
Demonstrating Proficiency 3	I can . . .	
Making Progress 2	I can . . .	
Working on the Basics 1	I can . . .	

Available for download at **http://resources.corwin.com/DeeperCompetencyBasedLearning**.

Appendix B

Hess Cognitive Rigor Matrices #1–#5D

The Hess Cognitive Rigor Matrices (CRMs) assist teachers in applying what cognitive demand might look like in the classroom and guide test developers in designing and aligning test items and performance tasks. Content-specific descriptors in each of the CRMs are used to categorize and plan for various levels of abstraction—meaning an analysis of the mental processing required of assessment questions and learning tasks. Today, many schools, states, and testing companies use these tools for professional development, curriculum work, and test item development. So where did the Cognitive Rigor Matrix come from?

ORIGIN OF THE HESS MATRICES

The CRM began to emerge in 2005, sparked by a thoughtful question from members of a state-level committee working with Karin on the design of their state's new large-scale assessment blueprint. Like many other states, this state and their testing contractor had been using Bloom's taxonomy to describe test item difficulty. "Isn't Webb's DOK model just another way to describe the same thing as what Bloom's six levels do?" teachers asked when Karin introduced and suggested a shift to using depth-of-knowledge (DOK) level descriptors instead of Bloom's taxonomy as the frame of reference for determining the complexity of test items and standards they were aligned with.

Karin knew these models were not specifically addressing the same characteristics of rigor or complexity, so she began to examine each model in greater depth and experimented with where the two models might intersect. Although related through their natural ties to the complexity of thought, she could see that Bloom's thinking levels and Webb's depth-of-knowledge levels differed in scope, application, and possibly intent. The result of her attempt to show where there was overlap resulted in a model that superimposed Bloom's taxonomy with Webb's depth-of-knowledge levels.

Starting with a blank matrix template and then putting Bloom's thinking levels along the vertical axis and DOK levels across the top (see Table B.1), Karin began to populate the cells with descriptions of what students might be doing when they were, for example, analyzing at a DOK 1, DOK 2, or DOK 3 level.

As she worked, it was becoming clear to her that higher-order verbs or thinking levels did not always result in learning tasks requiring deeper understanding or strategic thinking.

As the matrix evolved, she still had to resolve what to put in the cells at the lower DOK levels for *Evaluate* and at the upper DOK levels for *Remember*. As she thought more about describing *Remember* in terms of *depth,* it made no sense to put anything under DOK 2, 3, or 4. Either you know or remember something or you don't. It's as simple as that. Those cells were purposely left blank.

Deciding what to put next to *Evaluate* under DOK 1 and DOK 2 was a bit more perplexing. What do you call it when you evaluate something—state an opinion or try to make an argument—and have no supporting evidence, no elaboration, and cite no sources? Then, it came to her as a flashback to her past college days. These were "UGs"—a notation on the early papers that she wrote while in graduate school. If the professor put "UG" in the margin, it meant that you had an unsubstantiated (unsupported) generalization: You stated an opinion, claim, or a "truth" but provided no credible support for it. A UG sent you back to find a source to back up your idea.

We often give students prompts that can elicit unsupported opinions: Did you like the book? Is the character evil? Was this a good decision? We ask open-ended questions and then find ourselves giving the student credit for completing the assignment mostly because the handwriting was neat and it was handed in on time, not because their ideas and opinions were supported in a meaningful way. These essays either have not used criteria in making a judgment or the reasons used would not be ones we would generally agree are the criteria that should be used to evaluate a character archetype (e.g., who is the real hero?) or a viable mathematical solution to a real-world problem. UGs, therefore, are "low-level" (DOK 1–2) opinions— opinions without credible, justifiable support. Opinions supported by valid criteria and credible evidence rise to the levels of DOK 3 and 4.

Throughout this development process, Karin came to better understand that deeper learning/thinking was not simply about verbs, taxonomies, complex texts, or what we have generally accepted as "higher-order" thinking. There was a significant difference between "analysis lite" (DOK 1 or DOK 2) and deeper analysis of a topic or concept (DOK 3 or DOK 4).

TABLE B.1 Building a Cognitive Rigor Matrix to Describe Increasing Levels of Complexity

Building a Cognitive Rigor Matrix to Describe Increasing Levels of Complexity				
Bloom	**DOK 1**	**DOK 2**	**DOK 3**	**DOK 4**
Remember	Recall a fact, detail, or term	**Does anything go here????**		
Understand	Identify literary elements	Summarize a text	Identify a theme	
Apply	Apply rules of editing	Use context to determine meaning		Illustrate how multiple themes are interrelated
Analyze	Identify information in a text feature	Compare characters		
Evaluate	**What goes here????** **"UGs"**		Citing evidence, develop a logical argument for conjectures	
Create	Brainstorm ideas on a topic			Synthesize ideas across sources

TABLE B.2 Overview of the Hess Cognitive Rigor Matrix Tools

Overview of the Hess Cognitive Rigor Matrix Tools		
Tool		**Development and Possible Uses for Each Cognitive Rigor Matrix**
	1 **Close Reading and Listening CRM**	**Tool #1** identifies many ways that close reading of texts might be demonstrated across content areas, grade levels, and text types. It is also useful in thinking about tasks that require students to listen to or view nonprint texts (film, drama, podcasts, etc.). I've expanded upon Webb and Wixon's original DOK descriptors (Webb, 2002) for reading, drawing from my alignment study and test development work over the years.
	2 **Mathematics and Science CRM**	**Tool #2** identifies how mathematics and science skills and concepts might be demonstrated across grade levels, domains, or problem-solving situations. Math and science were combined in this matrix to illustrate the complementary nature of mathematics, science, and STEM activities. I've expanded upon Webb's original DOK descriptors for math and science (1997), drawing from my alignment study and test development work over the years.
	3 **Writing and Speaking CRM**	**Tool #3** identifies many ways that written and oral communication might be demonstrated across content areas, grade levels, text genre, and communication formats (plays, speeches, graphic novels, etc.). I've expanded upon Webb and Wixon's original DOK descriptors for writing (Webb, 2002), drawing from my alignment study and test development work over the years.
	4 **Social Studies and Humanities CRM**	**Tool #4** identifies ways that social studies (which can include history, civics, economics, and geography) and humanities skills and concepts might be demonstrated across units of study and in-depth inquiry activities. I've expanded upon Webb's original DOK descriptors for social studies (Webb, 2002), drawing from my alignment study and test development work over the years and my work with humanities assessments.
	5A **Fine Arts CRM**	**Tool #5A** was created and refined during my work with several states' development of standards and assessments for visual arts, music, dance, and theatre. This tool represents my interpretation of DOK when applied to the fine arts. To my knowledge, Norman Webb has not worked with DOK in the fine arts. You will notice right away that in this matrix, Bloom's taxonomy is not integrated with DOK. Instead, I worked with arts educators to identify common "arts practices" that could integrate with DOK descriptors. The result is the many ways that the fine arts might be demonstrated across arts disciplines and grade levels.
	5B **Health and Physical Education CRM**	**Tool #5B** was created and refined through my work with whole-school faculties. As with fine arts and world language, health and physical education (HPE) teachers struggled to see how DOK or Bloom applied to their curriculum and assessments. Tool #5B represents my interpretation of how DOK could apply to the national HPE standards. For this tool, I drew from Porter and Smithson's Cognitive Demand Categories (2002) rather than Bloom. To my knowledge, neither Webb nor Porter and Smithson have specifically described cognitive demand in health or physical education.
	5C **World Language CRM**	**Tool #5C** With input from world languages teachers Rachel Gilbert and Amy Flynn, we explored and refined curricular examples used in world language courses, identifying broad common expectations consistent with national standards. Then, I cross-referenced sources and expectations for English language learners (ELL) to create examples specific to world language content.
	5D **Career and Technical Education CRM**	**Tool #5D** closely resembles Tool #2, identifying how mathematics and science skills and concepts might be demonstrated across grade levels, domains, or problem-solving. Many career and technical education (CTE) teachers were already using Tool #2 but were looking for more specific examples that would more closely apply to courses they were teaching, such as building trades, health science, and auto mechanics. With input from Kirsten Soroko, who helped me gather CTE assessment examples and feedback from CTE teachers in New Hampshire, we refined Tool #2 to be more CTE-specific.

THE HESS CRMS

Hess Cognitive Rigor Matrix (Reading CRM): Applying Webb's Depth-of-Knowledge Levels to Bloom's Cognitive Process Dimensions

Tool 1

Revised Bloom's Taxonomy	Webb's DOK Level 1 Recall and Reproduction	Webb's DOK Level 2 Skills and Concepts	Webb's DOK Level 3 Strategic Thinking/Reasoning	Webb's DOK Level 4 Extended Thinking
	Use these Hess CRM curricular examples with most close reading or listening assignments or assessments in any content area.			
Remember Retrieve knowledge from long-term memory, recognize, recall, locate, identify	○ Recall, recognize, or locate basic facts, terms, details, events, or ideas explicit in texts ○ Read words orally in connected text with fluency and accuracy			
Understand Construct meaning, clarify, paraphrase, represent, translate, illustrate, give examples, classify, categorize, summarize, generalize, infer a logical conclusion, predict, compare or contrast, match like ideas, explain, construct models	○ Identify or describe literary elements (characters, setting, sequence, etc.) ○ Select appropriate words when intended meaning or definition is clearly evident ○ Describe or explain who, what, where, when, or how ○ Define or describe facts, details, terms, principles ○ Write simple sentences	○ Specify, explain, show relationships; explain why (e.g., cause/effect) ○ Give nonexamples or examples ○ Summarize results, concepts, ideas ○ Make basic inferences or logical predictions from data or texts ○ Identify main ideas or accurate generalizations of texts ○ Locate information to support explicit/implicit central ideas	○ Explain, generalize, or connect ideas using supporting evidence (quote, example, text reference) ○ Identify or make inferences about explicit or implicit themes ○ Describe how word choice, point of view, or bias may affect the readers' interpretation of a text ○ Write multiparagraph composition for specific purpose, focus, voice, tone, and audience	○ Explain how concepts or ideas specifically relate to other content domains (e.g., social, political, historical) or concepts ○ Develop generalizations of the results obtained or strategies used and apply them to new problem-based situations
Apply Carry out or use a procedure in a given situation; apply or use in an unfamiliar situation or nonroutine task	○ Use language structure (pre-, or suffix) or word relationships (synonym/antonym) to determine meaning of words ○ Apply rules or resources to edit spelling, grammar, punctuation, conventions, word use ○ Apply basic formats for documenting sources	○ Use context to identify the meaning of words or phrases ○ Obtain and interpret information using text features ○ Develop a text that may be limited to one paragraph ○ Apply simple organizational structures (paragraph, sentence types) in writing	○ Apply a concept in a new context ○ Revise final draft for meaning or progression of ideas ○ Apply internal consistency of text organization and structure to composing a full composition ○ Apply word choice, point of view, style to impact readers' or viewers' interpretation of a text	○ Illustrate how multiple themes (historical, geographic, social, artistic, literary) may be interrelated ○ Select or devise an approach among many alternatives to research a novel problem
Analyze Break into constituent parts, determine how parts relate, differentiate between relevant/irrelevant, distinguish, focus, select, organize, outline, find coherence, deconstruct (e.g., for bias or point of view)	○ Identify whether specific information is contained in graphic representations (e.g., map, chart, table, graph, T-chart, diagram) or text features (e.g., headings, subheadings, captions) ○ Decide which text structure is appropriate to audience and purpose	○ Categorize or compare literary elements, terms, facts or details, events ○ Identify use of literary devices ○ Analyze format, organization, and internal text structure (signal words, transitions, semantic cues) of different texts ○ Distinguish relevant/irrelevant information, fact/opinion ○ Identify characteristic text features; distinguish between texts, genres	○ Analyze information within data sets or texts ○ Analyze interrelationships among concepts, issues, problems ○ Analyze or interpret author's craft (literary devices, viewpoint, or potential bias) to create or critique a text ○ Use reasoning, planning, and evidence to support inferences	○ Analyze multiple sources of evidence, or multiple works by the same author, or across genres, time periods, themes ○ Analyze complex or abstract themes, perspectives, concepts ○ Gather, analyze, and organize multiple information sources ○ Analyze discourse styles
Evaluate Make judgments based on criteria, check, detect inconsistencies or fallacies, judge, critique	"UG" (unsubstantiated generalizations) = Stating an opinion without providing any support for it!		○ Cite evidence and develop a logical argument for conjectures ○ Describe, compare, and contrast solution methods ○ Verify reasonableness of results ○ Justify or critique conclusions drawn	○ Evaluate relevancy, accuracy, and completeness of information from multiple sources ○ Apply understanding in a novel way, provide argument or justification for the application
Create Reorganize elements into new patterns or structures, generate, hypothesize, design, plan, produce	○ Brainstorm ideas, concepts, problems, or perspectives related to a topic, principle, or concept	○ Generate conjectures or hypotheses based on observations or prior knowledge and experience	○ Synthesize information within one source or text ○ Develop a complex model for a given situation ○ Develop an alternative solution	○ Synthesize information across multiple sources or texts ○ Articulate a new voice, alternate theme, new knowledge or perspective

Hess Cognitive Rigor Matrix (Math/Science CRM): Applying Webb's Depth-of-Knowledge Levels to Bloom's Cognitive Process Dimensions

Tool 2

Revised Bloom's Taxonomy	Webb's DOK Level 1 Recall and Reproduction	Webb's DOK Level 2 Skills and Concepts	Webb's DOK Level 3 Strategic Thinking/Reasoning	Webb's DOK Level 4 Extended Thinking
Remember Retrieve knowledge from long-term memory, recognize, recall, locate, identify	○ Recall, observe, and recognize facts, principles, properties ○ Recall/identify conversions among representations or numbers (e.g., customary and metric measures)	*Use these Hess CRM curricular examples with most mathematics or science assignments or assessments.*		
Understand Construct meaning, clarify, paraphrase, represent, translate, illustrate, give examples, classify, categorize, summarize, generalize, infer a logical conclusion, predict, compare or contrast, match like ideas, explain, construct models	○ Evaluate an expression ○ Locate points on a grid or number on number line ○ Solve a one-step problem ○ Represent math relationships in words, pictures, or symbols ○ Read, write, compare decimals in scientific notation	○ Specify and explain relationships (e.g., nonexamples or examples; cause/effect) ○ Make and record observations ○ Explain steps followed ○ Summarize results or concepts ○ Make basic inferences or logical predictions from data or observations ○ Use models or diagrams to represent or explain mathematical concepts ○ Make and explain estimates	○ Use concepts to solve nonroutine problems ○ Explain, generalize, or connect ideas using supporting evidence ○ Make and justify conjectures ○ Explain thinking or reasoning when more than one solution or approach is possible ○ Explain phenomena in terms of concepts	○ Relate mathematical or scientific concepts to other content areas, other domains, or other concepts ○ Develop generalizations of the results obtained and the strategies used (from investigation or readings) and apply them to new problem situations
Apply Carry out or use a procedure in a given situation; apply or use in an unfamiliar situation or nonroutine task	○ Follow simple procedures (recipe-type directions) ○ Calculate, measure, apply a rule (e.g., rounding) ○ Apply algorithm or formula (e.g., area, perimeter) ○ Solve linear equations ○ Make conversions among representations or numbers or within and between customary and metric measures	○ Select a procedure according to criteria and perform it ○ Solve a routine problem, applying multiple concepts or decision points ○ Retrieve information from a table, graph, or figure and use it to solve a problem requiring multiple steps ○ Translate between tables, graphs, words, and symbolic notations (e.g., graph data from a table) ○ Construct models given criteria	○ Design an investigation for a specific purpose or research question ○ Conduct a designed investigation ○ Use concepts to solve nonroutine problems ○ Use and show reasoning, planning, and evidence ○ Translate between problem and symbolic notation when not a direct translation	○ Select or devise an approach among many alternatives to solve a problem ○ Conduct a project that specifies a problem, identifies solution paths, solves the problem, and reports results
Analyze Break into constituent parts, determine how parts relate, differentiate between relevant/irrelevant, distinguish, focus, select, organize, outline, find coherence, deconstruct	○ Retrieve information from a table or graph to answer a question ○ Identify whether specific information is contained in graphic representations (e.g., table, graph, T-chart, diagram) ○ Identify a pattern or trend	○ Categorize, classify materials, data, figures based on characteristics ○ Organize or order data ○ Compare/contrast figures or data ○ Select an appropriate graph and organize and display data ○ Interpret data from a simple graph ○ Extend a pattern	○ Compare information within or across data sets or texts ○ Analyze and draw conclusions from data, citing evidence ○ Generalize a pattern ○ Interpret data from a complex graph ○ Analyze similarities/differences between procedures or solutions	○ Analyze multiple sources of evidence ○ Analyze complex or abstract themes ○ Gather, analyze, and evaluate information
Evaluate Make judgments based on criteria, check, detect inconsistencies or fallacies, judge, critique	"UG" (unsubstantiated generalizations) = Stating an opinion without providing any support for it!		○ Cite evidence and develop a logical argument for concepts or solutions ○ Describe, compare, and contrast solution methods ○ Verify reasonableness of results	○ Gather, analyze, and evaluate information to draw conclusions ○ Apply understanding in a novel way; provide argument or justification for the application
Create Reorganize elements into new patterns or structures, generate, hypothesize, design, plan, produce	○ Brainstorm ideas, concepts, or perspectives related to a topic	○ Generate conjectures or hypotheses based on observations or prior knowledge and experience	○ Synthesize information within one data set, source, or text ○ Formulate an original problem given a situation ○ Develop a scientific or mathematical model for a complex situation	○ Synthesize information across multiple sources or texts ○ Design a mathematical model to inform and solve a practical or abstract situation

APPENDIX B

Hess Cognitive Rigor Matrix (Writing/Speaking CRM): Applying Webb's Depth-of-Knowledge Levels to Bloom's Cognitive Process Dimensions

Tool 3

Revised Bloom's Taxonomy	Webb's DOK Level 1 Recall and Reproduction	Webb's DOK Level 2 Skills and Concepts	Webb's DOK Level 3 Strategic Thinking/Reasoning	Webb's DOK Level 4 Extended Thinking
Remember Retrieve knowledge from long-term memory, recognize, recall, locate, identify	○ Complete short-answer questions with facts, details, terms, principles, etc. (e.g., label parts of diagram)	*Use these Hess CRM curricular examples with most writing and oral communication assignments or assessments in any content area.*		
Understand Construct meaning, clarify, paraphrase, represent, translate, illustrate, give examples, classify, categorize, summarize, generalize, infer a logical conclusion, predict, compare/contrast, match like ideas, explain, construct models	○ Describe or define facts, details, terms, principles, etc. ○ Select appropriate word or phrase to use when intended meaning or definition is clearly evident ○ Write simple complete sentences ○ Add an appropriate caption to a photo or illustration ○ Write "fact statements" on a topic (e.g., spiders build webs)	○ Specify, explain, show relationships; explain why, cause/effect ○ Provide and explain nonexamples and examples ○ Take notes; organize ideas or data (e.g., relevance, trends, perspectives) ○ Summarize results, key concepts, ideas ○ Explain central ideas or accurate generalizations of texts or topics ○ Describe steps in a process (e.g., science procedure, how to and why control variables)	○ Write a multiparagraph composition for specific purpose, focus, voice, tone, and audience ○ Develop and explain opposing perspectives or connect ideas, principles, or concepts using supporting evidence (quote, example, text reference, etc.) ○ Develop arguments of fact (e.g., Are these criticisms supported by the historical facts? Is this claim or equation true?)	○ Use multiple sources to elaborate on how concepts or ideas specifically draw from other content domains or differing concepts (e.g., research paper, arguments of policy—should this law be passed? What will be the impact of this change?) ○ Develop generalizations about the results obtained or strategies used and apply them to a new problem or contextual scenario
Apply Carry out or use a procedure in a given situation; apply or use in an unfamiliar situation or nonroutine task	○ Apply rules or use resources to edit specific spelling, grammar, punctuation, conventions, or word use ○ Apply basic formats for documenting sources	○ Use context to identify or infer the intended meaning of words or phrases ○ Obtain, interpret, and explain information using text features (table, diagram, etc.) ○ Develop a (brief) text that may be limited to one paragraph, précis ○ Apply basic organizational structures (paragraph, sentence types, topic sentence, introduction, etc.) in writing	○ Revise final draft for meaning, progression of ideas, or logic chain ○ Apply internal consistency of text organization and structure to a full composition or oral communication ○ Apply a concept in a new context ○ Apply word choice, point of view, style, rhetorical devices to impact readers' interpretation of a text	○ Select or devise an approach among many alternatives to research and present a novel problem or issue ○ Illustrate how multiple themes (historical, geographic, social) may be interrelated within a text or topic
Analyze Break into constituent parts, determine how parts relate, differentiate between relevant/irrelevant, distinguish, focus, select, organize, outline, find coherence, deconstruct (e.g., for bias or point of view)	○ Decide which text structure is appropriate to audience and purpose (e.g., compare/contrast, proposition/support) ○ Determine appropriate, relevant key words for conducting an Internet search or researching a topic	○ Compare/contrast perspectives, events, characters, etc. ○ Analyze/revise format, organization, and internal text structure (signal words, transitions, semantic cues) of different print and nonprint texts ○ Distinguish relevant/irrelevant information; fact/opinion (e.g., What are the characteristics of a hero's journey?) ○ Locate evidence that supports a perspective or differing perspectives	○ Analyze interrelationships among concepts, issues, and problems in a text ○ Analyze impact or use of author's craft (literary devices, or use of author's craft (literary devices, viewpoint, dialogue) in a single text ○ Use reasoning and evidence to generate criteria for making and supporting an argument of judgment (Was FDR a great president? Who was the greatest ball player?) ○ Support conclusions with evidence	○ Analyze multiple sources of evidence, or multiple works by the same author, or across genres, or time periods ○ Analyze complex or abstract themes, perspectives, concepts ○ Gather, analyze, and organize multiple information sources ○ Compare and contrast conflicting judgments or policies (e.g., Supreme Court decisions)
Evaluate Make judgments based on criteria, check, detect inconsistencies or fallacies, judge, critique	"UG" (unsubstantiated generalizations) = Stating an opinion without providing any support for it!		○ Evaluate validity and relevance of evidence used to develop an argument or support a perspective ○ Describe, compare, and contrast solution methods ○ Verify or critique the accuracy, logic, and reasonableness of stated conclusions or assumptions	○ Evaluate relevancy, accuracy, and completeness of information across multiple sources ○ Apply understanding in a novel way, provide argument or justification for the application ○ Critique the historical impact (policy, writings, discoveries, etc.)
Create Reorganize elements into new patterns or structures, generate, hypothesize, design, plan, produce	○ Brainstorm facts, ideas, concepts, problems, or perspectives related to a topic, text, idea, issue, or concept	○ Generate conjectures, hypotheses, or predictions based on facts, observations, evidence/observations, or prior knowledge and experience ○ Generate believable "grounds" (reasons) for an opinion or argument	○ Develop a complex model for a given situation or problem ○ Develop an alternative solution or perspective to one proposed (e.g., debate)	○ Synthesize information across multiple sources or texts in order to articulate a new voice, alternate theme, new knowledge, or nuanced perspective

Available for download at **http://resources.corwin.com/DeeperCompetencyBasedLearning** and **www.karin-hess.com/free-resources.**

© Karin Hess (2009, updated 2017). *A local assessment toolkit to support deeper learning: Guiding school leaders in linking research with classroom practice.* Permission to reproduce is given only when authorship is fully cited [karinhessvt@gmail.com].

Hess Cognitive Rigor Matrix (Social Studies/Humanities CRM): Applying Webb's Depth-of-Knowledge Levels to Bloom's Cognitive Process Dimensions

Tool 4

Revised Bloom's Taxonomy	Webb's DOK Level 1 Recall and Reproduction	Webb's DOK Level 2 Skills and Concepts	Webb's DOK Level 3 Strategic Thinking/Reasoning	Webb's DOK Level 4 Extended Thinking
		Use these Hess CRM curricular examples with most assignments, assessments, or inquiry activities in social studies, history, civics, geography, economics, or humanities.		
Remember Retrieve knowledge from long-term memory, recognize, recall, locate, identify	o Recall or locate key facts, dates, terms, details, events, or ideas explicit in texts			
Understand Construct meaning, clarify, paraphrase, represent, translate, illustrate, give examples, classify, categorize, summarize, generalize, infer a logical conclusion, predict, observe, compare/contrast, match like ideas, explain, construct models	o Select appropriate words or terms when intended meaning is clearly evident o Describe or explain who, what, where, when, or how o Define facts, details, terms, principles o Locate or identify symbols that represent ____ o Raise related questions for possible investigation	o Specify, explain, illustrate relationships; explain why (e.g., cause/effect) o Provide and explain nonexamples/examples o Summarize results, concepts, main ideas, generalizations o Make basic inferences or logical predictions (using data or text) o Locate relevant information to support explicit/implicit central ideas	o Explain, generalize, or connect ideas using supporting evidence (quote, example, text reference, data) o Support inferences about explicit or implicit themes o Describe how word choice, point of view, or bias may affect the reader's or viewer's interpretation o Write multiparagraph composition or essay for specific purpose, focus, voice, tone, and audience	o Explain how concepts or ideas specifically relate to other content domains or concepts (social, political, historical, cultural) o Apply generalizations to new problem-based situations o Use multiple sources to elaborate on how concepts or ideas specifically draw from other content domains or differing concepts (e.g., research paper, arguments of policy: Should this law be passed? What will be the impact of this change?)
Apply Carry out or use a procedure in a given situation; apply or use in an unfamiliar situation or nonroutine task	o Apply basic formats for documenting sources o Apply use of reference materials and tools for gathering information (e.g., key word searches)	o Use context to identify the meaning of words or phrases o Interpret information using text features (diagrams, data tables, captions, etc.) o Apply simple organizational structures (paragraph outline)	o Investigate to determine how a historical, cultural, or political context may be the source of an underlying theme, central idea, or unresolved issue or crisis	o Integrate or juxtapose multiple (historical, cultural) contexts drawn from source materials (e.g., literature, music, historical events, media) with intent to develop a complex or multimedia product and personal viewpoint
Analyze Break into constituent parts, determine how parts relate, differentiate between relevant/irrelevant, distinguish, focus, select, organize, outline, find coherence, deconstruct (e.g., for bias, point of view, approach/strategy used)	o Identify causes or effects o Describe processes or tools used to research ideas, artifacts, or images reflecting history, culture, tradition, etc. o Identify ways symbols and metaphors are used to represent universal ideas o Identify specific information given in graphics (e.g., map, T-chart, diagram) or text features (e.g., heading, subheading, captions)	o Compare similarities or differences in processes, methods, styles due to influences of time period, politics, or culture o Distinguish relevant/irrelevant information, fact, or opinion; primary from a secondary source o Draw inferences about social, historical, cultural contexts portrayed in (literature, arts, film, political cartoons, primary sources) o Explain, categorize events or ideas in the evolution of ____ across time periods	o Analyze information within data sets or a text (e.g., interrelationships among concepts, issues, problems) o Analyze an author's viewpoint or potential bias (e.g., political cartoon) o Use reasoning, planning, and evidence to support or refute inferences in policy or speech o Use reasoning and evidence to generate criteria for making and supporting an "argument of judgment" (e.g., Was FDR a great president? Is this a fair law?)	o Analyze multiple sources of evidence across time periods, themes, issues o Analyze diverse complex or abstract perspectives o Gather, analyze, and organize information from multiple sources o Analyze discourse styles or bias in speeches, legal briefs, etc., across time or authors o Compare and contrast conflicting judgments or policies (e.g., Supreme Court decisions)
Evaluate Make judgments based on criteria, check, detect inconsistencies or fallacies, judge, critique	o "UG" (unsubstantiated generalizations) = Stating an opinion without providing any support for it!		o Develop a logical argument for conjectures, citing evidence o Verify reasonableness of results of others o Critique conclusions drawn, evidence used, credibility of sources	o Evaluate relevancy, accuracy, and completeness of information using multiple sources o Apply understanding in a novel way, provide argument or justification for the application o Critique the historical impact on policy, writings, advances
Create Reorganize elements into new patterns, structures, or schemas; generate, hypothesize, design, plan, produce	o Brainstorm ideas, concepts, problems, or perspectives related to a topic, principle, or concept	o Generate testable conjectures or hypotheses based on observations, prior knowledge, and/or artifacts	o Synthesize information within one source or text o Develop a complex model or symbol for a given issue o Develop and support an alternative solution	o Synthesize information across multiple sources or texts o Articulate a new voice, alternate theme, new knowledge, or new perspective o Create historical fiction drawing on sources

Available for download at **http://resources.corwin.com/DeeperCompetencyBasedLearning** and **www.karin-hess.com/free-resources.**

© Karin Hess (2009, updated 2017). *A local assessment toolkit to support deeper learning: Guiding school leaders in linking research with classroom practice.* Permission to reproduce is given only when authorship is fully cited [karinhessvt@gmail.com].

APPENDIX B

Hess Cognitive Rigor Matrix (Fine Arts CRM): Applying (Hess's Interpretation of) DOK to Artistic Practices

Tool 5A

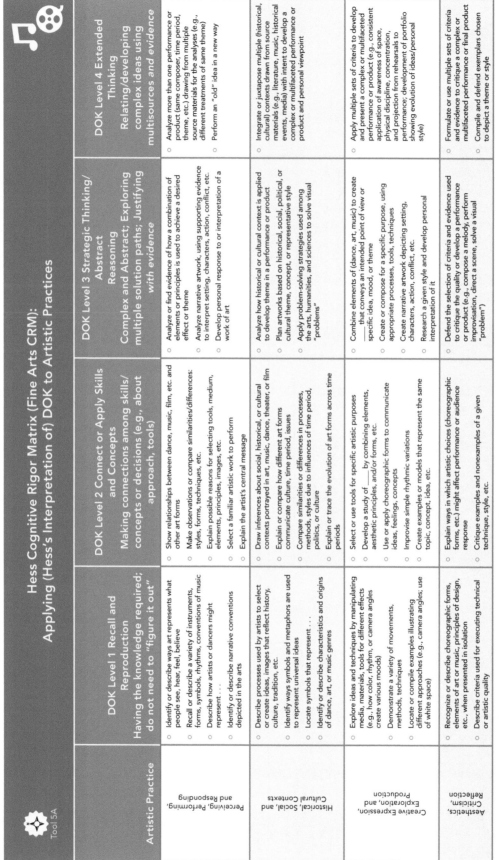

Artistic Practice	DOK Level 1 Recall and Reproduction — Having the knowledge required; do not need to "figure it out"	DOK Level 2 Connect or Apply Skills and Concepts — Making connections among skills/concepts or decisions (e.g., about approach, tools)	DOK Level 3 Strategic Thinking/Abstract Reasoning — Complex and Abstract; Exploring multiple solution paths; Justifying with evidence	DOK Level 4 Extended Thinking — Relating/developing complex ideas using multisources and evidence
Perceiving, Performing, and Responding	○ Identify or describe ways art represents what people see, hear, feel, believe ○ Recall or describe a variety of instruments, forms, symbols, rhythms, conventions of music ○ Describe how artists or dancers might represent . . . ○ Identify or describe narrative conventions depicted in the arts	○ Show relationships between dance, music, film, etc. and other art forms ○ Make observations or compare similarities/differences: styles, forms, techniques, etc. ○ Explain possible reasons for selecting tools, medium, elements, principles, images, etc. ○ Select a familiar artistic work to perform ○ Explain the artist's central message	○ Analyze or find evidence of how a combination of elements or principles is used to achieve a desired effect or theme ○ Analyze narrative artwork, using supporting evidence to interpret setting, characters, action, conflict, etc. ○ Develop personal response to or interpretation of a work of art	○ Analyze more than one performance or product (same composer, time period, theme, etc.) drawing from multiple source materials for the analyses (e.g., different treatments of same theme) ○ Perform an "old" idea in a new way
Historical, Social, and Cultural Contexts	○ Describe processes used by artists to select or create ideas, images that reflect history, culture, tradition, etc. ○ Identify ways symbols and metaphors are used to represent universal ideas ○ Locate symbols that represent . . . ○ Identify or describe characteristics and origins of dance, art, or music genres	○ Draw inferences about social, historical, or cultural contexts portrayed in art, music, dance, theater, or film ○ Explain or compare how different art forms communicate culture, time period, issues ○ Compare similarities or differences in processes, methods, styles due to influences of time period, politics, or culture ○ Explain or trace the evolution of art forms across time periods	○ Analyze how historical or cultural context is applied to develop theme in a performance or product ○ Plan artworks based on historical, social, political, or cultural theme, concept, or representative style ○ Apply problem-solving strategies used among the arts, humanities, and sciences to solve visual "problems"	○ Integrate or juxtapose multiple (historical, cultural) contexts drawn from source materials (e.g., literature, music, historical events, media) with intent to develop a complex or multifaceted performance or product and personal viewpoint
Creative Expression, Exploration, and Production	○ Explore ideas and techniques by manipulating media, materials, tools for different effects (e.g., how color, rhythm, or camera angles create various moods) ○ Demonstrate a variety of movements, methods, techniques ○ Locate or compile examples illustrating different approaches (e.g., camera angles; use of white space)	○ Select or use tools for specific artistic purposes ○ Develop a study of _____ by combining elements, aesthetic principles, and/or forms, etc. ○ Use or apply choreographic forms to communicate ideas, feelings, concepts ○ Improvise simple rhythmic variations ○ Create examples or models that represent the same topic, concept, idea, etc.	○ Combine elements of (dance, art, music) to create _____ that conveys an intended point of view or specific idea, mood, or theme ○ Create or compose for a specific purpose, using appropriate processes, tools, techniques ○ Create narrative artwork depicting setting, characters, action, conflict, etc. ○ Research a given style and develop personal interpretation of it	○ Apply multiple sets of criteria to develop and present a complex or multifaceted performance or product (e.g., consistent application of awareness of space, physical discipline, concentration, and projection from rehearsals to performance; development of portfolio showing evolution of ideas/personal style)
Aesthetics, Criticism, and Reflection	○ Recognize or describe choreographic forms, elements of art or music, principles of design, etc., when presented in isolation ○ Describe criteria used for executing technical or artistic quality	○ Explain ways in which artistic choices (choreographic forms, etc.) might affect performance or audience response ○ Critique examples and nonexamples of a given technique, style, etc.	○ Defend the selection of criteria and evidence used to critique the quality or develop a performance or product (e.g., compose a melody, perform improvisation, direct a scene, solve a visual "problem")	○ Formulate or use multiple sets of criteria and evidence to critique a complex or multifaceted performance or final product ○ Compile and defend exemplars chosen to depict a theme or style

 Available for download at **http://resources.corwin.com/DeeperCompetencyBasedLearning** and **www.karin-hess.com/free-resources.**

© Karin Hess (2009, updated 2017). *A local assessment toolkit to support deeper learning: Guiding school leaders in linking research with classroom practice.* Permission to reproduce is given only when authorship is fully cited [karinhessvt@gmail.com].

Tool 5B

Hess Cognitive Rigor Matrix (Health & Physical Education): Applying ((Hess's Interpretation of) Depth of Knowledge to Porter's Cognitive Demand Categories

Porter's Cognitive Demand Categories	DOK Level 1 Recall and Reproduction — Having the knowledge required; do not need to "figure it out"	DOK Level 2 Connect or Apply Skills and Concepts — Making connections among skills or concepts or decisions (e.g., about approach, tools)	DOK Level 3 Strategic Thinking/Abstract Reasoning — Complex and Abstract; Exploring multiple solution paths; Justifying with evidence	DOK Level 4 Extended Thinking — Relating or developing complex ideas using multisources and evidence
Memorize	○ Recall or identify basic facts, terms, definitions, skills, rules, principles, concepts, symbols ○ Acquire new terms, vocabulary, etc.	Use these Hess CRM Curricular Examples with most assignments, assessments, or learning activities for Health and Physical Education. See also the Hess CRM for Fine Arts with examples for dance.		
Communicate Understanding	○ Define terms, principles, concepts ○ Describe how to perform a routine skill or task ○ Use words, visuals, or symbols to represent basic ideas, movements, procedures, etc.	○ Explain concepts: show or predict relationships (if/then, cause/effect); provide examples and nonexamples ○ Observe and interpret teacher or student demonstrations ○ Summarize a concept, series of events, movements, or a result	○ Use evidence (data, examples, source, observations) to justify an interpretation of a result or performance ○ Locate or reproduce supporting evidence for results of effectiveness of a plan (e.g., exercise or diet routine) ○ Create a personal plan when given criteria	○ Share results of comparing different plans (e.g., compare exercise or diet routines) using data and evidence from multiple sources or data sets ○ Explain how a concept relates across content domains or to "Big Ideas" (e.g., systems, patterns)
Perform Procedures	○ Safely demonstrate or use appropriate tools or equipment ○ Execute or repeat basic skills or procedures (e.g., follow step-by-step directions or pattern) ○ Demonstrate a basic skill sequence, movement pattern, etc., with smooth transitions	○ Make observations; collect and record data and observations (e.g., health diary, skills progress) ○ Select and use appropriate tool or equipment for a given task ○ Complete routine tasks in a fitness assessment	○ Plan, execute, and evaluate multistep procedures (a dance routine, football play, rules of a new game, etc.) ○ Test effects and trends of using different activities by observing and collecting data (e.g., exercise or diet routines) ○ Select and plan how to use a combination of movements to achieve a desired effect	○ Design and conduct a performance (e.g., exercise or dance routine) using multiple sources or resources, and/or given constraints (e.g., use of space) ○ Test effects of different variables on performance (e.g., applied to a new situation)
Apply Concepts/Make Connections	○ Apply rules or score-keeping of a game or simple routine ○ Apply appropriate content-specific vocabulary or terms to tasks ○ Brainstorm ideas, problems, or perspectives related to a situation, scenario, or observation	○ Create an infographic or visual to show connections or to summarize key ideas (e.g., cause/effect, heart rate activity type, warm up/cool down, healthy/unhealthy) ○ Explain connections among concepts or skills in a given context (e.g., movement or open space concepts, health benefits)	○ Revise a plan (self, peer) based on feedback and evidence ○ Use concepts to explain phenomena or research or medical advances (e.g., use of steroids, drugs, food choices) ○ Investigate how an event or advancement led to a new perspective or outcome	○ Apply and adapt information and concepts to real-world situations ○ Integrate ideas from multiple sources to extend an idea or solve a problem with an alternative solution ○ Trace the evolution of (game, drug, etc.) from past to present, citing sources used
Analyze Information	○ Identify, describe, match, or name parts in a diagram or visual (e.g., muscle groups or skeletal system) or patterns ○ Determine which skill, rule, or principle applies to a given situation ○ Record performance data	○ Compare/contrast routines, skill sets, or qualities (e.g., use T-chart, graphic organizer for locomotor/nonlocomotor) ○ Generate questions and make predictions based on observations or information ○ Classify types of movements, sports, symptoms, examples, etc.	○ Analyze data in order to recognize patterns or draw conclusions based on evidence (e.g., batting averages, areas needing remediation) ○ Identify faulty arguments, strategies, or misrepresentations of data or media message ○ Defend the selection of criteria used to critique or develop a performance or product	○ Research a topic in-depth, evaluating relevancy, accuracy, and completeness of information from multiple sources or perspectives ○ Analyze evidence and recommend the most effective course of action for intended purpose (e.g., food, fitness)

Available for download at **http://resources.corwin.com/DeeperCompetencyBasedLearning** and **www.karin-hess.com/free-resources.** *A local assessment toolkit to support deeper learning: Guiding school leaders in linking research with classroom practice.* Permission to reproduce is given only when authorship is fully cited [karinhessvt@gmail.com].

© Karin Hess (2009, updated 2017).

APPENDIX B

Tool 5C

Hess World Language Cognitive Rigor Matrix

World Language Practices and Modes of Communication	DOK Level 1 Recall and Reproduction — Having the knowledge required; do not need to "figure it out"	DOK Level 2 Skills and Concepts — Making connections among skills/concepts or decisions (e.g., about approach, tools)	DOK Level 3 Strategic Thinking/Reasoning — Complex and Abstract; Exploring multiple solution paths; Justifying with evidence	DOK Level 4 Extended Thinking — Relating/developing complex ideas using multisources and evidence
Memorize and Recall	○ Reproduce, recall, and repeat vocabulary, grammar rules, facts, definitions, dictated statements, etc. ○ Describe cultural conventions ○ Recite in sequence (e.g., alphabet, counting, songs, rhymes)	Use these World Language CRM curricular examples for designing most language and communication assignments or assessment tasks.		
Interpersonal Communication Understand, Perceive, and Respond	○ Understand simple, familiar messages in social settings ○ Identify everyday objects ○ Follow simple oral directions or written procedures (recipe, etc.) ○ Convey simple messages, express feelings (e.g., I'm sad because . . .) ○ Ask or answer literal questions after reading, listening, or viewing	○ Explain how or why alternative responses may be correct (where do you live?) for different situations ○ Carry on a short conversation using familiar vocabulary and grammar ○ Paraphrase, summarize, or retell what was said, read, viewed (with cues) ○ Make logical predictions (e.g., what might happen next . . .); describe event	○ Prepare for an interview or develop survey on topic of interest, anticipating audience questions or possible responses ○ Initiate and extend a conversation about an unfamiliar topic, appropriately using language mechanics and tense throughout ○ Create a theme-based photo essay ○ Justify interpretation of purpose or tone (in media message, photo essay, etc.)	○ Carry on an extended conversation, responding appropriately to multiple speakers (e.g., using multiple tenses, asking and answering, elaborating on ideas, raising questions) ○ Deepen knowledge of a topic using multiple (oral, visual, textual) sources for an informational communication (e.g., "by the numbers" infographic)
Interpret and Apply	○ Match vocabulary (e.g., picture–word; synonyms); locate details ○ Apply a spelling or grammar rule (e.g., conjugate a verb, make plural) ○ Use resources to translate literally ○ Use nouns or verbs in familiar contexts	○ Infer and explain meaning using context, cognates, or structure in a familiar situation ○ Translate to identify use of nonliteral, figurative, or idiomatic language ○ Sequence events for given text or visual	○ Explain inferences or colloquial expressions using supporting evidence ○ Interpret symbolic or abstract meaning (from music, video, reading, art, etc.) ○ Interpret idiomatic or figurative language in context (poem, song lyric, media, etc.)	○ Make and justify conclusions based on 2+ ads for the same product or two political cartoons about the same event or person ○ Write, draw, perform in the style of a known author, artist, or cartoonist
Compare, Analyze, Critique, Evaluate, and Reflect	○ Edit a sentence or phrase ○ Select appropriate word or phrase for intended meaning ○ Answer what, when, and where questions using a source (map, calendar, schedule, visual, photo) ○ Connect words or phrases between languages (origins, meanings, etc.)	○ Categorize or compare (objects, foods, tools, people, etc.) using oral/physical/textual stimuli ○ Self-correct when speaking or reading ○ Evaluate message or cultural nuances (e.g., gestures, language) using listening and observational skills	○ Evaluate and correct inaccuracy of a message print or nonprint text (e.g., facts, sequence, cultural nuances) ○ Support an opinion, argument, or disagreement with evidence, reasoning ○ Determine if source can or cannot answer specific questions and why (e.g., websites)	○ Critique authentic literature, arts, or historical events from multiple sources: authors/perspectives/time periods ○ Evaluate relevancy, accuracy, and completeness of information ○ Keep a journal and use it to reflect on or evaluate personal progress
Presentational Communication Produce or Create	○ Represent vocabulary or common phrases in pictures, symbols, visuals, gestures, pantomime ○ Brainstorm related words, ideas, images, possible responses ○ Label information on a diagram, map, visual ○ Tell or select phrases as thumbnail sketch for a narrative text or story line	○ Perform a memorized dialog ○ Choose which tense to use in a less familiar context ○ Create an ABC book, connecting entries by central or organizing topic (e.g., animals, foods) ○ Create text messages or description (narration or voice-over) for a visual stimuli or "muted" video scene ○ Make or label a timeline of key events	○ Develop a vocabulary-based game to teach about geography, culture, etc. ○ Develop a new scene or ending, consistent with the original text ○ Create or perform a dialog based on visual stimuli or a current or cultural event (integrating academic vocabulary) ○ Co-plan website or event highlighting target culture (foods, traditions, places to visit)	○ Produce an "old" idea in a new way (e.g., multimedia, podcast) ○ Integrate ideas from several sources ○ Research a topic with evidence pro and con for debate, essay, or cartoon ○ Research and present performance or presentation using multiple sources ○ Design a theme-based café, including the menu, location, and décor and develop an ad for targeted clientele

Hess Cognitive Rigor Matrix Career and Technical Education (CTE CRM): Hess' Interpretation Applying Webb's Depth-of-Knowledge Levels to Bloom's Cognitive Process Dimensions

Tool 5D

Revised Bloom's Taxonomy	Webb's DOK Level 1 Recall and Reproduction	Webb's DOK Level 2 Skills and Concepts	Webb's DOK Level 3 Strategic Thinking/Reasoning	Webb's DOK Level 4 Extended Thinking
Remember Memorize, recognize, recall, locate, identify	○ Recall or locate key facts, terms, details, procedures (e.g., explicit in a technical manual)		Use these Hess CRM curricular examples with most assignments, assessments, or inquiry activities for Career and Technical Education.	
Understand Construct meaning, clarify, paraphrase, represent, translate, illustrate, give examples, summarize, generalize, infer a logical conclusion, predict, observe, match like ideas, explain, construct models	○ Select correct terms or graphics for intended meaning ○ Describe or explain who, what, where, when, or how ○ Define terms, principles, concepts ○ Represent relationships with words, diagrams, symbols ○ Solve routine problems	○ Specify and explain relationships (e.g., nonexamples/examples; cause/effect; if/then) ○ Summarize procedures, results, concepts, key ideas (paragraph) ○ Make and explain estimates, basic inferences, or predictions ○ Use models to explain concepts ○ Make and record observations	○ Explain, generalize, or connect ideas using supporting evidence (quote, example, text reference, data) ○ Justify your interpretation when more than one is plausible ○ Explain how a concept can be used to solve a nonroutine problem ○ Develop a multiparagraph manual or infographic for specific purpose or focus	○ Use multiple sources to outline varying perspectives on a problem or issue ○ Explain how a concept relates across content domains or to "Big Ideas" (e.g., patterns in the human or designed world; structure function) ○ Apply generalizations from one investigation to new problem-based situations, using evidence or data
Apply Carry out or use a procedure in a given situation; apply or use in an unfamiliar situation or nonroutine task	○ Apply basic formulas, algorithms, conversion rules ○ Calculate, measure ○ Use reference materials and tools to gather information ○ Demo safe procedures	○ Select and use appropriate tool or procedure for specified task ○ Use context to identify the meaning of terms or phrases ○ Interpret information using diagrams, data tables, etc.	○ Build or revise a plan for investigation using (new) evidence or data ○ Use and show reasoning, planning, and evidence to support conclusions or to identify design flaws ○ Conduct a designed investigation	○ Draw from source materials with intent to develop a complex or multimedia product with personal viewpoint ○ Conduct a project that specifies a problem, identifies solution paths, tests the solution, and reports results
Analyze Break into constituent parts, determine how parts relate, compare/contrast, differentiate between relevant/irrelevant, distinguish, focus, select, organize, outline, find coherence, deconstruct (e.g., for potential bias, point of view, technique, or strategy used)	○ Identify trend, pattern, possible cause or effect ○ Describe processes or tools used to research ideas ○ Identify ways symbols or metaphors are used to represent universal ideas ○ Retrieve data to answer a question (e.g., diagram, graph)	○ Compare similarities or differences or draw inferences about ___ due to influences of ___ ○ Distinguish relevant/irrelevant information; fact or opinion; primary from a secondary source ○ Extend a pattern ○ Organize and represent data ○ Categorize materials, data, etc., based on characteristics	○ Interpret information from a complex graph or model (e.g., interrelationships among variables, concepts) ○ Use reasoning, planning, and evidence to support or refute inferences or results stated ○ Use reasoning and evidence to generate criteria for making and supporting an argument ○ Generalize and support a pattern/trend	○ Analyze multiple sources of evidence (e.g., compare/contrast various plans, solution methods) ○ Analyze and compare diverse, complex abstract perspectives, models, etc. ○ Gather, organize, and analyze information from multiple sources to answer a research question
Evaluate Make judgments based on specified criteria, detect inconsistencies, flaws, or fallacies, judge, critique	"UG" (unsubstantiated generalizations) = Stating an opinion without providing any support for it!		○ Develop a logical argument for conjectures, citing evidence ○ Verify reasonableness of results or conjectures (e.g., of others) ○ Critique conclusions drawn or evidence used or credibility of sources	○ Evaluate relevancy, accuracy, and completeness of sources used ○ Apply understanding in a novel way, provide argument or justification for the application ○ Critique the historical impact of ___ on ___
Create Reorganize into new patterns or schemas, design, plan, produce	○ Brainstorm ideas, concepts, problems, or perspectives related to a given scenario, observation, question posed	○ Generate testable conjectures or hypotheses based on observations, prior knowledge, or artifacts	○ Generate testable conjectures or hypotheses based on observations, prior knowledge, or artifacts ○ Develop a complex model for a given concept and justify your reasoning ○ Develop an alternative solution and justify your reasoning	○ Synthesize information across multiple models, sources, or texts ○ Articulate new knowledge or new perspectives

 Available for download at **http://resources.corwin.com/DeeperCompetencyBasedLearning** and **www.karin-hess.com/free-resources**.

APPENDIX B

Appendix C

Recommended Resources to Support CBE Implementation

ASSESSMENT: FORMATIVE AND PERFORMANCE ASSESSMENT

Print

Ainsworth, L. (2014). *Common formative assessment 2.0: How teacher teams intentionally align standards, instruction, and assessment.* Corwin.

Burke, K. (2010). *Balanced assessment: From formative to summative.* Solution Tree.

Darling-Hammond, L., & Adamson, F. (2014). *Beyond the bubble test: How performance assessments support 21st century learning.* Jossey-Bass.

Hess, K. (2018). *A local assessment toolkit to promote deeper learning: Transforming research into practice.* Corwin.

Keely, P. (2008). *Science formative assessment: 75 practical strategies for linking assessment, instruction, and learning.* Corwin.

Keeley, P., Eberle, F., & Farrin, L. (2005). *Uncovering student ideas in science, Vol. 1: Formative assessment probes.* NSTA Press.

Keeley, P., & Tobey, C. (2017). *Mathematics formative assessment, Vols. 1–2: Practical strategies.* Corwin.

Rose, C., Minton, L., & Arline, C. (2007). *Uncovering student thinking in mathematics: 25 formative assessment probes.* Corwin.

Other

Defined STEM (www.definedstem.com) is a K–12 web-based curriculum and assessment tool that focuses on deeper learning and 21st century outcomes for all students. Empower your teachers with the tools they need to implement real-world project-based lessons that build future-ready skills.

Exemplars (www.exemplars.com) publishes standards-based performance assessment tasks for K–8 mathematics and science with annotated student work at four performance levels. Schools can find free examples at the website or purchase a subscription to use the assessments and scoring rubrics. It also provides professional development for teachers.

COMPETENCY FRAMEWORKS: ACADEMIC AND PERSONAL SUCCESS SKILLS

Print

CASEL. (n.d.). *CASEL guide to schoolwide SEL: Using interactive pedagogy.* https://schoolguide.casel.org/focus-area-3/classroom/integration-of-sel-and-instruction/using-interactive-pedagogy/.

Essential Skills and Dispositions Developmental Framework. (2015). National Center for Innovation in Education. https://www.inflexion.org/essential-skills-and-dispositions-development-frameworks/

Jones, S., Brush, K., Bailey, R., Brion-Meisels, G., McIntyre, J., Kahn, J., Nelson, B., & Stickle, L. (2017). *Navigating SEL from the inside out: Looking inside & across 25 leading SEL programs—A practical resource for schools and OST providers.* https://www.wallacefoundation.org/knowledge-center/Documents/Navigating-Social-and-Emotional-Learning-from-the-Inside-Out.pdf.

Social-emotional learning (SEL) values a whole-child approach in developing a positive school culture while supporting every child's success. An excellent resource to gain a deeper understanding of SEL has been produced by the Harvard School of Education.

Other

Building 21 Competencies (www.building21.org/open-resources/competencies/) provides nationally validated sample competencies in all core subjects.

The National Center for Innovation in Education (www.leadingwithlearning.org) at the University of Kentucky created a developmental continuum for the essential skills and dispositions needed for college and career readiness. This continuum, from *Beginner* through *Emerging Expert*, focuses on Collaboration, Creativity, Communication, and Self-Direction. Many schools and districts are using this framework as a foundational document in building the personal success skills needed for graduation.

The *New Hampshire Department of Education* (www.education.nh.gov) has been the pioneer in competency education with its breakthrough models in K–12 systems transformation and its state accountability system, including the New Hampshire Performance Assessment for Competency Education (PACE). All of the academic competencies developed in New Hampshire were created and validated by state educators. K–12 academic competencies in English/Language Arts, Mathematics, Science, and the Arts can be found at this site.

The *NEXT Charter High School* (www.nextcharterschool.org), a public charter school located in Derry, New Hampshire, has a unique structure. It is a competency-based, project-based high school that creates course equivalencies for its projects, ensuring that each project is multidisciplinary. It values the personal skills and competencies as part of its profile of the graduate.

Proviso East High School (www.pths209.org/east) in Maywood, Illinois, is a model turnaround urban school. The core values of the school guide the design of teaching and learning.

Vermont's (education.vermont.gov/student-learning/proficiency-based-learning) approach to proficiency-based learning focuses on flexible and personalized pathways set forth in Act 77 and the State Board of Education's Education Quality Standards. Vermont public schools must provide students with flexible and personalized pathways for progressing through grade levels and to graduation.

DEEPER LEARNING

Print

Bellanca, J. A. (2014). *Deeper learning: Beyond 21st century skills*. Solution Tree.

Chow, B. (2010). The quest for deeper learning. *Education Week, 30*(6), 1–3.

Conley, D. T., & Darling-Hammond, L. (2013). *Creating systems of assessment for deeper learning*. Stanford Center for Opportunity Policy in Education.

Farrington, C. A. (2013). *Academic mindsets as a critical component of deeper learning*. University of Chicago Consortium on Chicago School Research.

Fullan, M., Quinn, J., & McEachen, J. J. (2017). *Deep learning: Engage the world change the world*. Corwin.

Hess, K. (2018). *A local assessment toolkit to promote deeper learning: Transforming research into practice*. Corwin.

Huberman, M., Bitter, C., Anthony, J., & O'Day, J. (2014). *The shape of deeper learning: Strategies, structures, and cultures in deeper learning network high schools. Findings from the study of deeper learning opportunities and outcomes: Report 1*. American Institutes for Research.

Jensen, E., & Nickelsen, L. (2008). *Deeper learning: 7 powerful strategies for in-depth and longer-lasting learning*. Corwin.

Martinez, M., & McGrath, D. (2014). *Deeper learning: How eight innovative public schools are transforming education in the twenty-first century*. The New Press.

GRADING PRACTICES

These resources are helpful when working with teachers as they move from traditional grading practices to standards-based grading, and eventually to evidence-based grading and reporting.

Print

Dueck, M. (2014). *Grading smarter, not harder: Assessment strategies that motivate kids and help them learn.* ASCD.

Feldman, J. (2018). *Grading for equity.* Corwin.

Gobble, T., Onuscheck, M., Reibel, A., & Twadell, E. (2017). *Pathways to proficiency: Implementing evidence-based grading.* Solution Tree.

Guskey, T. R. (2008). *Practical solutions for serious problems in standards-based grading.* Corwin.

Guskey, T. R. (2013). The case against percentage grades. *Educational Leadership, 71*(1), 68–72.

Jung, L. A., & Guskey, T. R. (2011). *Grading exceptional and struggling learners.* Corwin.

Reeves, D. (2010). *Elements of grading: A guide to effective practice.* Solution Tree.

Stack, B., & VanderEls, J. G. (2017). *Breaking with tradition.* Solution Tree.

ORGANIZATIONS THAT SUPPORT CBE WORK

Achieve (www.achieve.org/resources) provides resources about competency-based pathways, graduation requirements, learning progressions, and college and career readiness.

Aurora Institute (formerly iNACOL; www.inacol.org) is a nonprofit organization with the mission to drive the transformation of education systems and accelerate the advancement of breakthrough policies and practices to ensure high-quality learning for all.

Center for Collaborative Education (www.cce.org) provides professional development to school teams in the areas of equity, personalization, and quality performance assessment.

Competency-Based Education Solutions (www.cbesolution.com) supports school-based programs in their continued transformation to a personalized competency-based system of teaching and learning through site-based coaching and professional development.

*Competency*Works (www.competencyworks.org) provides resources to support the understanding of competency-based education, personalization, and related policies.

Education Elements (www.edelements.com) provides help in planning for CBE, from initial steps at a few pilot schools to strategic planning for districtwide transformation.

Educational Research in Action (www.karin-hess.com) provides resources and professional development to school teams in the areas of rigor/depth of knowledge, personalization, CBE, and high-quality performance assessment.

Great Schools Partnership (www.greatschoolspartnership.org) offers resources for developing efficient standards-based systems that prepare all students for 21st century colleges, careers, and communities.

Innovative Lab Network (www.ccsso.org) is a collaborative effort among states that are taking action to identify, test, and implement student-centered approaches to learning.

Nellie Mae Education Foundation (www.nmefoundation.org/resources) offers a knowledge base of materials that provides evidence of student-centered learning, enabling every student to develop the skills and knowledge she or he needs for the future.

New Hampshire Learning Initiative (NHLI; www.nhlearninginitiative.org) is an educator-led team dedicated to helping teachers, administrators, and school district officials advance education and better prepare students for college, career, and life, offering resources and professional development.

William and Flora Hewlett Foundation (www.hewlett.org/programs/education) offers grants to support school transformation. They value student empowerment and future readiness while supporting open educational resources. They have been valued partners in promoting the work in performance assessment.

PERSONALIZED LEARNING: LEARNING PATHWAYS

Print

Cushman, K., & the students of *What Kids Can Do*. (2010). *Fires in the mind: What kids can tell us about motivation and mastery*. Jossey-Bass.

DeLorenzo, R. A., Battino, W. J., Schreiber, R. M., & Gaddy Carrio, B. B. (2008). *Delivering on the promise: The education revolution*. Solution Tree.

High Tech High School began as one of the first personalized competency-based and project-based learning schools in the country. Since its origin, its model for teaching and learning has been adopted by a number of schools, creating a network. This is an interesting look at this model:

David, S., & Goldberg E. (2013). *Profile: High Tech High network*. http://www.nmefoundation.org/getmedia/b1710b14-c1e5-48e4-afa6-e8017d2ed61d/PROFILE-HighTechHighNetwork-NMEF?ext=.pdf.

Mofield, E., & Parker, M. (2018). *Teaching tenacity, resilience, and a drive for excellence: Lessons for social-emotional learning for grades 4–8*. Prufrock Press.

reDesign. (n.d.). *Student agency*. https://www.redesignu.org/design-lab/mastery-learning/resource-bank/student-agency.

Smith, D., Frey, N., & Fisher, D. (2017). *Building equity: Policies and practices to empower all learners*. ASCD.

Other

Career Ladders Project (www.careerladdersproject.org) offers policy and tools for districts looking to design equitable, guided pathways that are rigorous and future focused in meeting the needs of students, as well as the capacities of the learning community. Career pathways maps clarify and align programs and services as high schools develop college and career readiness progressions into programs of study. Through the thoughtful development of career ladders and multiple pathways, schools can support students as they prepare for postsecondary learning and career experiences.

Competency Model Clearinghouse (CareerOneStop; www.careeronestop.org): In building multiple pathways that are aligned with college and career readiness skills as well as career ladders, the Employment and Training Administration (ETA) has developed a dynamic website to build competency-based models aligned to industries and various sectors of the economy. The goal of the effort is to promote an understanding of the skill sets and competencies that are essential to educate and train a globally competitive workforce.

The *New Tech Network* (newtechnetwork.org/resources/new-tech-network-agency-rubrics/) has shared much of its work in CBE. The Student Agency Rubric is one of its many rubrics, especially helpful as you think through student agency in personalization.

Next Generation Learning Challenges (NGLC), together with EdElements, has produced *The My Ways Learning Outcomes* (https://s3.amazonaws.com/nglc/resource-files/MW_LearningOutcomes_Preview.pdf). This is a wonderful tool for students to use as a pathfinder for their academic and personal learning.

PORTRAIT OF A GRADUATE: ARTICLES

Conley's work on college and career readiness provides you with the research-based foundation to begin your understanding of the profile of your graduate who is indeed ready for entering higher education and the workforce.

Conley, D. T. (2012). *A complete definition of college and career readiness*. http://www.epiconline.org/ccr-definition/.

Conley, D. T. (2012). *College and career ready: Helping all students succeed beyond high school*. Jossey-Bass.

Kuhlman, J. (2019). How aligning student of the month criteria to your portrait of a graduate increases transparency. https://knowledgeworks.org/resources/align-student-month-portrait-graduate-transparency/.

South Carolina Competencies Prototype (https://ed.sc.gov/instruction/personalized-learning/feature-box/competency-based-education/sc-competencies-prototype/) is designed to support local districts in making the South Carolina Portrait of a Graduate actionable. It identifies the critical components students will need for college, career, and citizenship as a collection of integrated learning indicators combining world-class knowledge and academic as well as life and career skills. Each component is broken down into levels of readiness as well as actionable steps to promote growth mindset and continuous improvement within students and the systems that support them.

Springpoint Schools partners with schools, districts, charters, networks, and foundations to create innovative school models that are designed for and responsive to the communities they serve.

Duffy, A. (2019). Portrait of a graduate: 5 things to keep in mind. https://www.springpointschools.org/blog/2019/07/portrait-of-a-graduate-5-things-to-keep-in-mind/.

Virginia is one of the pioneering states to develop its profile of a graduate as a guiding document for schools to anchor their future reforms.

Profile of a Virginia graduate. https://ttaconline.org/Resource/JWHaEa5BS74MV5HtpglDNA/Resource-profile-of-a-virginia-graduate-virginia-department-of-education-vdoe.

PORTRAIT OF A GRADUATE: SCHOOL EXAMPLES

Many schools/districts post descriptions of their portraits of the graduate as a way to communicate expectations to students, parents, and the wider community. We have included links to several school websites. Additional profiles of a graduate can be found at https://portraitofagraduate.org.

- Exeter Schools, Exeter, New Hampshire: www.sau16.org.

- Fraser School district, Fraser, Michigan: www.fraser.k12.mi.us/StrategicPlan.

- Oakes Public Schools, Oakes, North Dakota, aligns its "student of the month" awards with its POG: https://knowledgeworks.org/resources/align-student-month-portrait-graduate-transparency/?utm_source=LinkedIn&utm_campaign=website.

PROFESSIONAL LEARNING AND LEADERSHIP

Print

Bales, S. (2010). *Framing education reform: A frameworks message memo.* http://www
.frameworksinstitute.org/assets/files/PDF_Education/education_message_memo.pdf.

Burris, C. C., & Garrity, D. T. (2008). *Detracking for excellence and equity.* ASCD.

Duty, L., & Kern, T. (2014). *So you think you want to innovate.* www.gettingsmart.com/
2014/10/think-think-want-innovate. Beginning the innovation process can be overwhelming.
This tool allows your leadership team to self-assess on a variety of topics to help clear your
way forward with focus.

Elmore, R. F. (2004). *School reform from the inside out: Policy, practice, and performance.*
Harvard Education Press.

Other

Learn Next (www.2revolutions.net/opencontent) is an online professional resource
library designed by a consortium of organizations that includes all topics in
competency-based learning. All resources are open and free of cost.

Learning Commons (www.app.learning-commons.org) is a resource that can be
used for teachers to learn either as part of their collaborative learning time or even
independently to accelerate professional learning. Here, educators can create their
own customized playlist learning activities that provide "just in time" customized
learning opportunities.

Southern New Hampshire University (SNHU) and 2Revolutions have partnered in
designing a Masters/Certificate of Advanced Graduate Study program in CBE. This
program is unique in that it is a degree program in CBE that itself is competency-
based by design. School districts wishing to acquire additional information can
contact Adam Rubin of 2Revolutions at adam@2Revolutions.net.

Glossary

Academic Competencies: Academic competencies are explicit, measurable, transferable learning objectives drawn from established college- and career-readiness standards and course content.

Benchmark/Interim Assessment: Benchmark assessments are generally standards-based and designed to align with a pacing calendar and grade-level content standards. They are typically used to measure progress on large units of a district's curriculum and to determine which students are "on track" to meet specified annual academic goals. Interim assessments are designed to inform decisions at both the classroom level and beyond, such as at the school/grade level or district level. Thus, they may be given at the classroom level to provide information for the teacher, but the results can also be meaningfully aggregated and reported at a broader level.

Big Ideas: The concepts of Big Ideas and enduring understandings have been best operationalized by Wiggins and McTighe, 2005. Big Ideas are broadly defined as the domain-specific core concepts, principles, theories, and reasoning that *should* serve as the focal point of curriculum and assessment if the learning goal is to have students make broader and deeper connections among specific skills and concepts taught. Big Ideas tie together the learning from multiple units of study and are the unifying threads connecting the learning targets in learning progressions (e.g., proportional reasoning in mathematics; systems or patterns in science).

Blended Learning: Blended learning combines the use of online resources and technology tools with team-learning activities and traditional teacher-directed instruction. The hallmarks of blended learning are personalization, student agency, authentic audiences, connectivity, and creativity (Tucker, Wycoff, & Green, 2017).

Body of Evidence (BOE): High-priority assessments identified in the Assessment System Blueprint (Hess, 2018) are administered over an extended time in order to gather *sufficient* evidence that students are making progress toward achieving proficiency in a given content area. Best practices in developing the interpretations of student learning include use of common assessments, collaborative scoring, juried reviews of student work and portfolio products (e.g., involving experts, peers, community), and student self-assessment and reflection.

Cognitive Demand: Cognitive demand describes the potential range of mental processing required to complete a given task within a given context or scenario. Determining the intended cognitive demand of a test item or task requires more than simply identifying the verbs and the nouns describing the learning outcomes. Teachers must consider the reasoning and decision-making required to complete a task successfully. During instruction, the cognitive demand of highly complex tasks can be lessened using strategic scaffolding strategies (Hess, 2018) without significantly changing the constructs being assessed. This might include strategies such as "chunking" texts for a reading assessment, group data collection for a science investigation, and facilitated discussions as a prewriting activity.

Cognitive Labs/Think Alouds: Cognitive labs are used for determining how well a new or draft assessment will "perform"—meaning how effective is this assessment (test items, reading passages, and tasks) in eliciting the intended evidence of learning? A cognitive lab approach does not require the time and number of students that field testing and task piloting require; therefore, it is a good option for smaller schools with limited resources. (For specific strategies for conducting cognitive labs, see Hess, 2018, Module 3).

Cognitive Rigor: Cognitive rigor encompasses the complexity of the content, the cognitive engagement with that content, and the scope of the planned learning activity (Hess et al., 2009).

Cognitive Rigor Matrix (CRM): The Hess Cognitive Rigor Matrices (CRMs) are content-specific tools designed to enhance increasingly rigorous instructional and assessment planning and practices at classroom, district, and state levels. Descriptors in each CRM can guide a teacher's use of questioning during a lesson, shifting student roles to be more student-directed.

Common Assessment/Common Assignment: Common assessments are designed and used to collect *comparable* evidence of learning within and across grade levels, providing educators with predictions as to how students are likely to perform on similar summative assessment measures. They can include performance tasks (e.g., common writing prompts, parallel tasks with common scoring rubrics, such as internships or capstone projects), district interim/benchmark assessments (given at particular times during the school year to measure progress), and other district-level and state-level assessments. Administration guidelines must accompany common assessments (and common scoring guides) to ensure fidelity of implementation. If assessments are scored locally, calibration training and scoring practice are also essential.

Competency/Proficiency: The terms *competency* and *proficiency* are often used interchangeably. As defined by Achieve, Inc., competencies include explicit, measurable, transferable learning objectives that empower students. Competencies fall under two broad categories: academic and personal/soft skills.

Competency-Based Education (CBE): Competency-based education (also referred to as mastery-based, proficiency-based, or performance-based) is a school- or districtwide structure that replaces the traditional structure to create a system that is designed for students to be successful (as compared to sorted) and leads to continuous improvement. In 2019, the Aurora Institute fine-tuned an earlier definition of high-quality competency education, which now includes seven elements (Levine & Patrick, 2019):

1. Students are empowered daily to make important decisions about their learning experiences, how they will create and apply knowledge, and how they will demonstrate their learning.

2. Assessment is a meaningful, positive, and empowering learning experience for students that yields timely, relevant, and actionable evidence.

3. Students receive timely, differentiated support based on their individual learning needs.

4. Students progress based on evidence of mastery, not seat time.

5. Students learn actively using different pathways and varied pacing.

6. Strategies to ensure equity for all students are embedded in the culture, structure, and pedagogy of schools and education systems.

7. Rigorous, common expectations for learning (knowledge, skills, and dispositions) are explicit, transparent, measurable, and transferable.

Competency-Based Learning Pathways: Achieve, Inc. (Domaleski et al., 2015) developed this working definition to include these indicators:

- Students advance upon demonstrated mastery and can demonstrate their learning at their own point of readiness.

- Assessment is meaningful and a positive learning experience for students and requires students to actually *demonstrate* their learning.

- Students receive rapid, differentiated support based on their individual learning needs.

- Learning outcomes emphasize competencies that include the application and creation of knowledge.

- The process of reaching learning outcomes encourages students to develop skills and dispositions important for success in college, careers, and citizenship.

Conjunctive and Compensatory Accountability Models: Two methods for combining information from multiple assessments, subject areas, or grade levels (e.g., test scores, artifacts of learning) include using a conjunctive or a compensatory model, or a combination of both. A conjunctive model requires a minimum level of performance on each of several measures, meaning that poor performance on one measure may result in a failure to meet established targets. In a compensatory model, good performance on one measure may offset poor performance on another (NCME & ACE, 2006, p. 570).

Depth of Knowledge (DOK): Norman Webb's Depth of Knowledge Levels (Webb, 2002) describe the depth of content understanding and scope of a learning activity, which manifests in the skills required to complete a task from inception to finale (e.g., planning, researching, drawing conclusions). Webb's four DOK levels are

- Level 1: Recall and reproduction

- Level 2: Basic skills and concepts

- Level 3: Strategic thinking and reasoning

- Level 4: Extended thinking

Depth of Knowledge (DOK) "Ceilings and Targets": An important consideration in the development of test items/performance tasks is to use the highest depth-of-knowledge (DOK) demand implicit in an assessment blueprint as the "ceiling" for assessment, not a target. A "DOK target" has a narrower focus (e.g., only assess at DOK 2), whereas a "DOK ceiling" is the highest-potential depth-of-knowledge level to be assessed, as well as assessing DOK levels up to the ceiling. The DOK ceiling is determined by the intended cognitive demand of the combination of standards assessed (Hess, 2018).

Differentiated Learning/Assignment Menus: The essence of differentiation is to differentiate the content, differentiate the process/thinking, or differentiate the product and give students a choice about which assignments they want to do. Assignment menus are an effective strategy for varying the pace of learning and offering choice and challenge (Hess, 2018).

Differentiation: Differentiation choices (content, processes/thinking, or products) are designed by the teacher, based on the learning needs of a whole class or small groups of students. Teachers can differentiate by adjusting the curriculum materials, teaching strategies, and classroom environment to meet the needs of students.

Educational Equity: Educational equity, also referred to as equity in education, is a measure of achievement, fairness, and opportunity in education. The National Equity Project (www.nationalequityproject.org) states that educational equity means that each child receives what she or he needs to develop to full academic and social potential. Working toward equity involves

- Ensuring equally high outcomes for all participants in our educational system; removing the predictability of success or failures that currently correlates with any social or cultural factor.

- Interrupting inequitable practices, examining biases, and creating inclusive multicultural school environments for adults and children.

- Discovering and cultivating the unique gifts, talents, and interests that every human possesses.

Effect Size: An effect size is the magnitude, or size, of a given effect, as statistically determined by empirical research. An effect size of zero indicates no change in achievement. An effect size of 1.0 indicates an increase of one standard deviation on the outcome, such as reading achievement, and can be interpreted as a student making two- or three-years achievement (Fisher, Frey, & Hattie, 2016).

Evidence-Based Grading and Reporting: The primary goal of a CBE approach is to nurture a growth mindset that promotes personal efficacy, the belief or confidence that one's competencies will lead to the achievement of goals (Hattie, 2009). In a correctly implemented CBE grading model, teachers collect, monitor, and review student-produced evidence in essential course skills. Ultimately, each teacher assigns a final grade based upon the student's level of competence. Because "mastery" is the learning goal, if a student shows a higher level of proficiency on a more recent assessment, the teacher will consider giving more weight to the most recent scores in determination of the final grade.

Flipped Classroom: A flipped classroom approach is where a teacher provides access to a video or videotapes short lesson segments for students to access and view individually. Viewing these teacher-created segments can be done prior to the whole-class instruction as an option for students to move ahead at their own pace or as a review.

Formative Assessment: Formative assessment is as much a process or instructional strategy as it is a measurement tool. Also known as "short-cycle" assessment, formative assessment practices are embedded in instruction and used frequently during a teaching/learning cycle (e.g., to preassess readiness, to target mastery of specific skills, to check conceptual understanding). The primary purposes of using assessment data formatively are to (a) diagnose where students are in their learning along a learning progression; (b) identify gaps in knowledge and student understanding; (c) determine how to help some or all students move ahead in their learning; and (d) provide opportunities for peer and self-assessment as part of the learning process.

Individualization: In individualized instruction, the teacher customizes instruction for each student and uses accommodations that help the student meet the same learning objectives expected for all students. We might think of this as one-on-one teaching and support.

Intrapersonal Skills: Intrapersonal skills generally include skills such as goal setting, metacognition and self-reflection, and managing social and emotional skills (e.g., self-awareness, responsible decision-making).

Interpersonal skills: Interpersonal skills include the ability to work with others (collaboration and communication) and other social and emotional skills (e.g., relationship skills, social awareness).

Leadership Density: Leadership density is a term that refers to developing a broad group of leaders throughout the educational system, including school-based leadership councils composed of administrators, teacher leaders, content and curriculum specialists, and students. Leadership teams have the responsibility of developing and implementing new policies that expand their roles beyond the traditional role of school administrators. Leadership density is a proven strategy for implementing systemic change in schools (Hess, 2000).

Learning Goals/Outcomes/Objectives: Several terms are used interchangeably by educators to describe what students will understand and be able to perform with regard to the content and skills being taught. An effective learning goal is composed of a clearly stated progression of *learning targets* that demonstrate eventual attainment of the desired performance or proficiency. Smaller-grained learning targets guide day-to-day instruction and formative uses of assessment as a student makes progress toward the broader learning goal.

Learning Progressions (LP): Learning progressions, progress maps, developmental continuums, and learning trajectories are all terms that have been used to generally mean *research-based* descriptions of how students develop and demonstrate deeper, broader, and more sophisticated understanding over time. A learning progression can visually and verbally articulate a hypothesis about how learning will typically move toward increased understanding for most students. Learning progressions are based in empirical research and, therefore, are not the same as curricular progressions or grade-to-grade standards. This is because LPs often include typical misconceptions along the way to reaching learning goals.

When developing LPs, cognitive scientists compare *Novice* performers to *Expert* performers. Novice performers generally have not yet developed schemas that help them to organize and connect information. Novice performers use most of their working memory just trying to figure out what all the parts of the task are, not in engaging with the task/assignment.

Learning Sciences Research: According to Hoadley and Haneghan (2011), the core components of learning sciences research include the following:

- Research on thinking, including how the mind works to process, store, retrieve, and perceive information.

- Research on learning processes, including how people use "constellations of memories, skills, perceptions, and ideas" to think and solve problems, and the role that different types of literacies play in learning

- Research on learning environments, including how people learn in different contexts other than a direct-instruction environment with a core principle of creating learner-centered learning environments

Learning Target (LT): As defined by Moss and Brookhart (2012, p. 3), learning targets guide learning and therefore should use wording that students can understand and use for peer and self-assessment. LTs can be thought of as "lesson-sized chunks" of information, skills, and reasoning processes that students will come to know deeply over time. In proficiency-based systems, learning targets can be stated as short descriptive or bulleted phrases that create levels of a performance scale. A series of LTs detail the progression of knowledge and skills students must understand and be able to perform to demonstrate achievement of the broader learning goal/proficiency.

Local Assessment System (LAS): A comprehensive local assessment system includes multiple components, identifying high-priority local- and state-level assessments used in the educational system (Hess, 2018). The most important characteristic of an assessment system is that it is designed to provide cohesive and actionable information about student performance, using multiple measures. The various components of the system across the different educational levels provide complementary information so that decisions can be based on making valid inferences about demonstrating competency.

Moderation: The moderation method is a school-based assessment program wherein schools are responsible for collecting evidence of student work, judging that work based on the standards, and submitting sample work to external moderation panels (Allen, 2012). This method involves using a generalized (common) rubric with a representative collection of portfolios that include some common assessment tasks and some unique pieces of evidence. A "moderation" panel then creates sample portfolios that represent different performance levels (at, above, and below proficiency). The sample portfolios are used by teacher teams for calibration purposes when comparing their students' portfolios to the exemplar portfolios. Your school might consider using this method for one aspect of CB decision-making if students are required to develop digital portfolios, create capstone projects, or complete graduation exhibitions.

Performance Assessment/Performance Task: Performance assessments can be used for a variety of purposes—instructional/formative and evaluative/summative. Performance tasks are generally defined as multistep assignments with clear criteria, expectations, and processes that measure how well a student transfers knowledge and applies complex skills to create or refine an original product. Often, common assessments include a performance component because they are designed to integrate multiple skills and concepts within authentic contexts. Performance tasks produce a variety of real-world products such as essays, demonstrations, presentations, artistic performances, solutions to complex problems, and research/investigation projects. They are assessments that may be completed individually or with others (Hess, 2018).

Personal Success Skills/Dispositions/Soft Skills: Personal success skills are not content-specific and are best taught and assessed within the context of each content domain (Hess & Gong, 2014). In the CBE classroom, these skills are intentionally built into the teaching and learning every day and assessed within larger performance tasks or projects. Personal success skills are explicitly referenced in a school's vision of the graduate and often include a combination of workplace habits and self-management skills (e.g., goal setting, critical thinking, creative problem-solving) and skills for interacting effectively with others (e.g., developing empathy, collaboration, and communication skills).

Personalization: Personalization is tailoring a student's learning activities based on strengths, needs, and interests—including enabling student voice and choice in what, how, when, and where a student learns. Personalization strategies provide supports and guide a student to set personal learning goals, plan a learning pathway, maintain a record of explorations, and document evidence of competency.

Piloting: Piloting is one of three common strategies used for determining how well a new/draft assessment will "perform"—meaning how effective is this assessment (test items, reading passages, overall difficulty, and tasks) in eliciting the intended evidence of learning? An assessment piloting process requires fewer students than does field testing a new assessment and is therefore a time-efficient strategy for "trying out" new assessments. In a locally designed pilot, students from a minimum of two or three representative classrooms (within or across schools) will take an assessment. Then, educators collect and collaboratively review the results (student work, scoring rubrics, administration guidelines, etc.) to determine whether or not this assessment elicited the intended evidence and can be reliably scored. Student work analysis is used to refine both task prompts and rubrics. For strong assessments, scoring anchors may also be identified during the piloting phase.

Portfolios, Exhibitions, and Extended Learning Opportunities (ELO): These performance assessment models typically address a wide range of content area and cross-curricular learning, including both academic concepts and personal success skills (e.g., critical thinking and problem-solving, communication, teamwork, preparedness, responsibility, persistence). In course-based performance assessments, individual teachers use common, agreed-upon criteria to evaluate a body of work that students have completed over the course of an instructional period. For cross-curricular assessments, groups of content area teachers or review committees evaluate the work. It should be noted that portfolios do not have to require students to create new work, but they may require that students collect and present past work, evidence of growth, self-reflection, and accomplishments over time. Exhibitions may also incorporate examples of past work that has been used as a foundation for new products (Hess, 2018).

Prerequisite/Preassessment: Prerequisite (foundational) knowledge and skills encompass the discrete learning upon which more complex tasks are built; thus, they appear at the lower end of a CB performance scale. We recommend that preassessments begin with assessing the core prerequisite skills needed to build upon in order to be successful at completing more complex and cognitively demanding tasks.

Project-Based Learning (PBL): Project-based learning is designed to make learning more meaningful and relevant to students. Projects require that students go beyond the textbook to study complex topics based on real-world issues (e.g., examining water quality in their communities or the history of their town). Students often work in groups to gather and analyze information from multiple sources, including interviewing experts and collecting survey data. Project-based classwork is generally more demanding than traditional book-based instruction, where students may just memorize facts presented in a single source. Students are expected to use original documents and data, applying principles covered in traditional courses to real-world situations. Projects have multiple components and can last weeks or may cover entire courses. Student work is assessed in stages (e.g., gathering and analyzing information, integrating what was learned, presenting information) and presented to "authentic" audiences beyond the teacher, including parents and community groups.

Reliability: Test reliability is defined as the consistency of test scores over different test administrations, multiple raters, or different test questions. Reliability answers the question, How likely is it that a student would obtain the same score if she or he took the same test a second time (test-retest reliability) or if someone else scored this student's test (interrater reliability)? In statistics, interrater reliability/agreement—or concordance—is the degree of agreement or consistency with which two or more judges rate the work or performance of assessment takers. Strong interrater reliability is easiest to achieve with selected-response test items (questions having only one right answer). Interrater reliability for scoring more complex assessments (projects, portfolios, observations, and/or performance tasks) is strengthened by the use of clear scoring guides, annotated student work, and periodic calibration practice. Assessments can be reliable and still not be valid (assessing what is intended to be assessed).

Rubrics/Scoring Guides: Rubrics and scoring guides provide a set of rules or guidelines for assigning scores to test takers. Rubrics are often used to elaborate on how to score longer-constructed response items, performance tasks, and extended projects. More simplified scoring guides tend to be used for shorter, open-ended test items. (For a detailed discussion on strengths and weaknesses of rubric types [e.g., analytic, holistic] and scoring criteria, see Hess, 2018, Module 3.)

Scaffolding Strategically: Scaffolding is the purposeful use of supports to achieve a balance between cognitive complexity and student autonomy as the overall cognitive demand of the task increases. Strategic scaffolding means the intentional steps designed into the instruction that ensure that all students can eventually complete the same complex task independently. The primary difference between scaffolding and differentiating is that differentiating means different—different assignments, different options, student choice. Differentiation is achieved by changing the content, the process skills, and/or the products of learning.

Scales—Performance, Proficiency, Scoring, Analytical: Various terms are used to describe a continuum of performance descriptors that articulate distinct levels of demonstrated knowledge and skills relative to a learning outcome or proficiency-based statement. Scales can be used to plan instruction, develop scoring guides, monitor progress over time, and guide the development of artifacts to be included in a student's body of evidence. We use the term *performance scale* (not *proficiency* scale) so as not to imply this is only for scoring or grading, and we recommend developing scales for each competency (not for each standard). A **holistic scale** combines several criteria to yield one generalized—or holistic—score. While these scores can be used to describe overall performance, they are not as useful in providing specific feedback to students on strengths and weaknesses of the performance (Hess, 2018).

Social Emotional Learning (SEL): Social Emotional Learning includes a number of skills, attitudes, or behaviors that can be demonstrated by learners as they develop interpersonal, intrapersonal, and cognitive competence. For example, in the CASEL model, "self-awareness" is described as the ability to accurately recognize one's own emotions, thoughts, and values and how they influence personal behavior. See Also Competency Frameworks, Appendix C.

Standard Setting: Standard setting is a verification method typically used when there is one assessment, such as a state assessment or a common local benchmark assessment (e.g., end-of-course exam). Educators collaboratively review scores from the range of scores generated by the test and then set "cut" scores to denote score ranges for performance levels, such as *Advanced*, *Proficient*, *Approaching*, and *Basic*. Using this method for every CB assessment would be too time consuming and unmanageable. However, standard setting could be included as part of a school district's overall approach to CB decision-making when all students might be taking a small number of common assessments in academic courses that will be included in a larger BOE.

Station Rotation: Station rotation is a differentiation strategy that can be used to reinforce a variety of skills and the development of conceptual understanding during a unit of study. Different "stations" are designed by a teacher to offer small groups of students a variety of resources (e.g., online, text-based), direct instruction, or more independent group explorations.

Student Agency: Student agency—or "ownership"—is central to ensuring equity, empowerment, and authenticity in classroom learning communities. For students to learn how to advocate for themselves, they need to understand and apply the skills and habits associated with a particular social or academic situation or problem. The opportunity and the challenge for teachers in developing student agency is to concurrently integrate learning mindsets with strategies and subject matter instruction (academic competencies) so that they are supporting each other.

Student-Centered Learning (SCL): Student-centered learning involves shifting the traditional role of teacher and student so that students are more engaged and more responsible for their own learning. The Nellie Mae Education Foundation has supported schools and districts in implementing SCL practices. In contrast to more traditional, adult-directed approaches to instruction, SCL adheres to four broad principles (Hess & Gong, 2014):

1. *Learning is personalized.* Each student is well known by adults and peers and benefits from individually paced learning tasks, tailored to his or her needs and interests. Collaboration with others and engaging, authentic, increasingly complex tasks deepen learning.

2. *Learning is competency-based.* Students move ahead when they demonstrate competency, and they have multiple means and opportunities to do so. Differentiated supports ensure that all students have what they need to achieve college and career readiness goals.

3. *Learning takes place anytime, anywhere.* Students learn outside the typical school day and year in a variety of settings, taking advantage of learning technologies and community resources, and receiving credit for learning, wherever it happens.

4. *Students exert ownership over learning.* Students understand that they improve by applying effort strategically. They have frequent opportunities to reflect on and understand their strengths and learning challenges. They take increasing responsibility for learning and assessment, and they support and celebrate each other's progress.

Success Criteria: Success criteria are the established learning targets for a given task, performance, or project. Success criteria are stated using "kid-friendly" wording that students can understand and use for peer and self-assessment. Success criteria are incorporated into scoring rubrics using several broad criteria (e.g., use of research skills) with performance indicators that further define expectations specific to the given task (e.g., conduct a key word search, check validity of sources).

Summative Assessment: A summative assessment is given at the end of a period of learning (e.g., unit of study, end of semester), and generalizes how well a student has performed. Summative assessments are typically used for grading and making high-stakes decisions, such as when evaluating a body of evidence to determine competency.

Systematic Observation: Systematic observation is a formative assessment strategy used to document knowledge and skills of students over a period of time rather than assessing all students at the same time (on-demand). This approach works well for areas that are difficult to assess with pencil-and-paper tests or when multiple opportunities are provided for students to demonstrate acquisition of skills and knowledge over time. Systematic observation captures the often "missed opportunities" for collecting assessment data during an instructional activity and can document progress being made over time in meeting broader learning goals for the school year (Hess, 2018).

Team Learning: Team learning can take many different forms (e.g., within short-term station rotations, longer-term project-based learning). Team-learning activities are structured by teachers for small groups of students to work collaboratively, such as to solve a problem or conduct an investigation of an issue or topic.

Transfer: "In cognitive theory, knowing means more than the accumulation of factual information and routine procedures; it means being able to integrate knowledge, skills, and procedures in ways that are useful for interpreting situations and solving problems" (National Research Council, 2001, p. 62). The ability to transfer knowledge and skill effectively involves the capacity to take what is known and use it creatively, flexibly, and fluently in different settings or novel problems.

Universal Design Principles (UDL): The idea of universal design in assessment comes from architectural practices. Think about how a person might get from the first floor to the second floor of a building. A ladder would only provide access for some people. A set of stairs would work for more people, but not for those using wheelchairs or crutches. An elevator is the most accessible structure and therefore more "universally designed" for access to all who want to get to the second floor. Thompson, Johnstone, and Thurlow (2002) lay out guidelines to ensure that large-scale tests meet the principles of universal design. Application of those guidelines in the construction of assessments ensures that all students have a fair and equitable opportunity to demonstrate their learning. (Hess's PLC Tool 9 incorporates the application of these principles when developing high-quality local assessments.)

Validity: Validity refers to the degree to which tests measure what they purport to measure. Alignment studies are designed to examine how well an assessment design and test items match the intent (standards to be assessed). For example, does this writing assessment actually assess a student's ability to compose and communicate ideas in writing or simply to edit a composition? Assessments can be valid (assessing what is intended to be assessed) and still not be reliable in terms of scoring.

Verification of Body of Evidence: Determining proficiency using a body of evidence requires a review and evaluation of student work and assessment scores. The review and evaluation process may vary in both format and intensity, but verifying proficiency requires that educators use common criteria to evaluate student performance consistently from work sample to work sample or assessment to assessment. For example, teachers working independently may use agreed-upon criteria to evaluate student work, a team of educators may review a student portfolio using a common rubric, or a student may demonstrate proficiency through an exhibition of learning that is evaluated by a review committee using the same consistently applied criteria.

Bibliography

Allen, R. (2012). *Developing the enabling context for school-based assessment in Queensland, Australia.* The International Bank for Reconstruction and Development/The World Bank.

Anderson, L., Krathwohl, D., Airasian, P., Cruikshank, K., Mayer, R., Pintrich, P., Raths, J., & Wittrock, M. (Eds.). (2001). *A taxonomy for learning, teaching, and assessing: A revision of Bloom's taxonomy of educational objectives.* Addison Wesley Longman.

Bray, B. (2019). *The teaching and learning continuum to learner agency.* https://barbarabray.net/2019/02/17/teaching-and-learning-continuum-moving-to-learner-agency/.

Casey, K. (2018). *Moving toward mastery: Growing, developing and sustaining educators for competency-based education. Competency*Works. https://www.competencyworks.org/wp-content/uploads/2018/11/Moving-Toward-Mastery.pdf.

Casey, K., & Sturgis, C. (2018). *Levers and logic models: A framework to guide research and design of high-quality competency-based education systems.* iNACOL.

Cave, C. A. (2016). *Progress report on the board of education's development of a profile of a Virginia graduate.* http://www.doe.virginia.gov/boe/committees_standing/accountability/2016/06-jun/june-2016-profile-of-a-graduate-presentation-final-draft.pdf.

Coburn, C. E. (2003). Rethinking scale: Moving beyond numbers to deep and lasting change. *Educational Researcher, 32,* 3–12.

Colby, R. L. (2017). *Competency-based education: A new architecture for K–1 schooling.* Harvard Education Press.

Collaborative for Academic, Social, and Emotional Learning (CASEL). (2017). *CASEL core competencies for SEL.* https://casel.org/core-competencies/.

Competency Model Clearinghouse. (2020). *Building blocks model.* https://www.careeronestop.org/competencymodel/competency-models/building-blocks-model.aspx.

Corwin. (2019). *Visible Learning™ 250+ Influences on Student Achievement.* https://us.corwin.com/sites/default/files/250_influences_chart_june_2019.pdf.

Domaleski, C., Gong, B., Hess, K., Marion, S., Curl, C., & Peltzman, A. (2015). *Assessment to support competency-based pathways.* http://www.karin-hess.com/free-resources

Dweck, C. S. (2006). *Mindset: The new psychology of success.* Random House.

Feldman, J. (2018). *Grading for equity.* Corwin.

Fisher, D., Frey, N., & Hattie, J. (2016). *Visible learning for literacy: Implementing the practices that work best to accelerate student learning.* Corwin.

Frey, N., Hattie, J., & Fisher, D. (2018). *Developing assessment-capable visible learners, grades K–12.* Corwin.

Fullan, M., Quinn, J., & McEachen, J. J. (2017). *Deep learning: Engage the world change the world.* Corwin.

Glowa, L., & Goodell, J. (2016). *Student-centered learning: Functional requirements for integrated systems to optimize learning.* https://www.inacol.org/resource/exploring-integrated-learning-systems-to-optimize-student-centered-learning/.

Gobble, T., Onuscheck, M., Reibel, A., & Twadell, E. (2017). *Pathways to proficiency: Implementing evidence-based grading.* Solution Tree Press.

Goddard, R. D., Hoy, W. K., & Hoy, A. W. (2004). Collective efficacy beliefs: Theoretical developments, empirical evidence, and future directions. *Educational Researcher*, 3–13. ASCD.

Guskey, T. R., & Brookhart, S. M. (2019). *What we know about grading.* ASCD.

Hattie, J. (2009). *Visible learning: A synthesis of over 800 meta-analyses relating to achievement.* Routledge.

Hess, K. (2000). *Beginning with the end in mind: A cross-case analysis of two elementary schools' experiences implementing Vermont's framework of standards and learning opportunities.* University of Vermont: Unpublished Dissertation.

Hess, K. (2018). *A local assessment toolkit to promote deeper learning: Transforming research into practice.* Corwin.

Hess, K., Carlock, D., Jones, B., & Walkup, J. (2009). *What exactly do "Fewer, clearer, and higher standards" really look like in the classroom? Using a cognitive rigor matrix to analyze curriculum, plan lessons, and implement assessments.* Educational Research in Action. http://www.karin-hess.com/free-resources.

Hess, K., & Gong, B. (2014). *Ready for college and career? Achieving the common core standards and beyond through deeper, student-centered learning.* Nellie Mae Education Foundation. http://www.karin-hess.com/free-resources.

Hoadley, C., & Haneghan, P. V. J. (2011). *The learning sciences: Where they came from and what it means for instructional designers—Trends and issues in instructional design and technology* (3rd ed., pp. 53–63). Pearson.

Horn, C. M., Christensen C. W., & Johnson, M. B. (2010). *Disrupting class: How disruptive innovation will change the way the world learns* (expanded ed.). McGraw-Hill Education.

Jones, C. (2018). *Just let it go.* CompetencyWorks. https://www.competencyworks.org/insights-into-implementation/classroom-practice/just-let-it-go/#more-17983.

Kettle Moraine PM Team Revision. (2018). *Kettle Moraine personalized learning look fors.* https://www.kmsd.edu/cms/lib/WI01919005/Centricity/Domain/468/KMSDPersonalizedLearningLookFors.pdf.

Klein, A. (2015). No Child Left Behind: An overview. *Education Week.* http://www.edweek.org/ew/section/multimedia/no-child-left-behind-overview-definition-summary.html.

Kohn, A. (2011). *Feel-bad education and other contrarian essays on children and schooling.* Beacon Press.

Levine, E., & Patrick, S. (2019). *What is competency-based education? An updated definition.* Aurora Institute.

Marzano, R. J. (2006). *Classroom assessment & grading that work.* Association for Supervision & Curriculum Development.

Marzano, R. J., & Kendall, J. S. (2008). *Designing and assessing educational objectives.* Corwin.

McTighe, J. (2018). Measuring what matters. *Association for Supervision and Curriculum Development, 75,* 4.

Moss, C., & Brookhart, S. (2012). *Learning targets: Helping students aim for understanding in today's lesson.* ASCD.

National Council on Measurement in Education (NCME) and American Council on Education (ACE). (2006). In R. L. Brennan (Ed.,), *Educational measurement* (4th ed.). American Council on Education and Praeger.

National Research Council (NRC). (2001). Knowing what students know: The science and design of educational assessment. In J. Pellegrino, N. Chudowsky, & R. Gaser (Eds.), *Board on testing and assessment, center for education, division of behavioral and social sciences and education.* National Academy Press.

New Tech Network. (2017). *New Tech Network agency rubrics.* https://www.jff.org/resources/educator-competencies-personalized-learner-centered-teaching/.

New York Performance Standards Consortium. (n.d.). *How it works: The essential components.* http://www.performanceassessment.org/how-it-works.

O'Connor, K. (2009). *How to grade for learning, K–12.* Corwin.

Patrick, S., & Sturgis, C. (2011). *Cracking the code: Synchronizing policy and practice for performance-based learning.* iNACOL. https://www.inacol.org/resource/cracking-the-code-synchronizing-policy-and-practice-for-performance-based-learning.

Patrick, S., Worthen, M., Truong, N., & Frost, D. (2017). *Fit for purpose: Taking the long view on systems change and policy to support competency education.* iNACOL. https://www.inacol.org/wp-content/uploads/2017/06/CompetencyWorks-FitForPurpose-TakingThe LongViewOnSystemsChangeAndPolicyToSupportCompetencyEducation.pdf.

Porter, A., & Smithson, J. (2001). *Defining, developing, and using curriculum indicators: CPRE research report series RR–048.* Consortium for Policy Research in Education.

reDesign. (n.d.). *Student agency.* reDesign Institute. https://www.redesignu.org/design-lab/mastery-learning/resource-bank/student-agency.

Rubin, S. C., & Sanford, C. (2018). *Pathways to personalization.* Harvard Education Press.

Smith, D., Frey, N., Pumpian, I., & Fisher, D. (2017). *Building equity: Policies and practices to empower all learners.* ASCD.

South Carolina Department of Education. (2020). *Profile of the South Carolina graduate.* Website. https://ed.sc.gov/about/profile-of-sc-graduate/.

Stack, B. (2012). *Assessment of learning with competency-based grading.* CompetencyWorks. http://www.competencyworks.org/how-to/assessment-of-learning-with-competency-based-grading/.

Stack, B., & VanderEls, J. G. (2017). *Breaking with tradition.* Solution Tree.

Sturgis, C. (2014). *A conversation with Adams 50.* CompetencyWorks. https://www.competencyworks.org/uncategorized/a-conversation-with-adams-50/#more-6255.

Sturgis, C. (2015). *Six trends at Lindsay Unified School District.* CompetencyWorks. https://www.competencyworks.org/insights-into-implementation/six-trends-at-lindsay-unified-school-district/.

Sturgis, C. (2016). *Chugach School District: A personalized, performance-based system.* iNACOL. https://www.inacol.org/resource/chugach-school-district-a-personalized-performance-based-system/.

Sturgis, C., & Casey, K. (2018a). *Designing for equity: Leveraging competency-based education to ensure all students succeed.* iNACOL.

Sturgis, C., & Casey, K. (2018b). *Quality principles for competency-based education.* iNACOL.

Thompson, S. J., Johnstone, M. J., & Thurlow, M. L. (2002). *Universal design applied to large scale assessments (Synthesis report 44).* University of Minnesota, National Center on Educational Outcomes. http://education.umn.edu/NCEO/OnlinePubs/Synthesis44.html.

Truong, N. (2019, December). *Special update to a snapshot of K–12 competency-based education state policy across the United States.* Aurora Institute. https://www.inacol.org/news/special-update-to-a-snapshot-of-k-12-competency-based-education-state-policy-across-the-united-states.

Tucker, C., Wycoff, T., & Green, J. (2017). *Blended learning in action: A practical guide toward sustainable change.* Corwin.

VanderArk, T. (2017). *How schools develop student agency.* CompetencyWorks. https://www.competencyworks.org/insights-into-implementation/how-schools-develop-student-agency.

Webb, N. (1997). *Research monograph number 6: Criteria for alignment of expectations and assessments on mathematics and science education.* CCSSO.

Webb, N. (2002). Depth-of-knowledge levels for four content areas. White paper shared via personal email (K. Hess).

Whan Choi, Y. (2019). *Oakland's graduate profile: A spotlight on what matters most.* Education Week. http://blogs.edweek.org/edweek/next_gen_learning/2019/06/oakland's_graduate_profile_a_spotlight_on_what_matters_most.html.

Wolfe, R., & Poon, J. (2015). *Educator competencies for personalized, learner-centered teaching.* The Council of Chief State School Officers (CCSSO) and Jobs for the Future (JFF). https://www.jff.org/resources/educator-competencies-personalized-learner-centered-teaching/.

Wormeli, R. (2006, April). Differentiating for tweens. *Educational Leadership, 63*(7), 14–19.

Wormeli, R. (2018). *Fair isn't always equal.* Stenhouse.

Index

A SAGE Publishing Company

Solutions YOU WANT | Experts YOU TRUST | Results YOU NEED

EVENTS

>>> **INSTITUTES**

Corwin Institutes provide large regional events where educators collaborate with peers and learn from industry experts. Prepare to be recharged and motivated!

corwin.com/institutes

ON-SITE PD

>>> **ON-SITE PROFESSIONAL LEARNING**

Corwin on-site PD is delivered through high-energy keynotes, practical workshops, and custom coaching services designed to support knowledge development and implementation.

corwin.com/pd

>>> **PROFESSIONAL DEVELOPMENT RESOURCE CENTER**

The PD Resource Center provides school and district PD facilitators with the tools and resources needed to deliver effective PD.

corwin.com/pdrc

ONLINE

>>> **ADVANCE**

Designed for K–12 teachers, Advance offers a range of online learning options that can qualify for graduate-level credit and apply toward license renewal.

corwin.com/advance

Contact a PD Advisor at (800) 831-6640 or visit www.corwin.com for more information